Shrimp & Spey
FLIES for SALMON

Chris Mann & Robert Gillespie

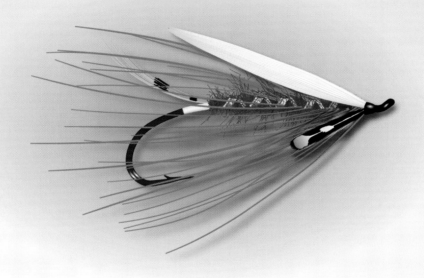

MERLIN UNWIN BOOKS

First published in Great Britain by Merlin Unwin Books, 2001

ISBN 1 873674 52 X

Published by
Merlin Unwin Books
Palmers House
7 Corve Street, Ludlow
Shropshire SY8 1DB, U.K.

The authors assert their moral rights to be identified as
the authors of this work.

British Library Cataloguing-in-Publication Data:
A catalogue record for this book is available from the British Library

Book design by Chris Mann
Printed in China by Leo Paper Products

Contents

Introduction and Acknowledgments

he concept of this book arose from a series of long discussions about fly style and fly design between the two authors. During these discussions we became very interested in our respective specialised areas of knowledge. Robert is a recognised expert in tying and fishing traditional Irish shrimp patterns while Chris has a wide ranging knowledge of the development of both traditional and modern Spey and Dee flies. Both of us had dabbled in each other's areas of expertise and we wished to know more. As these areas of common interest were explored, we soon came to recognise that we shared the same basic approach to salmon fly design.

Before we got into the details, we had both assumed that shrimp flies were a specialized aspect of fly fishing for salmon, albeit an important one. However, the more we delved into the distribution and use of shrimp flies in many countries, the more it became clear to us that this was not true - the use of shrimp patterns is a major and continuing theme that runs through the history of salmon fly fishing. At the present time, shrimp flies (even if they are not always called shrimps) are, as a group, probably the most widely used type of salmon and steelhead fly. Our intention here is to provide a service to anglers and flytyers throughout the world by gathering together in one book as much information as possible on the freshwater patterns and their use. We hope that this material will bridge the information gap between Europe and North America and also between regions within these areas. This is probably the first book to fully compare Atlantic salmon flies (on both sides of the Atlantic) with those of the steelhead fisheries of North America. There are parallel traditions and history behind these two major fishing styles and we consider that such an exercise is long overdue. There is no doubt in our minds that both sides have much to gain by such an interchange.

The selection of flies in this book is inevitably a little arbitrary and personal. We have chosen to include patterns on grounds of their relevance to modern fishing practice and if they are intrinsically

interesting or original. We have, of course, sought local advice whenever possible, but the responsibility for any errors or omissions lies entirely with us and not with the contributors.

We have set out the book in what we consider to be a straightforward and logical manner:

Part One traces the development of shrimp flies from their earliest beginnings up to the present day. This is intended to present shrimp flies in a historical perspective, but not a definitive, scholarly history.

Part Two is a regional guide to the shrimp flies in many of the major fishing areas of Europe. Part Three considers the flytying traditions of North America.

Part Four is a catalogue of dressings for all of the flies mentioned in the text - in total approximately 480 different flies. Each fly is illustrated and a full dressing recipe is given.

The last part of the book consists of an extensive, cross-referenced index of all the fly patterns, books and flytyers mentioned in the text.

ne of our most important tasks is to acknowledge the help and assistance which has been provided by fishermen and flytyers from countries throughout the world. This we now do with pleasure. It is surely stating the obvious that a book such as this would be impossible without the contributions of others. No single person, however knowledgeable, could possibly come into the vast range of local information and expertise presented in these pages. We would like to give heartfelt thanks to all our contributors for their willingness to share their expertise and experience with us, and via this book, with a wider audience. Our experience in researching this book has proved that there is indeed an international brotherhood of fly fishermen and we feel proud to be a small part of it.

Special thanks are also due to our publisher, Merlin Unwin. It goes without saying that to produce a book like this is a team effort and Merlin, Karen, Tina and Gillian have been unfailingly helpful, courteous and patient. We have also quoted widely from Merlin's other publications, particularly *Trout & Salmon Flies of Ireland*, *Trout & Salmon Flies of Scotland* and *Trout & Salmon Flies of Wales*. Special thanks are also due to the authors of these books: respectively,

Peter O'Reilly, Stan Headley and Moc Morgan.

We have been privileged to have received fly patterns from some of the great flytyers of the world. We were constantly amazed and humbled whenever we opened yet another package to find more breathtaking examples of the flytyer's art. The levels of skill and inventiveness shown in these flies is simply stunning. Gentlemen, we salute you!

What follows is a list of names, some very well known, others less so. What they all have in common is a willingness to share their expertise with others. If ever you get the opportunity to see, listen to or to talk to any of the people in this list - at a trade show, flytying convention or country fair - do so! You will only gain from the experience.

IRELAND
Paddy Bonner
Michael Roulston
Peter O'Reilly
Joe McDonald
Albert Atkins

ICELAND
Skúli Kristinsson
Kristjan Gislason

SCANDINAVIA
Mikael Frodin
Ismo Saastamoinen
Nestor Dupo
Martin Jørgensen

ENGLAND & WALES
Davy Wotton
Malcolm Greenhalgh
Tony Jones
Malcolm McKenzie
Michael Evans

SCOTLAND
Alexander Keachie
Davie McPhail
Stan Headley
Tam Wescott

NORTH AMERICA
Trey Combs
Bob Veverka
Bob Blumreich
Steve Schweitzer
Troy Bachmann
Brian Silvey
Bill Hunter
Bryant Freeman
Marvin Nolte
Rick Whorwood
Gerald Bartsch

We also wish to thank an army of other flytyers, past and present, who have unwittingly made their contribution to this book by continuing the rich tradition of fly development.

Chris Mann and Robert Gillespie
August 2001

The History and Development of the Shrimp Fly

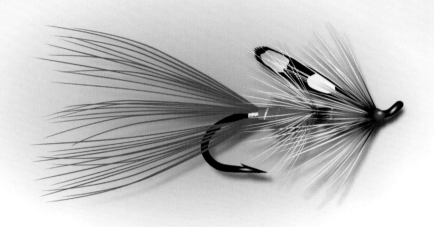

he origin of shrimp flies, as with many other aspects of the development of salmon flies is open to much speculation. If we look at the early development of salmon flies after the primitive and drab flies after the primitive and drab patterns that were based upon trout flies, there are three distinct types that can be identified. Firstly there are the Spey and Dee patterns which may be characterised by their subdued colouring, short wings and long flowing hackles, normally of heron. Secondly there are the complex and colourful fully dressed salmon flies with mixed and built wings, typified by such creations as the Jock Scott. The third strand is represented by the wingless Grub patterns made popular on the Usk and Wye rivers. Of these three types, there is no doubt that the Spey and Dee flies are the oldest. The first recorded patterns of these types date from the beginning of the 19th century, although it is fairly certain that they were well established even at that time. In contrast, the brightly coloured creations,

known appropriately as 'gaudy flies' when they were introduced, which have come to represent the classic salmon fly, did not come into widespread use until the second half of the 19th century. If we look at the construction and overall design of the Spey and Dee flies, can we conclude that these are shrimp flies? Their appearance alone would suggest so. They bear no resemblance to the kinds of natural insects that they were claimed to imitate and were tied on large hooks that would seem make this even more unlikely. Certainly Francis Francis, in his *A Book on Angling* first published in London in 1867, thought so. He comments that the flies in common use at the time could be divided into those which represented shrimps and crustaceans and those which represented butterflies and dragonflies. The division was quite clear: the older, more subdued patterns from the Spey and Dee represented the shrimps. Whilst we now know that the comparison with butterflies and dragonflies was based upon false premises, we still consider that the Spey and Dee flies do represent crustaceans.

The common features of both Spey and Dee patterns are the low set, simple wings and the use of long flowing hackles along the body or throat. These features, taken together, give the flies a very hump-backed appearance compared to built wing salmon flies and the hackling gives a very convincing imitation of the legs and feelers of shrimps or prawns. The flies that we have illustrated in Plates 1 & 2, show just how convincing these early shrimp flies could be. The main difference in the construction of the Spey and Dee flies lies in the configuration of the wings. In the Spey flies, the wing is normally brown mallard, tied short and low over the body. In the Dee flies, the wings consist of two feather strips which are tied in a low vee-configuration, spreading out sideways from the body. It is sometimes held that the heron hackling of the Spey flies should be longer than those employed on the Dee flies, but the difference is difficult to quantify. The hackle length varies so much, depending upon the hook size, the size of feathers available and the individual preference of the tyer, that is it impossible to lay down hard rules. Suffice it to say that the hackling is, by comparison with other flies, extremely long, almost always extending well beyond the length of the hook.

The other type of hackles used on many Spey flies came from a type of fowl known as a Spey cock which were specially bred in the Spey valley for their feathers. These feathers are long, although not to be compared to heron hackle, and are usually a mid red or grey in colour. They are normally tied in by the stalk at the rear of the body and then wound forward, producing a hackling that is longer at the rear than at the head of the fly.

The difficulty entailed in getting an accurate picture of these early patterns may be well illustrated by quoting Pryce-Tannatt on the subject of Spey flies. Talking about his indebtedness to Messrs. William Brown of Aberdeen for obtaining him samples of these flies tied by Speyside gillies, he wrote: *'From them I elicited the information that there was no such thing as a constant dressing of any Spey fly, for the reason that every dresser had a different rendering for each pattern, and, moreover, subjected his own rendering to considerable variation.'*

The history of the earliest Spey and Dee patterns is hard to trace, there being few published records before the latter quarter of the 19th century.

The main source of information and patterns for the early Spey flies is the book called *Autumns on the Spey* by Knox, first published in 1872. This book gives sixteen fly patterns for the Spey, including such classics as the Gold Reach and the Black Heron. Earlier books, such as William Blacker's *Fly making, Angling and Dyeing* (1855), concentrated heavily on introducing and publicising the colourful, new classic flies and it is not surprising that little mention was made of the more subdued flies that they were to replace. The strip wing Dee flies are mentioned by both Francis Francis (*A Book on Angling*, 1876) and Kelson (*The Salmon Fly*, 1895). One of the reasons why both the Spey and Dee patterns fell out of favour later may lie with the fact that Kelson and Francis Francis, who were both very influential, were of the opinion that these flies were only suitable for their home rivers and then only for particular water conditions. By the time Pryce-Tannatt published his book *How to Tie Salmon Flies,* in 1914, the relegation of these flies to a subordinate position, suitable only for special circumstances, was complete. Attempts were made to develop new Spey and Dee patterns such as the Moonshine, which incorporated features taken from the fully dressed salmon flies, thus losing the simplicity and purity of line which made the classic tyings so effective. The largely unsuccessful re-vamping of the Spey and Dee patterns by introducing features such as butts, veilings and complicated wings from the 'new' fully dressed feather wing flies, simply had the effect of pointing up the difference in philosophy enshrined within the earlier patterns. A few of the classic patterns such as the Lady Caroline and the Akroyd continued to be used, mainly as low water tyings, but it is only in more recent times that there has been any resurgence in their popularity.

A further special group of Dee flies are also of relevance to the development of shrimp flies. These flies are collectively known as 'Eagles' because they were hackled with the downy feathers from the legs of Golden Eagles. They were in fact the first 'marabou' flies. There are a series of these flies but two patterns are representative of the style: the Grey Eagle and the Yellow Eagle. In both cases, they are tied in the typical Dee fashion, as previously described. The main difference between them is that the Grey Eagle is hackled with the natural grey

Akroyd

Gardener

Moonshine

Glentana

PLATE 1: Strip Wing Dee Flies

feather, whereas for the Yellow Eagle the hackle is dyed a bright yellow. We will see later that many of the modern Spey flies from North America are in direct line of descent from these flies.

Grey Eagle

Yellow Eagle

Another, less typical fly in this group is the White Avon Eagle. The pattern illustrated is as given by Buckland and Oglesby and is unusual in that the body is of tinsel. In this case the eagle hackling is restricted to the throat rather than palmered along the whole body.

White Avon Eagle

The third major major group of early patterns that influenced shrimp fly development is that of the wingless Grubs or Bugs. Many of these patterns were popularized, if not invented, by George M. Kelson. His explanation that they imitated grubs and caterpillars is, however, unconvincing. Even allowing for the fact that it was believed at that time that salmon still fed whilst running the rivers to spawn, these flies do not lead one to believe that they were really tied to imitate these creatures - they look nothing like caterpillars! It is much more reasonable to suppose that having found a style of fly that was effective, anglers then sought some kind of rational explanation as to why this should be. It may not be coincidence that the grub patterns were particularly effective in warm, low water, mid-summer conditions, exactly the time at which many grubs and caterpillars are to be found in abundance.

The effectiveness of the flies themselves is however, not in doubt. Kelson himself recommended that all the standard winged patterns should also be dressed in a grub version and, by his own results, found them highly effective in the summer, particularly in low water conditions. Pryce-Tannatt gave tying details for a range of these grubs, including one called the Brown Shrimp, so we know that at least one of these flies was considered to be a shrimp. The tying style of this shrimp is in no way different to that of the other Grub patterns: all share the common features of a split body and three hackles, wound at the tag position, the centre of the body and at the head, respectively, increasing in size towards the front. We believe that it is justifiable to say that if one of these patterns is a shrimp, then all of them are shrimps.

Brown Shrimp with hackles reversed

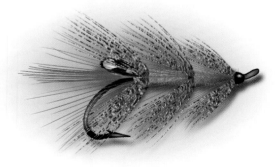

Lady Caroline

Black Heron

Carron Fly

Gold Riach

Gold Reeach

PLATE 2: Spey Flies

In their book *A Guide to Salmon Flies,* John Buckland and Arthur Oglesby also agree that the Grubs are the logical forerunners of the shrimp flies and make the point that by merely reversing the sizes of the hackles, putting the largest at the tail and the smallest at the head, the more familiar modern shrimp design can now be clearly seen.

The Grub patterns spread to waters outside the UK at a fairly early stage. Flies such as the Moisie Grub were recorded in Canada as early as 1887 and their use in Norway is also well documented. Later, in the chapters on shrimp flies worldwide, you will find shrimp patterns from Sweden and Norway, such as the Chillimps and Ullsock, which are directly based on the shape and tying style of the early grub flies. In Denmark, a whole range of modern sea-trout patterns such as the Omoe Brush, the Dalby Dribbler and the Umbrella, are also clearly based on the style of the Grubs.

The wingless grubs, together with the Spey and Dee flies, were therefore the starting points for the development of modern shrimp patterns. Almost all modern shrimp flies use one or more of the features of these old flies in various combinations. The long mobile hackling of the Spey and Dee flies is reflected in the wound tail hackles of the Irish shrimps, or in the palmered body hackles of the more literal imitations. The golden pheasant tippet and jungle cock of the grubs may be found in many modern shrimp patterns as winging. The body, divided by collar hackles, is a characteristic of the Irish shrimp patterns but this influence has extended well beyond the shores of Ireland.

Shrimp flies in Ireland were first popularized around the late 1930s and have been in general use throughout the North and West of Ireland since the early 1940s. Among the earliest patterns are the Curry's Red Shrimp tied by Pat Curry of Coleraine, the Agivey Wye bug (also known as the Wye Bug or simply the Bug), and the Secret Weapon (or Jock Scott shrimp) tied by E.C. Heaney, from the Faughan Valley. It may be speculated that the Irish shrimp style was simply designed as improvements on other earlier well known flies, such as the Welsh Usk Grub in particular, and other grub or wingless patterns of the Victorian era, such as the Wye Grub. The Wye Bug is an Irish shrimp pattern that certainly pre-dates both the Curry's Red Shrimp and Heaney's Secret Weapon. It is more than likely

that this fly, which is a combination of features present in the Usk Grub and the Wye Grub, owes its name and tying details to a confusion between the two flies.

Original Irish Wye Bug

Colonel Cristie Shrimp

An interesting example is a fly which we obtained which was tied by Curry himself. This fly is a previously unknown variant of the Bug and has a black rear body and an orange front body, both of seal's fur. The tail is of wound golden pheasant red breast feather, the centre hackle is cream and the front hackle is of red game. Veilings of white pheasant neck feathers dyed ruby red are mounted on the sides of both front and rear bodies.

Curry's Bug

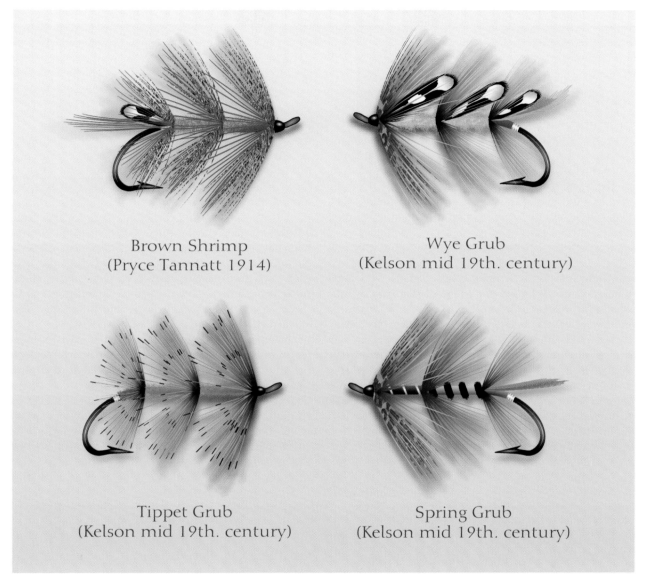

Brown Shrimp
(Pryce Tannatt 1914)

Wye Grub
(Kelson mid 19th. century)

Tippet Grub
(Kelson mid 19th. century)

Spring Grub
(Kelson mid 19th. century)

PLATE 3: Wingless Grubs

It is known that E.C. Heaney was influenced by the Bug when he produced the Secret Weapon, now more commonly known as the Jock Scott Shrimp. The Usk Grub, in the guise of the Wye Bug, is still a very popular and effective shrimp pattern in Ireland and has at least five commonly used variants. Its resemblance to the Usk Grub is clear to see.

The Usk Grub shows many of the features that were to be used in the further development of the Irish patterns. It has a head hackle and a mid-hackle, a divided body, large jungle cock wings and a golden pheasant breast feather tail. The overall appearance of the fly can be made to look quite different by altering the relative sizes of the hackles and the heaviness of the body, and the tying of the Usk Grub has varied a great deal over the years. From its very grub-like origin it has been tied in many styles but the 'modern' appearance, similar to the current Irish shrimp patterns, appeared as early as the turn of the 19th century. The modern Welsh version, which was a speciality of Lionel Sweet, has lost its head hackle somewhere along the way. Plate 4 shows a range of the various tying styles which have been used for the Usk Grub over the years. Modern tyings include a version from the USA which looks like a kind of Spey version of an Irish shrimp. It is certainly most attractive. This fly is particularly interesting, coming as it does from the Great Lakes area of America. As can be seen from the illustration, the tying is heavily influenced by the Spey style. Spey flies are commonly used in this area with notable success for steelhead, and the Usk Grub, with its swept back throat hackle is very much in this vein.

The Red Shrimp, devised by Pat Curry of Coleraine, uses elements of the Usk Grub combined with the Tippet Grub and the red and black colours, which were a feature of many of the successful classic salmon flies. The use of a wound golden pheasant body feather as a tail has been thought to be innovative, but we now know that his use of this feature was pre-dated by more than fifty years. It is hard now to imagine a shrimp fly without a long mobile tail, so popular has this feature become. The Red Shrimp was quickly followed by other similar patterns such as Curry's Gold Shrimp. The fact that Pat Curry did not actually invent the modern style of shrimp pattern, as has often been thought, does not belittle his achievement in re-defining an old style and devising a more effective version. The Red Shrimp and its descendants first appeared in the 1930s on the River Bann and its fame soon spread throughout Northern Ireland and westwards into Donegal and then to the Moy via the constant exchange of information which takes place on the association and day ticket waters in those areas. This rapid spread may not have taken place had the introduction occurred on private waters in Scotland or England for example. It is hard to keep a fly secret when a river is shared with many other anglers. Since then it has proved over the years that it is a superb pattern and is still as good today as when it was first developed.

The Secret Weapon developed by E.C. Heaney is another Irish shrimp of the modern type which was devised at almost the same time as Curry's Red Shrimp. This fly is clearly a combination of two traditions. The colours of the body are taken from the classic Jock Scott and the overall shape is borrowed from, or at least heavily influenced by, the Usk Grub and the Irish Wye Bug. It is not suprising therefore that their offspring proved to be highly effective. As far as can be ascertained, both Heaney and Curry were unaware of the fly style being developed by the other. This may seem to be more than a coincidence, but history shows that when a particular development is 'in the air' and a general discussion is taking place, it is not unusual for two people to pick up on these ideas and to come up with similar answers at almost the same time.

Reds and oranges been very influential colours for many of the subsequent shrimp patterns and have proved their attractiveness to salmon, particularly in coloured water. Apart from the fact that red and orange are effective, there does however seem to be a curious leaning towards these colours as being especially suitable for shrimp patterns. This must surely derive from the traditional colours of shrimps used in bait fishing. Certainly, the natural shrimp does not have this bright colouration unless it is cooked, dyed or treated.

Since these first patterns were introduced in Ireland, many variations and refinements have been added, most of them being local variations to solve particular local problems. It should not be thought that there was a clear goal and a logical, ordered sequence to these developments, on the contrary they proceeded on an *ad hoc* basis, in no particular order and in a geographically disparate manner. Patterns were introduced by experimentation, driven here and there by talented local flytyers and fishermen. Patterns were rarely documented and tyings spread normally by word of mouth - a constant source of variations of all kinds. The rich diversity of colour variations in hackles and bodies together with the sheer numbers of Irish shrimp patterns (over 120 in this book alone) bear witness to this.

It may be useful to explore the development of salmon flies in more general terms. Most salmon flies have been developed almost by accident. Classic salmon flies were given complex and colourful wings because it was believed in past times that salmon ate butterflies. Modern tyings use simple hairwings rather than feather but, basically, the hair simply replaces the complex feather

Victorian Usk Grub
ca. 1900

Usk Grub (Bates)
mid19th.cetury

Modern Usk Grub: U.S.A.

Modern Usk Grub: Wales

PLATE 4: Usk Grubs

wing of the traditional fly - it is still a wing. The modern type of hairwing pattern was developed for three main reasons. Firstly, it is easier to tie than a feather wing, secondly it does not require the use of almost unobtainable (not to mention illegal) exotic materials and thirdly it was developed against the background that salmon were becoming scarcer and harder to catch.

It should be remembered that most of the famous classic salmon fly patterns were developed between 1850 and 1940. These years were bonanza years, with salmon running the rivers of western Europe in numbers that are scarcely credible today. Pollution was not a problem, rod fishing pressure was light and large scale commercial fishing for salmon on their feeding grounds did not exist. The fishermen who designed the classic patterns fished waters that were prolific, even at the worst of times.

Gentlemen anglers fished these waters at the best times of the season and had almost unlimited access to the best water conditions by residing, sometimes for months on end, in lodges situated directly next to the river. In these circumstances, one might suppose that almost any fly that was correctly presented would take enough fish to satisfy the angler. Even today, it is not uncommon for anglers to take tens of fish per day from the best beats on the famous rivers.

In more recent times, the numbers of fish running our rivers have, with a few notable exceptions, been drastically reduced. Abstraction from rivers to produce water for the fast growing conurbations, lack of summer rainfall and increasing pollution from both agricultural and industrial sources have all combined to make the task of the modern salmon fisherman vastly more difficult. The increasing numbers of anglers, together with the fact that only a few anglers can afford to fish the best beats on the best rivers mean that the effectiveness of the fly patterns and fishing techniques are more important than they have ever been.

In these circumstances, it is not suprising that a lot more thought has gone into fly design. Hairwing designs that are more mobile and active than traditional feather winged patterns, particularly in low water conditions, have almost swept the board. Most modern European hairwing patterns are tied on double or treble hooks but a significant number of anglers prefer tube flies.

Other modern approaches have included the use of softer, more mobile hair such as arctic and silver fox hair, marabou and, in the USA and Canada, the use of bear and polar bear hair. Some types of classic flies, such as those used on the Scottish Dee and Spey, were tied with long, flowing body hackles of heron which are highly mobile and work well in the current. These types of flies, although they have been superceded in Scotland by modern hairwings, have always been effective fishing flies and have never gone out of fashion in Scandinavia and North America. Although they were originally developed for fast flowing waters, they do in fact work well in a variety of water conditions, from low flows right through to heavy fast water.

Although we now know that salmon do not feed in freshwater, they nevertheless continue to take a well presented fly. Amongst the many other factors that may be involved, this has led to the theory that a salmon takes a fly because of a conditioned reflex based on hunting instincts and a memory of feeding at sea. Flies have therefore been devised which seek to imitate small fish, shrimps and prawns with the purpose of awakening this reflex. Whilst all styles of salmon fly may create this image intentionally or otherwise, the shrimp fly category defines for us those patterns which specifically set out to represent a crustacean by intentionally highlighting some crustacean features and movements. Shrimp flies range from simple to very complex designs but they all share some obvious common characteristics that suggest a crustacean.

While the conditioned reflex theory is not susceptible to proof, it remains as plausible as anything yet proposed and offers us the comfort that we are doing something on a rational basis. It may be thought that if a salmon takes our fly as a real shrimp, prawn or fish, then the more accurate the imitation, the better would be the results. We could discard our Curry's Red Shrimp and General Practitioner and replace them with meticulous, naturalistic representations of the creatures in question. Such imitations do exist, of course, and with modern tying techniques and materials, together with accurate photographic evidence, we can produce very convincing representations. The problem is that in real fishing conditions these accurate representations come a very poor second to the more impressionistic patterns. The close copy approach would seem to lead us down a blind alley. An exception may be found on the west coast of North America where accurate imitations seem to be more effective on Steelhead than on Atlantic salmon. This may have to do with the fact that Steelhead continue to feed, at least for some time, in freshwater. It may also be connected with the fact that the Steelhead sea feeding grounds may not be so far away from the river estuaries and that the fish may therefore be fresher when they enter the rivers. Certainly, these patterns seem more effective nearer to salt water. Some supporting evidence for this view may be gleaned from experience in Iceland. It is not uncommon here to find Atlantic salmon that have entered the rivers still retaining their sea teeth and it may be no coincidence that the Francis prawn fly, which is substantially a realistic imitation, is by far the most popular and effective of the shrimp or prawn imitations.

In such matters we consider that the pragmatic view is the best approach. The fact that the

Crane Fly

Bluebell

Spider

Orange & Grouse

PLATE 5: Idiosyncratic Irish Flies

theory may be flawed should not divert us from the fact that designing flies on this principle has produced some very effective fishing patterns indeed - we may be doing things for the wrong reasons, but we must be doing the right things! Salmon certainly do take shrimp patterns. Perhaps if we take the features of Irish shrimps as an example and look at them in detail we can draw some conclusions about them:

• Irish shrimps, although the colours them-

selves may not always be very bright, are tied with sparkling hackles and often with transluscent seals fur

• The flies have a silver or gold tag and silver or gold ribbing to add glints of light and reflections under water

• The two mobile hackles and a long wound tail promote lifelike movement and 'kick' in the water.

The overall effect of these features is to produce a

fly which flickers with movement and life – known to be killing features for any salmon fly. Shrimps are proven fish takers in almost all water conditions, at almost all times of the season. Experience, not just in Ireland but in waters throughout the world, seems to suggest that the illusion of life is more persuasive to a salmon than a slavish static representation of its prey. This may be why the Irish shrimp flies are so effective: they convey a strong impression of the moving shrimp as it would be seen by the salmon in its familiar marine environment.

Development of the Shrimp Fly

hen it comes to discussing the development of the shrimp fly, we make no apology for starting with Ireland. Judged purely on the number of patterns alone, Ireland can be justly called the home of the shrimp fly.

Why should it be that so many shrimp patterns have been designed and are used in Ireland? Firstly, there is the fact that by accident or not, some of the earliest and most effective patterns were developed in Ireland. With these patterns to build upon, it is no surprise that many anglers, having used them and found them to be effective, developed local variations that were even more effective for their own waters. Success breeds success and the more that shrimp patterns became known and used, the more anglers used them. This in turn led to them becoming the most successful flies for many fishermen, simply because they were used so much. This factor alone cannot, however, explain their widespread use and success. Secondly, one could ask if there is something special about Irish fish or Irish rivers that makes shrimps particularly effective in Ireland? Certainly there are factors such as the warmer water temperatures and the fact that many Irish rivers have a prolific grilse run. Irish rivers certainly have their own characteristics and peculiarities, but there are no features that are not shared by waters in many other countries.

Shrimp patterns, albeit of different constructions, are highly effective in Scottish, Norwegian, Icelandic and North American waters, viz patterns such as the Ally's Shrimp from Scotland and the Francis and Raeken from Iceland. Those anglers who have taken the Irish shrimp patterns to Scotland, the north of England, Scandinavia, Iceland and elsewhere, can testify to their effectiveness in other rivers in other countries.

Perhaps too, the fishing culture in Ireland may have something to do with the development of these patterns. Salmon fishing in Ireland has never had the connections with wealth and privilege that it has had in England and Scotland. Access to prolific rivers has always been more readily available to the average man and therefore fishing for salmon has never been just the preserve of the rich. In consequence, there is a much greater degree of interaction between anglers and a much greater exchange of information. In the days before the widespread dissemination of information via the angling press, this factor is not to be underestimated.

There is a long tradition of invention in the development of Irish salmon fly patterns, which seem peculiarly suited to the waters of Ireland. It should also not be forgotten that the forerunners of the brightly coloured, fully dressed classic salmon flies had their origin in Ireland. Flies such as the Parson series, developed in 1830s by Pat McKay are amongst the most well known of these. Apart from the development of the classic salmon flies, there is also a great tradition in Ireland of aberrant patterns. The flies that we have illustrated in Plate 5, such as the Crane, the Spider, the Orange & Grouse and the Bluebell are typical of the unusual forms of these early Irish flies. In Scotland and England, the development of later patterns was concentrated on devising ever more complex and colourful versions of the built wing flies, the influence of Kelson being overwhelming. The idiosyncratic nature of Irish flies remains to this day.

Many of the features that make an effective trout pattern are shared by salmon flies. In Ireland, it is not uncommon to take one species on flies that were intended for another. This has had the consequence that the separate development of salmon patterns as against trout patterns, common in some other traditions, has never been total in Ireland. There are probably more examples in Ireland than in any other country, of fly patterns which are used successfully for both salmon and trout angling.

The Red Shrimp of Pat Curry and the Secret Weapon of E. C. Heaney defined the modern Irish shrimp style and led to the myriad of patterns now in use. These patterns have now spread overseas and have been used with great success in Scotland, Norway, Iceland, the USA and Canada.

Curry's Red Shrimp

General Practitioner (Drury)

Compared to the huge numbers of shrimp patterns developed in Ireland, comparatively few shrimp and prawn flies have their home in England and Wales. Nevertheless, the few that they have produced have been very influential.Two of the important forerunners of the modern shrimp flies, the Usk Grub and the Wye Grub, have their roots on the borders of England and Wales, coming as they do from the Rivers Usk and Wye. The Usk & Wye Grubs were very influential in the development of the early Irish patterns, as acknowledged by the inventors of these flies. Although these patterns are now little used in their home waters they continue to be used with success, in modified form, in both Scandinavian and North American waters.

In more modern times, the General Practitioner (sometimes also called the Drury Shrimp), devised by Colonel Esmond Drury on the River Test around 1953, has also had a lasting influence and is still a popular pattern. In terms of its tying style, the General Practitioner is a fairly straightforward attempt to mimic the appearance of a prawn as used in bait fishing. The use of long hair for the feelers and a palmered body hackle does, however, give the fly a mobility in the water, which, added to the lifelike silhouette, probably explains its long lasting effectiveness. The original and variants of this fly are exceedingly popular in North America and it has been one of the most influential patterns in the development of modern North American steelhead flies.

Peter Deane's Francis Shrimp, which dates from around 1965, has also proved to have a lasting

influence, curiously more so in Iceland than in the UK. The Icelandic versions of this fly are by far the most commonly used flies in Icelandic waters although the tying has varied slightly from the original. It should be noted that Frances is the correct spelling for the name of this fly as it was named after an assistant of Peter Deane called Frances, who due to the popularity of the fly, spent nearly all her time tying it. Icelanders altered the name to the masculine form of Francis, and it is this spelling which is now usually seen. A later addition of eyes to the pattern led to the pattern also being known as Deane's Black Eyed Prawn.

Black Francis Tube (Deane)

Modern developments have tended to be based very much on the hair wing types, typified by the Ally's Shrimp from Scotland, although more recently, tyers among the steelhead anglers of North America have devised effective new patterns using long, mobile feather hackles, combined with hair.

Scotland has been important for the development of shrimp patterns in several ways. Firstly, it was the home the Spey and Dee styles of dressing

that have been picked up and extended in other countries, particularly in North America. These flies form an extremely important group in both these areas, but ironically, these styles of dressing are now rarely used in Scotland. Secondly, it is the home of the Ally's Shrimp, devised by Alastair Gowans. This pattern has proved to be one of the most effective flies of modern times, figuring in the lists of successful patterns in nearly every salmon angling country. This fly alone has certainly introduced more fishermen worldwide to the use of shrimp patterns than the rest put together. So important has been the wildfire spread of the Ally's Shrimp that in the chapter *European Shrimp & Spey Flies* we have devoted a complete section to it and its variants. The Stewart Shrimp was one of the early Scottish patterns that maintained its popularity for many years. Simply tied, it nevertheless has all the hallmarks of more modern patterns. The tail is golden pheasant tippet and the body is split red and black, a feature that is popular to this day. The front hackle, long and swept back, is golden pheasant red breast feather.

Stewart Shrimp

In Sweden and Norway, modern patterns that are hugely successful include the Mörrum, named after the Mörrum River on which it was developed.

The Chillimps fly, although it may not look like a typical shrimp, was certainly intended to be a shrimp imitation according to the fishermen who developed it. First devised in 1942, it is a pattern that has stood the test of time. The record Mörrum sea-trout of 28 lb was caught on this pattern in 1993, breaking a 46-year-old record, also held by the Chillimps.

Some of the classic Dee and Spey flies are also still in use in Scandinavia and whilst they

Mörrum Fly

Chillimps

cannot be considered as a major group, a small band of enthusiastic fishermen still use them regularly and with a deal of success. Among other successful flies have been the Dunt, the Akroyd and the Glentana.

Dunt

There is a huge variety of shrimp patterns in use throughout North America. Most of these patterns have made little impact on salmon fishing in Europe up until now, but we think that this will change. One of the most important aspects of the use of shrimps in North America is the continued use and development of Spey and Dee type patterns and derivations. The effectiveness of Spey and Dee flies is not to be underestimated and we would not be suprised to see this style of fly re-emerge in popularity in Scotland and other European waters. It should be noted that many North American anglers are totally unaware that these patterns are not widely used in Europe and were very suprised when they found this out. Also important in the development of shrimp flies is the use of modern synthetic materials. Combined with the sheer breadth of the inventiveness of flytyers from the American continent means that the fly patterns developed there can only become more influential in the future, particularly when it is realised just how effective the patterns which are primarily tied for steelhead can be for Atlantic salmon.

The present day popularity of Spey and Dee type flies in North America, particularly for Steelhead, was largely due to the influence of a flytyer called Sydney Glasso who lived in the Northwest of the USA He was the person who first adapted the traditional Spey patterns for steelhead and his flies have a continuing impact up to the present day. Modern north American Spey and Dee flies are recognisably derived from their Scottish ancestors but there are differences of style and emphasis. Firstly, there are the differences in materials. The classic patterns were very often tied with heron hackles which are now difficult to obtain or illegal. Many of the modern north American Spey patterns use marabou as a substitute for heron hackle. Apart from the fact that this material is easy to obtain, it has some other advantages as well. When the fly is not under pressure from the water flow it presents a large profile. Marabou is even more mobile than heron and the slightest water movement will give life to the fly. Conversely, when the fly is under tension, as when it is fished 'on the swing' the materials sleek back very easily which avoids the problem of the fly skating upwards in the water. Body material is another area where the patterns have changed. The old Spey and Dee flies were never particularly bright in colour, relying upon the hackle movement for their effectiveness. This has changed so that the new patterns are tied in much brighter colours and the use of flashy artificial materials for the body is quite normal.

Secondly, there are the differences in style. One of the major differences lies in the winging. Modern patterns often incorporate a mixture of Spey and Dee style features and it is not unusual to see a fly tied as a Spey pattern but using Dee style winging.

The influence of Sydney Glasso is also strong and his use of hackle tips for winging is often seen on modern Spey flies. Other flies may have hair-wings or even no wings at all. The multiple, complex ribbing of the Spey flies has largely disappeared. Another feature which is often very noticeable is the shortness of the fly compared to the hook length. The body on many modern Spey patterns starts well inside the hook point and may be no longer than half the total hook length. It is not certain whether this was adopted to try and avoid the perceived problem of short takes, or whether it is because the flies simply look good when tied in this manner. The humpbacked but streamlined look of a typical Spey fly is certainly exaggerated when the fly body is tied short.

The hooks used and the size of fly have also changed. Most flies are tied on modern 'Spey' hooks such as the Alec Jackson or curved shank salmon irons such as the Bartleet. Standard fishing sizes vary from size 10s up to hooks about 2" (50mm) long. The 3" to 6" long Dee hooks of yesteryear are no longer used.

Glitter Shrimp

Among the more usual type of shrimp flies there are two main strands. Firstly, there is a range of flies which are more realistic imitations of shrimps than the Spey flies. These flies are often loosely based on the General Practitioner and the derivation is normally obvious. Examples of this type of fly can be found in use on the east coast, the

Great Lakes and the west coast. Secondly, there is a range of realistic shrimp imitations, a typical example being the Squamish Poacher. These flies are often used in estuaries and in salt water and are generally fished when intercepting steelhead and salmon early in their run before they reach any distance into their home rivers. With certain exceptions, these flies tend to be mainly orange and red - the 'normal' colour for shrimps.

Flies such as Curry's Red Shrimp have also had an influence, particularly in the east of Canada. It is said that the first examples of the fly reached Canada during the Second World War via the crews of submarines who came from Northern Ireland with the Royal Navy to ports such as Halifax.

The Irish Tippet Shrimp is another pattern that is well known on rivers such as the Miramichi and it is possible that the introduction occured in the same manner. Whilst neither of these flies is used much these days, there is no doubt that they had an influence on the development of later patterns such as Hunter's Tippet Shrimp and Barnett's Shrimp.

Irish Tippet Shrimp

One of the most interesting aspects of the development of shrimp flies over the years, is the decline in realistic imitations. In fact, we believe strongly that the future lies in the illusionistic direction. It may well prove to be more fruitful to consider a shrimp fly, not as a shrimp as such, but more as a style of dressing. If the aim of a successful fly is to provide an illusion of life and movement, then we know that the various shrimp styles of dressing, whether it be the double hackled forms of the Irish shrimp, the long tailed form of the Ally's or the long mobile hackled form of the

modern Spey, are some of the most promising avenues that we can pursue.

Each of these styles of fly has its own strengths, depending upon the conditions for which it was designed. The easiest way to think of mobility in a fly is to see it as a function of water flow. The Ally's Shrimp and similar styles can be seen as possessing a longitudinal mobility which makes them particularly suitable for fast flowing water. Longitudinal mobility is produced by a combination of long, slim tail fibres and sleek, sparse hackling. The effect of these features is to produce a fly in which the mobility in the water substantially consists of a sinuous movement along the axis of the fly, with little tendency for the fly to rise and skate. Compared to these flies, the Irish Shrimp can be classed as having three dimensional mobility. The tail and hackles are tied much more 'in the round' and stand off from the axis of the fly much more. This has the effect of producing a fly in which the fibres and the fly itself are much more mobile in slower water flows. The action produced is a series of three-dimensional movements of the hackle and tail fibres, even in moderate or low flows. The disadvantage of such a style is that there is a tendency for the hackles and tail to collapse if the water flow is too heavy, or for the fly to be lifted to the surface and skate.

Carron Fly

The Spey style combines elements and advantages of both these styles. The body dressing is very sparse and the hackles long. This produces a fly which sinks and stays down in the fast flows for which it was originally designed, but nevertheless retains the mobility of the hackles even in slower flows. It should be noted, however, that among the steelhead fishermen of the north west of America who have more experience of actually fishing Spey flies than anybody else, there are those who consider that Spey flies are more suited to slack water flows. They believe that because of the long hackling underneath the hook shank, Speys are unstable in fast water with a tendency to swim on their side. The mobility of the flies in slack water is also improved by the use of marabou hackles as is often the case in modern tyings from north America.

It cannot be accidental that more and more traditional patterns are being tied as shrimp flies. This tendency includes the Scottish hairwing patterns which are very often tied in long-tailed versions and north American steelhead patterns which are now being tied in the Spey style. We would advise any angler or flytyer who wishes to develop effective new patterns, to look to the shrimp patterns. They are amongst the most successful styles of dressing that have ever been developed.

We are certain that this process is already taking place. The new generation of fly dressers, grounded in the tying of trout patterns, especially patterns for rainbow trout in the large stillwaters, are bringing their experience to the tying of salmon flies. They have no reticence in using flashy and fluorescent materials and have already proved that salmon, when taking a fly, have no hang-ups about the traditions of flytying. Maintaining a tradition is also about movement and new ideas, not just about keeping things as they are. The effectiveness of modern patterns means that we cannot afford to be reactionary about the use of new materials. If Pat Curry, Esmond Drury, Alastair Gowans and many other anglers and flytyers had been content with the existing patterns of their day, our fishing today would be much the poorer.

Another aspect of modern salmon fishing that has had a great influence on the spread of patterns is that anglers travel more than ever before. Modern travel, the availability of fishing water, and the fact that the average fisherman has more free time and the prosperity to indulge his hobby, mean that this tendency can only increase. The cross fertilisation of ideas was apparent as we were preparing this book. When looking at the patterns from the various countries it was sometimes very difficult to decide where to place them. Under which country should a new pattern, devised by an

Englishman for use on Scottish waters, which later proved to be one of the most effective patterns on Icelandic waters, best be placed? This book, which pulls all the various aspects of shrimp patterns from throughout the world together, may also play a role in this process. There are many patterns in this book which have all the credentials to be successful far from their home waters.

Another factor which should be considered is the role that hook choice plays in the development of fly patterns. Throughout North America catch restrictions and catch-and-release are normal, sometimes voluntary and, in many places, legally required. Hook restrictions play an important part here. The use of barbed, double and treble hooks is often illegal. The vast majority of flies from North America are therefore tied on large single hooks, often barbless. The introduction of catch-and-release in European waters, often voluntary but increasingly becoming a legal requirement, means that this trend can only increase. Catch and release restrictions, if extended, as may well be the case, will probably mean that the hairwing tube flies so commonly used in Europe may fall from favour even if multiple hooks are not banned. Tubes are not so well suited to single hooks which is probably the reason why they are seldom seen in North America. It should be said, however, that in Scandinavia on rivers such as the Mörrum where single hooks are now mandatory, tubes are still used with single hooks. These hooks are normally of the short shank, wide gape, heavyweight type, such as those designed for carp fishing. Shrimp patterns, whether they be of the Ally's Shrimp style, the Spey style or the Irish style are extremely well suited to single hooks.

The colour of flies is another interesting aspect that, until now, has only been explored on an empirical basis. The number of anglers and fly tyers who are aware of the scientific studies that have been done on the visual system of salmon is very few. The colours used in salmon flies have very often been based on folklore and speculation - early season patterns should be of bright, light colours, late season patterns should be darker and redder. In fact these 'rules' which have been developed by experience and observation do reflect, at least partly, some of the scientific evidence. It has been shown that fish that live in a marine environment have a visual system in which the sensitivity

of the eye is heavily biased towards green. In freshwater fish, this bias is towards the red end of the spectrum. Migratory fish, such as salmon have been shown to have the capability to change this bias during their progression from salt to fresh water. This change of visual sensitivity is a gradual process, moving from green, through yellow and orange and finally to red. Based on these findings, we should therefore use green and yellow flies in the lower stretches of a river or for fresh fish, gradually changing to orange and red as the fish spend more time in freshwater.

CLASSIC COLOUR PROGRESSION FOR FLIES THROUGH THE YEAR

Spring   Summer   Autumn

An interesting case which helps to illustrate this point is the River Moy in Co. Mayo in the west of Ireland. On this river, there is a very clear progression of effective colour patterns through the course of the season. The season starts with flies having a blue-silver combination, moves on to those which are predominantly yellow, then orange, then claret and ends with brown-red. Before any one is tempted to bombard us with the thousand exceptions which occur, we quite accept that this is not a hard and fast rule. There does however remain a general tendency which is quite valid. An exception to the 'green early' rule is the Fluorescent Green Shrimp from Ireland. This fly is generally used in August and September and is a brilliant fly in a dirty flood. Curiously, it is not recommended for use early in the season.

Fluorescent Green Shrimp

The general idea that flies should follow this kind of colour progression is, with one major exception, borne out in practice. The exception being the fact that green is rarely used for salmon flies - the number of well known patterns that are predominantly green can be numbered on the fingers of one hand. This tendency even extends to the Irish shrimps, where only a few of the hundreds of colour combinations that exist use green. The use of green-yellow combinations is therefore one aspect of fly development that could be usefully explored. The effectiveness of these colours is certainly confirmed by the few patterns that are widely used.

Scandinavian Tube Shrimp

One colour tendency that is quite marked in North America and Ireland is the use of purple. The purple used is normally quite dark and is very often used to replace black, particularly for steelhead flies. The explanation that we were given is that anglers wished to retain the density of image given by black but at the same time offer a fly with a bit more colour interest. One can well imagine that as such a fly moves in the water and the light conditions change, the fly presents a constantly changing appearance, varying from a near black silhouette to showing flashes of colour.

European Shrimp & Spey Flies

he easiest way to get an overview of the distribution of shrimp patterns world-wide is to look at the most popular patterns in the main salmon angling countries - Ireland, England & Wales, Scotland, Scandinavia, Iceland and North America. In this chapter we shall look at the range of shrimp and Spey flies currently being used in the major European countries, including Scandinavia and Iceland. In the succeeding chapter we shall look at Canada and the USA. Russia is a special case as its history of salmon fly fishing is very recent. Flies from other countries which are effective in similar conditions are generally used and we can therefore be confident that they will also work in Russia. The only problem with judging fly patterns in Russia is that many rivers are so prolific that a catch of several hundred fish to a party of anglers in a week is not uncommon. We have no doubt that in due

course a catalogue of flies developed or adapted specifically for Russian rivers will emerge. Indeed, the first evidence of this can already be seen.

The flies described in the following sections are intended to give a representative view of shrimp patterns in the countries mentioned. Whilst it is not possible to cover all the known patterns and their variants, we have nevertheless taken great care to include all the major patterns. Where possible we have obtained these from their inventors or else from expert local anglers, so as to ensure that dressing details are as correct as possible. Lesser known patterns that have proved their effectiveness have also been included when we considered them worthy of note. Whilst we have taken note of the views and advice of local anglers and fly tyers, the final selection of patterns was ours and any errors and omissions are entirely for our account.

IRELAND

he traditional Irish shrimp fly style produces patterns of great intrinsic beauty and effectiveness for salmon and grilse angling and are the most commonly used style of salmon fly in Ireland. Whilst they are popular in almost all areas and on most rivers of the country, they are most extensively used in Northern Ireland where the style originated. They are also widespread in the North West and West of Ireland.

Traditional Irish shrimp flies are not meant to be exact or close copy representations of shrimps in the same way that a General Practitioner is a fair representation of a prawn, but are tied to be highly mobile flies producing a caricature or image of life in the water. The dressing style with its emphasis on mobility, colour and translucency are important in creating this life-like image. The real genius of the design however is the ability of the style to be 'worked' in the water. In order to fully appreciate the design of Irish shrimps they must be looked at in the water, not in the hand. Put an Irish shrimp into the water and it immediately comes alive. If you hold an Irish shrimp stationary in a moderate flow you will see that jungle cock wings are very noticeable and that the tail and hackles constantly flicker. If the tip of the rod is moved in a steady to and fro motion, the fly will pulsate in the water as the hackles open and close. If, at the same time, you move the rod upstream or handline slowly, you will that see the fly both pulsates and darts, becoming extremely lifelike indeed. In faster flows the current alone is enough to work the fly by flickering its tail and hackles. In a more moderate current the fly may be moved attractively across the flow by moving the rod tip alone, whereas a combination of rod 'tipping' and handlining allows an Irish shrimp to be pulsated attractively across even very slack water. The Irish shrimp fly can be fished in any direction, including upstream across slower water, provided you retrieve it to work the fly. There is no question but that the Irish shrimp is a very versatile and deadly salmon fly.

If you asked any salmon angler or fly tyer in Northern Ireland who was the most important person in the history of Irish salmon fly tying, they

would most likely answer Pat Curry of Coleraine. The Irish shrimp style and the myriad of Irish shrimp patterns we know and use today owe their existence and popularity to Pat Curry tying his original Red Shrimp. The Bug, Wye Bug or Agivey Wye Bug as it is also known, is the oldest known popular Irish shrimp pattern. Although its origins are not documented, it may be reasonably supposed that it derived from the Usk Grub. An important further confirmation of this may lie in the fact that the many variants are almost exactly the same as those found on the Usk Grub. There is no doubt that the Bug was influential in the development of Curry's Red Shrimp. Although Curry may not have invented the shrimp fly, as such, he certainly defined and popularized a new style and thus may be fairly considered to be the father of the modern Irish shrimp fly. In addition to the Red Shrimp, Curry also devised other patterns such as the Gold Shrimp as well as popularizing the Bug.

Curry himself stated that although he tied many different shrimp patterns for his customers, he used only three himself and that on one of them, the Curry's Red, he took 95% of his salmon. We cannot be sure, but it seems likely that the other two flies that he used were his Gold Shrimp and the Bug or Wye Bug. These early Bugs usually had tails of game cock hackles, normally furnace.

Curry's Red Shrimp - modern tying

Whilst researching the original dressing for Curry's shrimps we were fortunate enough to obtain about a dozen flies tied by Curry himself. These patterns include several examples of the Curry's Red shrimp, one example of the Curry's Gold shrimp, as well as a previously unrecorded pattern.

Because of its importance in the development of Irish salmon angling it is worth taking a look at the Curry's Red Shrimp in some detail. In Curry's original pattern, shown in the illustration below, the tail is of wound golden pheasant red breast feather. The slim rear body is usually of floss with fine oval tinsel ribbing, although two examples of a brighter red colour are tied with wool. There are rear body side veilings of crimson hackle tips or white ringneck pheasant feathers dyed crimson. The body is in two halves, but the rear body is often slightly longer than the front body. The middle hackle is kept quite short and sparse. The slim front body is floss or wool, again with a fine rib. The front body again has side veilings, similar to the rear veilings, or slightly shorter. The winging is of roofed Jungle cock which is quite large and the front hackle is noticeably longer and fuller than the middle hackle.

Curry's Red Shrimp - original tying

Curry's original pattern is almost always quoted as having Indian Crow veilings, sometimes only at the rear. Looking at the veilings on Curry's own flies, however, this is not the case. He always uses front and rear veilings and in most of the examples these are of dyed white ringneck pheasant feathers, although one example uses hackle tips. Curry makes no attempt to imitate Indian crow with the pheasant ringneck feathers but simply dyes them plain colours to suit the dressing of the fly. Surely if he had wanted to imitate Indian crow he would not have dyed the feathers a deep, blood red crimson. The form of the veilings is also interesting in that they are markedly spade shaped, again no attempt has been made to modify the feather shape to match that of an Indian crow. Based on the evidence we have of Curry's own tyings, we think it unlikely that the veilings

were ever normally Indian Crow. This is not to say that examples were never dressed using Indian crow, but that if they were they were likely to be 'specials' using the diminishing stocks of feathers held for tying the classic fully dressed salmon flies. All the evidence suggests that the every day fishing flies were tied using the dyed pheasant neck feathers, as mentioned above. Indian crow was specified for the veilings on E.C. Heaney's Secret Weapon and it is also possible that this caused the confusion with Curry's Shrimp. If we wish to remain true to the original when tying modern versions of Curry's Red Shrimp, the veilings should also be dyed crimson rather than the scarlet usually quoted.

Curry's Gold Shrimp - Original dressing

Curry's Gold Shrimp (as given by E. J. Malone)

An interesting point, which has some relevance to the chapter on North America, is the tale of how this pattern crossed the Atlantic during the Second World War to Nova Scotia in Canada via British submarine crews from Northern Ireland. It is not absolutely certain that this story is true, but certainly the Curry's Shrimp was known in Canada

at quite an early date and is mentioned in *Atlantic Salmon Flies and Fishing* by Col. J. D. Bates.

Pat Curry's original Gold Shrimp has a yellow golden pheasant rump feather for a tail. Both sections of the body are of broad oval gold tinsel in touching turns and the centre and front hackles are golden olive. From this example there seems little doubt that oval gold tinsel is correct for the body, and not silver as has often been given in later dressings. In the example, tied by Curry himself, there is again no attempt to imitate Indian Crow for the veilings. The veilings are pheasant neck feathers dyed golden olive to match the hackles.

Although Curry himself liked and used the original dressing, some of his customers preferred an orange hackle in the middle and a red breast feather as the tail. Others wanted the standard red tail and two orange hackles. This version is the most used today. According to our evidence, provided by Curry's fishing partners and contemporaries, Curry was perfectly happy to tie variants if his customers wanted them.

Curry's Blue Shrimp (E. J. Malone)

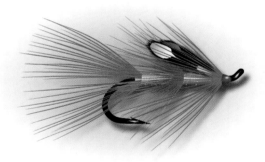

A little known early shrimp fly is the Curry's Blue Shrimp which is given in E.J. Malone's *Irish Trout & Salmon Flies*. According to Malone, this fly was devised by Joseph Curry, Pat Curry's brother. Despite the fact that it is not widely known, it is one of the most successful flies for the river Finn in County Donegal where a particular shade of rich blue is used for the centre hackle.

E.C. Heaney, also known as Clarkey Heaney, was an angler from the Faughan Valley and in August 1940 he first used a fly called the Secret Weapon. The Secret Weapon is similar to Curry's Red Shrimp but Heaney always maintained that he

developed it while completely unaware of Curry's fly. He does, however, say that he was influenced by the Bug. Heaney's fly uses yellow floss on the body instead of red floss but otherwise is very similar to Curry's Red shrimp. The veilings on the original Secret Weapon were Indian crow, later becoming either orange or red hackle points or swan strips. The Secret Weapon with the red veilings later became known as the Jock Scott Shrimp, no doubt due to its yellow and black body. Two well known variants emerged from the Jock Scott Shrimp: the Colonel Cristie and the Ghost Shrimp. The Colonel Cristie is identical to the Jock Scott Shrimp, other than that the veilings are yellow instead of red. The Ghost Shrimp has orange veilings and the centre hackle is white rather than badger. The Ghost Shrimp is a very effective fly for bright days and is an excellent fly for fresh run grilse at any time.

Secret Weapon (Heaney)

Ghost Shrimp

In *Irish Trout & Salmon Flies*, E.J. Malone gives several shrimp patterns, most of which are no longer commonly used. These flies are nevertheless of historical interest and, given the right conditions, could still be effective. The Dancer Shrimp is a case in point. This dark fly which was often tied

Judy of the Bogs

Dancer Shrimp

Kingfisher Shrimp

Bessie Bell

Gold Shrimp

Grey Thunder Shrimp

PLATE 6: Shrimp Flies from E. J. Malone

by Rogan's during the 70s is predominantly claret in colour, relieved only by veilings of yellow toucan.

Judy of the Bogs is an odd mixture of styles. The tail is unusual in that it consists of a wound grey heron feather combined with a golden pheasant topping dyed orange. The front hackle is of soft hen, so as to give maximum mobility.

The Bessie Bell is also known as the Purple Tailed Shrimp. The colour combination of a white rear body, old gold front body and purple tail is quite unusual. This might well be worth a try when

everything else has been tried, the fish certainly won't have seen anything similar.

The Grey Thunder Shrimp is noted as a personal dressing from Malone. The body colours of the fly are dark, the grey refers to the front hackle of duck flank.

It is important to realise that in the early days of their use, the traditional style of shrimp fly was fished on ungreased silk lines, in other words sunk. The modern equivalent would be intermediate or slow sinking lines such as a Wet Cel 1. As the fly was sunk, skating was not a problem and the large front hackle probably helped create water disturbance to flutter the tail. Over the years many new patterns in this style emerged and minor changes to the style occurred. Veilings were moved from the sides to top and bottom and swan strips were often used. Jungle cock was often used as cheeks or eyes as well as roofed. Jungle cock wings were often tied in a 'V' formation rather than roofed and this became standard after the emergence of trebles in the 1970s. This style of winging was often referred to as 'split winging' as the tips were not stuck together as in roofed jungle cock.

Shrimps tied in the traditional manner are still the standard fly in Northern Ireland where most of the fishing is with sinking, intermediate or sink tip lines for large summer and autumn salmon or late summer grilse during spates. Larger sizes are generally used for autumn fishing and on flies of size No.6 and upwards, tails are often tied using two feathers in order to maintain the proportion of the fly. During summer spates, the traditional dressing style serves very well.

With easier travelling for salmon angling, the decline of summer and autumn salmon stocks in the north, the popularity of smaller trebles and the more frequent use of shrimps with the floating line, changes were made to the traditional styles. Anglers travelling to the west for summer grilse fishing were often fishing over earlier runs of spring salmon and grilse in low water conditions with the floating line. The standard patterns used in the north, while fine in normal water or spate conditions, would often not be effective during prolonged periods of low water. Finer, sparser tyings were called for. Smaller sizes of shrimp fly would be used and the sparser styles of dressing

and patterns emerged in the west of Ireland as they became necessary. An overly large front hackle would often be undesirable or unnecessary. Fur bodies would be tied much slimmer or changed to floss. Following these tendencies, two main styles of adaptation emerged from the traditional patterns: the Paddy Bonner style and the Robert Gillespie style.

Paddy Bonner is a professional flytyer from Northern Ireland and is a very experienced and successful salmon angler. In his adaptation of the traditional style, Bonner usually dispensed with veilings completely. The hackles on his shrimp flies are soft genetic saddles and are kept smaller than on traditional tyings. The front hackle is still larger than the middle hackle, but only slightly so. Although both hackles are smaller, the mobility of the fly is actually increased as both hackles can work independently without the front hackle masking the middle hackle. Bonner's flies are mainly tied on trebles and almost always use floss for the bodies. Instead of two jungle cock wings, he uses a single jungle cock feather folded and tied on top in the centre. When tying cheeks or eyes, two jungle cock feathers are still used. The bodies of Paddy Bonner's flies are divided half and half, as were the traditional tyings. Paddy has three significant, well-proven flies in the traditional Irish shrimp style to his credit: the Finn Gold Shrimp, the Red and Gold Shrimp and the Silver Shrimp.

Finn Gold Shrimp (Bonner)

Irish shrimp flies are one of the most effective types of fly for use in coloured water, particularly peat stained water where there is colour, but no muddy sediment. The general construction of an

Silver Shrimp (Bonner)

Red & Gold Shrimp (Bonner)

Irish shrimp gives a much better image in peat stained conditions than hairwing patterns and Irish shrimps can be recommended for these conditions everywhere, not just in Ireland. One of the best examples of a fly which excels in peat stained water is the Finn Gold Shrimp.

There are two variants to the traditional style developed by Robert. Firstly, the front hackle size was reduced so that the two hackles were of equal size and both were small so enabling the two hackles to work independently of each other in the water. This progressed to a style in which a larger hackle was used in the middle and a smaller hackle at the front, in effect swapping the traditional style around. This proved to be very successful as the fly was even more streamlined. In this style, the rear body is made slightly longer than the front body in approximately a 3/5 to 2/5 ratio. Fur is still used if it is specified in the dressing, but it is finely dubbed. Veilings top and bottom on both front and rear bodies are also retained on those patterns requiring them. Jungle cock wings in either roofed or 'V'

form are retained but often cheeks or eyes, tied over the front hackle, replace the wings. Both the Bonner and Gillespie styles retain a wound tail of soft mobile fibres, which is considered vitally important in creating an effective shrimp fly.

Most of the modifications mentioned above reduced the overall bulk and water resistance of the shrimp flies, making them more suitable for low water or floating line fishing. The extra mobility provided by distinctly separating the two hackles proved more effective in low water than simply miniaturizing a traditionally proportioned shrimp. The styles not only proved very effective when a slimmer fly was essential ,but remained as effective as flies tied in the traditional proportions in all water conditions. Many Irish shrimp flies are now tied in Robert's style not only because they are very effective, but also because his style of fly was prominently featured in Peter O'Reilly's *Trout and Salmon Flies of Ireland*. Robert is happy to use the older traditional style for sunk line or lough fishing and uses his own styles or Paddy Bonner's style for low water summer or floating line fishing.

Robert has also popularized the use of some very effective patterns such as the Foxford or Fiery Brown Shrimp, Ballina Grey Shrimp, Faughan Shrimp (dark) and White Shrimp, that otherwise would have remained largely unknown. These flies are particularly effective on the River Moy, Robert's home waters, but have been used throughout Ireland with success.

The most popular of these is the Foxford Shrimp. This is a pattern of subdued but rich colouring, being predominantly black and fiery brown. The Foxford Shrimp has proved itself to be one of the great all-round flies.

It is effective in spate conditions, low, clear water and in heavily coloured water in the late season. It takes fresh fish, jaded resident fish and will produce fish when little else will. Truly a fly for all seasons. We consider that the colour of the front body and hackle are most important. We would recommend anybody who wishes to tie this fly to obtain materials from Ireland which are dyed the correct colours. A superb range of dubbings in the true Irish colours, developed by Frankie McPhillips is now available from a range of suppliers. The use of fiery brown goes back deep

Foxford Shrimp

Faughan Shrimp

Ballina Grey Shrimp

White Shrimp

PLATE 7: Irish Shrimps popularized by Robert Gillespie on the Moy

into the tradition of Irish salmon angling. Michael Rogan, of Ballyshannon, was renowned for producing this colour in a way that no other fly tyer could. It is said that he used donkey's urine in the dying process to obtain the richness of colour. The process may have been welcomed by anglers, what his neighbours thought about it is less clear! The use of rich, glowing colours has always been a feature of Irish salmon flies, giving them a unique appearance unlike flies from any other country. For those interested, we would refer you to *Irish Trout & Salmon Flies* by E. J. Malone. A series of plates of superb flies tied by Frankie McPhillips shows these colours perfectly.

The Ballina Grey Shrimp is named for the town of Ballina on the River Moy, home of the world famous Ridge Pool. The fly is particularly successful here and on the lower tidal stretches and is regarded as one of the best flies to use on dull, rainy days.

The Faughan Shrimp is a fly used often on the River Moy, particularly on the Swinford stretch. It is generally at its best on dull days and is regarded as a spring fly par excellence for resident fish and is just as effective in this role later in the summer and autumn.

The White Shrimp is unusual in appearance and probably owes its success to this fact - fish are unlikely to have seen anything similar. It can be successful at all times of the year and in all water conditions. Its advocates regard this fly as absolutely deadly for fresh run fish. We would recommend that all anglers have one of these in their box. Try it as a total change when other flies have failed. First tied by Eddie Doherty, of Ballina, with a yellow hackle, this fly first proved its effectiveness when a fly with defective dying caused the colour to leech away, leaving the hackle white. After this somewhat fortuitous discovery new versions were purposely tied with white or cream

Agivey Wye Bug #1

Agivey Wye Bug #2

Agivey Wye Bug #3

Agivey Wye Bug #4

Agivey Wye Bug #5

PLATE 8: Agivey Wye Bugs

hackles and proved to be much more effective than the original yellow version.

Apart from Curry's Red Shrimp and the Secret Weapon, the Agivey Wye Bug was one of the most important early shrimp patterns. Unfortunately, the origins of this pattern are not known, except for the fact that it was developed on the River Agivey. The name Wye Bug tends to indicate that it was derived from the Welsh Wye Grub,

although the tying is far more reminiscent of the Usk Grub. We feel sure that this was simply a case of mis-identification of the original pattern and that the Usk Grub is the true forerunner.

A whole family of dressings have developed from the original, each of which are simply known by a number. Taken as a group, the Agivey Wye Bugs are probably the most widely used shrimp patterns in Ireland. The Agivey Wye Bug #I is

generally accepted as the original pattern. The Agivey Wye Bug #2 is popular in Northern Ireland. Number 3 has a non-standard body in that it has no divisions. Together with the #5 it is popular in the west of Ireland. The version most commonly available as a commercial tying is the #4 and is probably the most widely used for this reason. The Donegal Wye Bug is yet another variant from the same stable. It is essentially the same as the Agivey Wye Bug #1, except that there are red veilings over the rear body.

McHaffie Wye Bug #1

McHaffie Wye Bug #2

Donegal Wye Bug

An important variant of the Wye Bug from Robert McHaffie is very similar to Lionel Sweet's version of the Usk Grub. This fly has a body which is red at the rear and black at the front. The centre hackle is of orange over white and the front hackle is hen furnace or dark Greenwell's over orange. It is very popular throughout Northern Ireland. Another of Robert's patterns is the McHaffie Wye Bug which has a rear body of orange seal's fur and a front body of black seal's fur. The centre hackle is orange and the front hackle is red game over orange.

Before looking at the next groups of flies, it may well help the reader if we give an explanation of the Foyle, one of the major river systems of Northern Ireland, because it can be rather confusing. The main system is generally known as the Foyle system, the confusion arises because the main freshwater length of the parent river is called the Mourne, the name Foyle being reserved for the lower tidal stretches and Lough Foyle into which it decants. The rivers Roe and Faughan, which are considered as part of the Foyle system, also decant into Lough Foyle.

The Foyle system was once the most prolific salmon system in Ireland (and thus, probably one of the best in the world) and was known as the Spey of Ireland. Stories are legendary of its fly fishing for spring fish, large grilse and autumn salmon, particularly in the 50s and 60s. These huge runs were largely destroyed by drift netting in the 1970s. Those that experienced its heyday, experienced some of the best Atlantic salmon fishing ever seen. One angler from Newton Stewart is said to have taken 830 fish to the fly in one season. Although only a shadow of its former self, good fishing for large fish is still to be had on occasion.

Note that the fishing in this area is not typical of that in the rest of Ireland. Fishing with shrimp flies here is mainly done towards the back end of the season, often in heavy water conditions with a sinking line. for large fish generally between 3.5 to 7.5 kg (10 to 16 lb). The flies tend to be tied in larger sizes, certainly larger than the size tens and twelves used for the west coast grilse fisheries. The bodies are normally of seal's fur, whatever the size of the fly.

A very distinctive group of patterns is that of the Mourne shrimps. All of these dressings are charac-

Mourne Claret Shrimp

Mourne Orange & Gold Shrimp

Mourne Purple & Gold Shrimp

Mourne Red Shrimp

PLATE 9: Mourne Shrimps

terized by the use of richly coloured seal's fur for the bodies and differently coloured ribbings at the front and rear. Some of the colours used in these patterns are more subdued than other shrimps, particularly the reds and oranges. This does not seem to reduce their effectiveness. and they are amongst the most beautiful of all the Irish shrimps. The Mourne Purple and Gold Shrimp is a great fly for late running fish and may well be of interest to steelhead fishermen. The Mourne Claret Shrimp is particularly dark in colour and is a fly for clear water conditions. The Mourne Red Shrimp has the dark red preferred by the Mourne anglers to the bright reds used in other shrimp patterns. The colour of the body and middle hackle is really a ruby wine red. This is a killing pattern on the Mourne, but has also worked well throughout Ireland, Scotland and England.

The Mourne Red Shrimp is an original dressing by professional fly tyer Joe McDonald of Co. Tyrone and has been around and remained effective for a long time. Joe has been dressing flies for over fifty years and has been responsible for a whole range of successful shrimp flies which we have illustrated in Plate 9.

The Mourne Gold Shrimp was first tied about 1955 when Joe worked for White Bros. in Omagh. The fly was one of the first tinsel bodied shrimp flies and the gold and orange colour combination has remained popular to this day. The front hackle is a special brown, achieved first by dying an off-white hackle red and then brown. The Mourne Gold is effective for a wide range of rivers, from the Finn, the Mourne and the Foyle to the Moy. It works at all times of the year in both low and high water conditions. Fishermen have been known to

Mourne Gold Shrimp

Mourne Silver Shrimp

Purple Shrimp #1

Purple Shrimp #2

Donegal Blue Shrimp

Lemon Grey Shrimp

Purgatory Shrimp

The Bishop

Paddy Shrimp

Rat Shrimp

PLATE 10: Joe McDonald Patterns from Northern Ireland

take 40 or 50 fish per season with this fly. This fly is also known as the Gold Bug.

Joe considers the Mourne Silver Shrimp to be his best all round fly. It can be fished successfully in any water and has taken hundreds of fish all over Ireland. It can be tied as large as a size 2 and as small as size 16. A fly which every fisherman in Ireland should have in his box.

The Purple Shrimp was developed by Joe from the Purple Peewit, an old classic salmon fly from the Mourne which was dressed by Rogans. The dressing of this fly varies in the winging but all versions have a body of purple floss. The Purple Shrimp is at its best for resident fish, particularly in the late season.

A second version of the Purple Shrimp has a purple tail hackle, a purple head and winging of jungle cock which has been dyed fiery brown. This version is recommended for low water and has been particularly effective on the rivers Strule, Derg and Glenelly.

The Donegal Blue Shrimp was originally tied by Joe about ten years ago for the River Dearg and other Donegal rivers. The fly came about because seatrout fishermen, using the Donegal Blue seatrout fly, were taking lots of salmon. Its use has now spread to many other rivers including the Finn, Mourne, Faughan and Roe. It is a great fly for fresh run fish and is particularly good in low water conditions when tied in sizes 10 to 16. An alternative tying, nearer to the original, would have a black head hackle rather than white badger.

The Lemon Grey Shrimp is Joe's derivation from the old Irish classic Lemon Grey salmon fly which dates back to around 1830. With its muted body tones of grey and grizzle it is not a fly which hits you in the eye. This, however, does not seem to deter the salmon. A good fly all year round, it is at its best when the water has a bit of colour. As a contrast we have a Spey style version of the Lemon Grey (also shown) which originates from the west coast of North America

The Purgatory Shrimp was designed as a fly for spring fish and has proved to be effective and popular on the rivers Finn and Mourne. It also fishes well for grilse in high water conditions and may be tied as large as a size 2.

The Paddy Shrimp is a very recent pattern

based upon the old Irish fly called the Fenian. It is used on the rivers Derg and Mourne and also on the Moy at Foxford. It is a good fly for spring fish.

Lemon Grey Spey

The Bishop fishes well in both high and low water conditions. In low water, the smaller sizes are recommended. The Bishop has proved to be very effective on the Mourne, the Strule, the Glenelly and the Finn.

The Rat Shrimp is a low water fly for small rivers such as the Drowes, Glenelly or Derg. It is normally tied in sizes from ten down to sixteen, the smaller the better.

Irish General Practitioner

The River Mourne is also the home of the Irish General Practitioner, a variant of the standard G.P. which we consider to be more effective than the original. It combines the main features of the G.P. with a typical Irish shrimp tail of wound golden pheasant breast feather. For smaller sized flies, the body may be tied in one piece, rather than being jointed. The fly illustrated is tied in hot orange, a colour considered at its best in coloured water conditions or for fresh run fish. More often the fly is tied with body and hackles of fiery brown,

claret or golden olive, which are held to be more effective for resident fish and for clear water conditions. Maybe there is a tip here for anglers in North America looking for a change of pace from the more usual orange and black variants. Having seen the number of G.P. variants in use in North America and knowing their effectiveness for steelhead, we think that this fly should be of interest to all steelhead fishermen.

A point of interest is the number of successful shrimp patterns that are dressed in relatively sombre colours. As the season progresses, it is noticeable that many of the most widely successful shrimp patterns tend to be dressed with dark reds rather than fire-engine bright reds and burnt orange rather than hot orange.

Their more flashy relatives obviously have their place in particular water conditions and at particular times of year, but at other times the more sober dressings seem to have the edge. The Foxford Shrimp being a very good example of a sombrely coloured fly that nevertheless shines (both literally and figuratively) in coloured water conditions. Perhaps this is an indication that the underwater visibility of a fly is perceived quite differently by a salmon - many anglers believe that a black fly shows up particularly well in dirty water conditions. The evidence offered by the dark claret flies of the Foyle system and the dark purple flies of the west coast steelhead fisheries of North America would seem to support this view.

Scientific evidence has been offered that the colour vision of salmon alters with the length of time that they have spent in fresh water. The longer they spend in the river, the less they are able to see the greener, lighter colours. In other words, resident fish will be more likely to take flies dressed in the sombre colours towards the red end of the spectrum. This can be important as the season develops and the number of resident fish grows proportionally larger as a percentage of the total salmon population in the river. The fact that the brighter patterns tend do well in the first half of the season and again from September onwards may be connected with the fact that on many rivers the salmon tend to enter in distinct runs and that at these times of year the proportion of fresh fish is at its highest.

Another shrimp fly from the same area is the Claret Shrimp, a dressing from Robert McHaffie

Claret Shrimp (McHaffie)

on the River Roe. This fly shares the same dark, rich colouring which is to be found in the Mourne Shrimps. Seal's fur should always be used for the body segments, even when the fly is tied in small sizes.

The Claret Shrimp is successful for both fresh and resident fish, at all times of the season and in all conditions. Peter O'Reilly notes that it is particularly effective on rainy days with flashes of sunshine. Robert considers this fly to be probably the best of all claret shrimp patterns and it is certainly the most popular.

Another extremely popular claret fly is Howard's Claret Shrimp, also from the River Roe. First tied by Howard Reilly, this fly is also very well used on the River Moy. The fly is particularly effective in autumn, and excels in peaty water. The dark bulk of the fly is relieved by oversized wings of jungle cock, making the fly extremely visible even in dark water conditions. The front hackling on the fly illustrated is of hair, but feather hackle may also be used.

Howard's Claret Shrimp (Reilly)

Both of these flies were popularised by Robert McHaffie who is a well respected fly tyer

from the Foyle system and who has had a considerable influence in the development of Irish shrimps. Apart from his own patterns he was also one of the pioneers of the short dressed low water patterns, for which he coined the term 'within the hook'. This style, where the tail is moved forward to the centre joint is the basis of the low water patterns from Albert Atkins which are discussed below.

The Faughan Dark Shrimp has been widely popularized by Robert throughout the west of Ireland, particularly on the River Moy. A lighter version of the Faughan Shrimp is very popular on the River Roe as well as more generally throughout the Foyle system. This is one of the few Irish shrimp patterns that does not use jungle cock as a wing, the front veiling or wing being of golden pheasant tippet. The Faughan Light Shrimp is at its most effective towards the back end of the season.

Faughan Shrimp Light

The River Bann in Northern Ireland is the home of two patterns that have proved to be successful in a wide range of conditions.

The Bann Special originated on the Carnroe beat of the lower Bann. It is regarded by many anglers as one of the most effective of all shrimps for fresh grilse, perhaps bettered only by the Glenties Shrimp. The Bann Special can be used throughout the season, in all types of water conditions for both fresh and resident fish. In recent times the fly is often tied without the jungle cock and with a red head. The Bann Special is a most popular shrimp on rivers as varied as the Cork Blackwater and the Moy. The Orange & Gold shrimp is a significant variant of the Bann Special

which has become a very popular fly in its own right (see page 46).

Bann Special Shrimp

The second pattern, the Claret Tail Bann Special, is very similar except that the tail of golden pheasant red breast feather is dyed claret. The body is always tied in floss rather than seal's fur, exactly the opposite as for the normal Bann Special. The claret tail version is ideally suited to a spate river or for jaded and sullen back-end fish. It is one of the best shrimp flies when tied in the low-water version and fished in slow pools by stripping back across the current. Peter O'Reilly records that this fly once took twelve salmon for one angler in one afternoon.

Claret Tail Bann Special Shrimp
tied low-water style

One of the main low water styles of dressing is shown in the illustration above. Firstly, the fly is tied on a low water iron, most usually on a double hook. The tail will usually consist of a bunch of hackle fibres tied above and below the hook shank, or it will be wound very sparsely. The body will usually retain the standard colours, tied in two joints, as in the fully dressed fly, but the material will normally be slimly tied floss. The centre and

front hackles will not be wound but are tied beard-style with bunches of hackle fibres above and below the hook shank. The winging is reduced to one jungle cock feather which is normally split into several sections using a needle. These are tied in as a bunch, under the hackle.

Albert Atkins is a well known commercial fly tyer from Northern Ireland. He has been responsible for a wide range of shrimp patterns for rivers such as the Roe, Faughan and Bush. Albert also produces a range of low water patterns which use a slightly different style of dressing, as shown in Plate 12. In this style the centre hackle disappears and the tail, which is tied more sparsely than usual, is moved forwards and tied in at the centre joint. In the last two examples in the plate, the tail is reduced even further to just four strands of Krystal Flash. We have illustrated the patterns that Albert supplies most often to his customers, but this technique could be applied to any of the Irish shrimps. This style of low water dressing was originally popularised by Robert McHaffie.

This style of dressing can also be seen in a shrimp pattern given by John Todd in the December 1994 issue of *Trout & Salmon*. This fly has proved to be effective on rivers such as the Lower Bann.

Todd's Shrimp

Irish shrimps can also be dressed, as droppers as shown in the illustration below. The fly is tied on a low water hook, usually a double. The tail consists of a bunch of hackle fibres tied above the hook shank rather than being wound as a hackle. The body will usually retain the standard colours, tied in two joints, as in the fully dressed fly, but will normally be of floss. If there are two different hackle colours in the original fly, hackles of both

these colours will normally be tied in at the head, but far more swept back and shorter than would normally be the case.

Claret Tail Bann Special Shrimp
tied dropper style

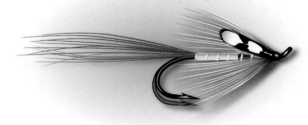

It probably won't have escaped your notice that flies tied in this manner have more than a passing resemblance to the form of the Ally's Shrimp. Curiously, flies like this were never developed in Ireland for use in fast water conditions.

Many of the following group of flies are either Albert's own inventions or they are flies which he has popularized through his fly tying business. An interesting point about Albert's shrimp patterns is that he rarely uses jungle cock eyes or wings on them. The strong colours and also the use of sparkle material in Albert's flies may have much to do with the fact that many of his flies are designed for use on the Lower Bann. This part of the river flows from Lough Neagh and for long periods in the summer is subject to a fine green algal bloom. This means that effective patterns are needed which rely on their intrinsic colour combinations to stand out in the water. There is, of course, no reason why jungle cock eyes cannot be added to these flies, the salmon, however, seem to find them quite satisfactory just as they are..

Among the most popular and widespread shrimp flies invented by Albert Atkins is the Apache Shrimp, notable for its striking use of strong primary colours.

This fly was originally used on the Lower Bann and the Lackagh rivers but has since spread all the way to the Moy and beyond. Albert has recently released a new version of this fly tied in the style of a Bonner Shadow Shrimp (see page 51). This fly promises a great deal, the Shadow

Yellow Shrimp

Apache Shrimp

Badger Shrimp

Bann Special Shrimp

Black Shrimp

Blue Shrimp

Finn Gold Shrimp

Crystal Tail Gold Shrimp

Crystal Tail Agivey Red Shrimp

PLATE 11: Low water flies from Albert Atkins

Shrimps have been extremely successful and the combination of this style of dressing with the proven track record of the Apache Shrimp should produce a fly which is very effective.

Apache Shrimp (Atkins)

Apache Shadow Shrimp (Atkins)

The Faughan Purple is a bright combination of yellow, purple, orange and red. Although the fly is called purple, only the front body is actually purple. As you can see from the illustration, the overall impression is much more of red-orange than of purple.

Faughan Purple Shrimp (Atkins)

The Roe Purple Shrimp provides an interesting contrast, combining as it does yellow and purple, with a front hackle of claret magenta. This unusual colour is obtained by dying a rich magenta over a ginger hackle which produces claret on the dark side and magenta on the light side of the hackle fibres. The effect is most interesting and

quite different to that obtained by dying a white hackle, as is normal.

Roe Purple Shrimp (Atkins)

Both the Faughan and Roe Purple flies are shrimp versions of the old fully dressed salmon flies once popular on these rivers.

The Roe Gold Shrimp is rather similar to the Mourne Gold Shrimp, but again there is a contrast in style. The Roe Gold has a bright head hackle of purple, whereas the Mourne Gold uses a more subdued brown hackle. The purple colour traditionally used on the Foyle system was produced using the old potato dye which resulted in a brilliant violet-purple rather than a dark purple. Whilst it is only speculation, it seems probable that the brighter hackle is used to give impact to the front of the fly, a function which is fulfilled by the jungle cock winging on the Mourne version.

Roe Gold Shrimp (Atkins)

The Roe Royal is a predominantly claret fly, this time combined with a hot orange middle hackle. The front hackle is also dyed claret magenta as used for the Roe Purple Shrimp, illustrated above.

Albert has also devised his own version of the perennial General Practitioner. This fly generally

Roe Royal Shrimp (Atkins)

General Practitioner (Atkins)

The Bush Special Shrimp uses a colour combination of red body with blue and hot orange hackles and is again unusual and striking.

Bush Special Shrimp (Atkins)

Atkins' Millennium Shrimp is a new fly for 2000 which has yet again an unusual combination of colours, in this case yellow and blue.

Millennium Shrimp (Atkins)

follows the style of the original but the body is a fifty-fifty mixture of magenta and orange seal's fur and the body hackling is a golden pheasant red breast feather. The tail consists of orange bucktail and a few strands of pearl Krystal Flash, veiled by a golden pheasant red breast feather. The shellback is in three sections, each of a tippet feather veiled by a red breast feather.

The Bush Red Shrimp is a variant of Curry's Red Shrimp which again hails from the Bush. Both the middle and front hackles are a combination of red and silver badger. This gives added impact to the fly but still retains the same colouration as the original. Veilings have been replaced by the red under hackles. Many anglers on the Bush prefer this fly to Curry's original.

Bush Red Shrimp

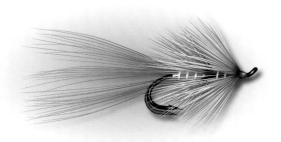

The Wheatsheaf Shrimp was devised by Frank Mullen, a fly tyer and gillie on the Carnroe beat on the River Bann. This is another fly which combines the yellow and golden colours so popular in Ireland.

Wheatsheaf Shrimp (Mullen)

Badger & Orange

Badger & Golden Olive

Badger & Red

The Badger Shrimps are a series of shrimp flies which all share the use of badger hackles at both mid-body and at the front of the fly and have no eyes or winging. They are comparatively simple to tie but are nevertheless extremely effective. All these flies are at their best in dull weather, or in a dropping spate. The colour of the badger hackle tips should be a dark cream, not white. The badger shrimps come in three colour variations: red, orange and golden olive - the colour refers to the rear body.

The Moy is one of the most prolific grilse rivers in Europe. Even in these depressed days we estimate the catch to range from 10,000 to 12,000 fish per season (the declared return is, of course, less than this). Even allowing for the fact that the

Moy is a heavily fished river, there are few other rivers in Ireland, or indeed Europe for that matter, which can offer a run of these proportions. The majority of the fish caught are small grilse in the range of 1.5 to 2.5 kg (3 to 5 lb) but larger fish up to 16lb are seen in the early spring and sometimes towards the end of the season. It should be noted that on the River Moy fish are classified as grilse if they are 3kg (7lb) or under, the length of time spent at sea is not considered. The Moy also has some other peculiarities - the river drains through two loughs and has a long tidal estuarial stretch which reaches up as far as the town of Ballina (including the famous Ridge Pool). The Moy often fishes at its best in low water conditions, and this, combined with the fact that the majority of the fish are small grilse caught in the early summer months, means that the flies used tend to be small, in the general size range of 8 to 12, most often on treble hooks. Irish shrimps are probably at their most effective in low water conditions and it is no surprise, therefore, that the vast majority of anglers fish the Moy with shrimp flies. Apart from patterns such as the Ballina Grey Shrimp, the Foxford Shrimp and the Faughan Shrimp which have been popularized by Robert, the following flies have proved effective on the Moy at different times and under different conditions.

The Black & Silver Shrimp has its origins in Northern Ireland. It is an excellent fly for fresh grilse and is known to be effective in the evening. It is useful throughout the season, but has also gained a good reputation on the lower estuary beats of the River Moy in late summer.

Black & Silver Shrimp

The Blue Shrimp, also known as the Blue Hackle Shrimp, has a blue centre hackle, in this case combined with a rear body of orange floss and a front body of black floss. It is another fly which is at its best for fresh fish. This is the fly which was used when two anglers, fishing the Ridge Pool on the Moy in 1991, took so many fish (45) in one afternoon session that the pictures in the angling press caused an immediate outcry. Be that as it may, this fly can be absolutely deadly for fresh run fish when the conditions are right.

Blue Hackle Shrimp

The Octopus Shrimp is unusual in that it was devised by a Frenchman. It is good in both in coloured and clear water conditions and is most effective for fresh fish. Peter O'Reilly reports that this fly took seventeen fish for one angler over two days of a dirty, late summer spate on the Ridge Pool when nothing else was successful.

Octopus Shrimp

The Nephin Shrimp is a simple shrimp fly with a one piece body. It is a subdued pattern which is most effective in coloured water on a bright day. The Nephin Shrimp is also used on Carrowmore Lake and the rivers of northern Mayo.

Nephin Shrimp

The Yellow Shrimp is a universally popular pattern which has a reputation as a good catcher of spring fish on the Moy, but it is also effective late in the season and at any time when the water has a peaty stain. The yellow can very from a pale lemon yellow all the way through to a deep, rich golden olive. It is important, however, that the same shade is used for both the body and hackle. Modern versions of the fly often omit the jungle cock.

Yellow Shrimp

Another popular Moy fly which shares the yellow theme is the Yellow and Silver Shrimp. This fly also takes many spring fish and is highly recommended for coloured water and bright days. Both this and the Silver Shrimp are often tied without the jungle cock.

Yellow & Silver Shrimp

The Swinford Blue Shrimp, from the late Seamus Mularkey, is named after the town of Swinford. It is an good fly for spring salmon and a great grilse fly. The blue of the front hackle can vary quite a lot depending upon the tyer. Robert prefers a medium Kingfisher blue.

Swinford Blue Shrimp

Following on with the theme of flies that are most effective in the early season, the Juner Shrimp is a pattern devised by Chris Downey of Foxford. The Juner, so called because it is most effective in June, is another excellent pattern for fresh fish, particularly in cold conditions.

Juner Shrimp

Many of the shrimp flies used in Ireland are derived or inspired by the fully dressed salmon flies of the classic era. Most of these derivations are named for their colours and thus it is not always possible to trace their parentage. There are, however, exceptions, such as the shrimp flies derived from the classic Silver Wilkinson fully dressed salmon fly.

The dark version is popular on the Moy where it has a reputation for taking fish on bright, glaring days. It is not a fly that is widely used in other areas. The lighter version is better known and used throughout Ireland. This fly has proved to be an all round pattern, effective in most conditions, particularly for fresher fish, on bright days, or when there is a bit of colour in the water. .

Dark Wilkinson

Light Wilkinson

Quinn Shrimp

Gold Wilkinson

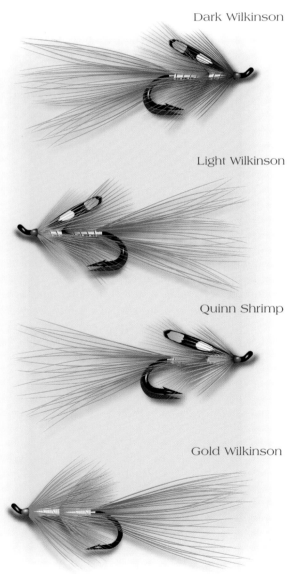

The Gold Wilkinson is a pattern from Albert Atkins, in Northern Ireland. This fly is a combina-

tion of blue and gold, with a front hackle of hot orange. The Gold Wilkinson is popular in the north on rivers such as the Roe but has not spread to the west of Ireland. The Quinn Shrimp, which is given in *Irish Trout & Salmon Flies* by E.J. Malone is another derivation which is quite clearly from the same source. The Quinn Shrimp is not widely used these days, the Light Wilkinson being preferred.

A more widely used version of the Quinn Shrimp has a magenta hackle at the centre and a magenta hackle with badger over at the front. The rear veilings of bright blue hackle tips are dispensed with. This fly is used on both the river Moy and Mourne.

Magenta Shrimp

The Golden Olive Shrimp comes in two forms: one with a body of silver tinsel and one with a body of golden olive seal's fur. The silver bodied version is preferred for clear water and bright days. Both of these flies are extremely effective in the early season. Note that on the silver bodied version, the tail consists of the yellow rump feather of the golden pheasant rather than the red breast feather used on the vast majority of the Irish shrimp flies. Obtaining long feathers of this type is a problem when tying flies in the larger sizes.

Quinn Shrimp - modern

The Purple Bug is a late summer and autumn fly for clear water conditions. When tied in larger sizes, veilings of hackle tips or calf hair are often tied in above and below the body. They may be the same colour as the centre hackle or a complementary colour such as red or hot orange. Red veilings, as illustrated, are particularly effective.

The Gold Bug is a fly for coloured water at any time of the season. A teal breast feather with one dark eye marking, as illustrated, may be used for winging as an alternative to jungle cock. The colour of the gold tinsel used on these flies can vary quite a lot. Paddy Bonner uses a darker shade of old gold tinsel, on many of his flies and reports that it can often be more effective than the lighter tinsel colours.

The Magenta Shrimp is another fly which excels in bright weather. Peter O'Reilly reports that this fly once took nineteen fish from one pool on a bright, windy day. An excellent pattern which should always be in your fly box.

Golden Olive Shrimp

Golden Olive Shrimp - silver body

Orange & Gold Shrimp   Donegal Purple & Gold Shrimp

Purple & Gold Shrimp   Red & Gold Shrimp

Gold Bug   Purple Bug

PLATE 12: Gold bodied shrimps

The next group of shrimps, shown in Plate 12, are variations on a gold theme. The construction of these flies varies somewhat, but one common feature is that at least one part of the body consists of gold tinsel. Many of these flies do not have jungle cock, either as eyes or wings.

The Orange & Gold Shrimp is regarded as a super spate river fly which suits faster water flows because of its slim, heavy body. The orange/gold colouration really glows in peaty water conditions. A good all round fly, effective for both fresh and resident fish. The Orange & Copper Shrimp is identical, except that the gold tinsel is replaced throughout by copper tinsel. Although copper tinsel is not often used, there are those who think that it can be even more effective than gold, particularly on extremely bright days when gold may be too garish. The fact that it is not more popular may be due to nothing more than that it is often difficult to obtain.

The Purple & Gold Shrimp is regarded as a late season fly which will take stubborn fish in

difficult conditions. A version from Co. Donegal has a red front body and red head. Russell Whiteman, the well known fly caster and gillie from Derry, prefers this fly and considers that it is better for fresh fish whilst being just as effective for resident fish.

The Red & Gold Shrimp has a shorter one piece body and a double hackle at the front. Red hackle tip veilings are usually tied in above and below the body. It is held by its adherents to be irrisistable to late-running fish. It is at its best on dull days but is just as effective in clear as well as coloured water.

The next very popular fly is simply called the Shrimp Fly. This is confusing because anglers tend to call any shrimp pattern a shrimp fly. Nevertheless, this is a particular pattern which is an excellent all-round fly. It is effective when the water has a dark peat stain and also has a good reputation for difficult fish.

Shrimp Fly

The Easkey Gold Shrimp is named after the Easkey River in Co. Sligo. It is another gold bodied shrimp with orange hackles that excels in the spate rivers and when there is a bit of colour in the water, as do many other patterns with this colouration.

Easkey Gold Shrimp

County Donegal has a rich history of fly development and it is no surprise, therefore, that a whole range of shrimp flies has its origin in this beautiful region.

The Owenea Shrimp, as the name suggests, hails from the Owenea River. The configuration of this fly is slightly unusual because the tail is tied in at the middle joint rather than at the rear of the fly (see also Todd's Shrimp on page 40 for another fly tied in this manner). The veiling of the tail feather over the rear gold body gives a most interesting effect. A variant has a tail of dyed orange hackle.

Owenea Shrimp

The Glenties Shrimp is named after the town of Glenties on the River Owenea. This is one of the very best shrimp flies, excelling in peaty water conditions and is considered by Robert to be the best Irish shrimp fly of all. Although it is not so widespread as the Bann Special Shrimp, this is primarily because of the difficulties for commercial fly dressers (the tail feathers are dyed and there is a double hackle at the head). To those anglers in the know, it is the preferred fly and one never to be without. The secret is out!

Glenties Shrimp

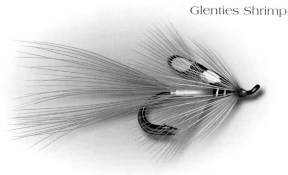

John O'Donnell from Glenties was the originator of the John Anthony Shrimp. During his lifetime he was probably the most successful angler on the Owenea River and this was his favourite fly, taking the majority of the thousands of fish that he caught in his career. The John Anthony is one of those unusual patterns that look totally nondescript in the hand, but which are absolute killers in the water. It has proved to be very effective for those anglers who have been confident enough to use it, despite its lack of any outstanding features.

The fly has also been effective on the Moy, where it continues to catch fish. An early variant of this fly from John Anthony was identical except that the rear body was of oval gold tinsel. A later variant has a tail of purple dyed, golden pheasant red breast feather and a rear body of embossed gold or silver tinsel.

John Anthony - original

John Anthony - variant

The Roy Wilson Shrimp is a modern Northern Ireland pattern devised by Roy Wilson. With its bright, fresh colours it is well suited to low water flows on bright days and is primarily a fly for spring fish and fresh run grilse. The tail on this fly is a wound cock hackle and is not as long as tails made from golden pheasant feathers. This is no great disadvantage because the fly is normally tied small, sizes 8 to 12 being typical. The front hackle is normally made longer so as to blend in with the yellow fibres of the centre hackle. It is now one of the most popular flies on the river Moy.

Roy Wilson Shrimp

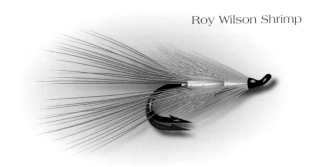

Shrimp flies in Ireland have seen a rapid and continuing state of development in recent times, mainly by varying the proportions, the introduction of modern synthetic materials and the trend towards using hair for tails. The newer patterns have mostly emerged from the west of Ireland or from anglers or tyers from the north who have experimented and fished in the west. They have been designed mainly as flies for summer grilse fishing, although they also adapt well to larger sizes.

Amongst those worthy of note are the range of patterns devised by Michael Roulston of Easkey, Co. Sligo. These include McCormick's Folly (also known as the Claret Coolraw Killer or McCormick's Shrimp), the Red Peacock Shrimp and the Yellow Peacock shrimp. More slimly dressed than the traditional Irish shrimp and using bucktail for the tail, the last two of these flies also make good use of the blue neck feathers from the peacock as veilings. It is surprising that so little use is made of these feathers in other salmon flies. These flies are designed for use on the Easky, which is a spate river, and are generally at their most effective from summer through to autumn in peaty, coloured waters. They are usually tied small and sparse.

McCormick's Folly or Claret Coolraw Killer

Red Peacock Shrimp

Yellow Peacock Shrimp

The history of McCormick's Folly is extremely interesting as it is one of the few flies whose ancestry can be traced with a degree of certainty. In this case we can trace the development through each stage of a series of six flies. The story starts with the Parson Shrimp (Figure 1 of Plate 13, page 50). This fly, which is documented by E.J. Malone in *Irish Trout and Salmon Flies,* is basically a yellow shrimp. The only unusual features are the cheeks of kingfisher feathers. Being composed of hen hackle, the tail of this fly was usually fairly short due to the difficulty of obtaining long hen hackles. A variant of this fly, ribbed with silver tinsel rather than gold and without the cheeks, was popular on the Moy around 1994 and was fished with some success by Eddie Preston of Co. Down (Plate 13, Figure 2). A friend of Eddie's, Stephen Bailie, tied a further variant of this fly (Figure 3). In this version, yellow dyed squirrel hair was substituted for the hen

hackle in the tail and was further enhanced by the addition of six or eight strands of Krystal Flash, tied in under the squirrel hair. Most significantly the body material was changed to wound yellow ostrich herl. This last alteration seemed to make the fly much more effective. The next stage was the addition of an orange hackle wound over the front yellow hackle (Figure 4). This fly became known as the Coolraw Killer, so named after the pool on the Moy on which it was first regularly used. In order to make this pattern suitable for faster water flows a further variant used a longer tail (Figure 5). The last stage was the addition of a long wound Chinese hackle to the tail, in other words a combination of both hair and hackle. The body was changed to floss and divided into two sections and the hackles were moved so that the yellow hackle was now between the body segments, the orange hackle being retained at the head. In this form (Figure 6) the fly is known as the Long Coolraw Killer. With the McCormick's Folly, the fly retains the identical dressing details of the Coolraw Killer except that all the yellow elements are changed to claret and the ribbing is changed to gold. A popular variant of McCormick's Folly, uses gold Krystal Flash in the tail and has a front hackle of orange dyed badger.

For a new shrimp pattern to raise an eyebrow in Northern Ireland, which is serious shrimp fly country, it needs to be something very special indeed. This happened with the introduction of a range of new shrimp flies called Shadow Shrimps, developed in Northern Ireland by the well known fly tyer, Paddy Bonner of Co. Tyrone, and first introduced in 1997. We regard these new flies as probably the most effective and important shrimp patterns yet developed in Ireland and believe that they will prove to be just as successful in other countries.

The background to their development can be traced back many years to Ireland's most famous salmon fishery at Ballina, Co. Mayo – the renowned Ridge Pool on the River Moy. Before this fishery was bought by the Irish government it was owned by the Moy Fishery Company. Fishermen, like Paddy, who were privileged to fish it during that period had the opportunity to experience fishing a pool which was ideally suited to the

1 - Parsons Shrimp

2 - Moy variant

3 - Yellow Coolraw Killer

4 - Orange Coolraw Killer

5 - Long tailed variant

6 - Long Coolraw Killer

PLATE 13: Parsons Shrimp to Coolraw Killer

fly and during periods of low water was stocked with a head of fish unheard of elsewhere. This gave Paddy an almost unique opportunity to study the reaction of fish to various types of fly in varying water levels. The Shadow Shrimps are the culmination of many hundreds of hours of such study and experimentation, brought together with the experience of mobile materials gained by Paddy whilst making fox winged tube flies for customers in Norway.

In the last two seasons these flies have come to prominence simply because of the astounding success that they have had on Irish rivers. Three Shadow Shrimps in particular have achieved almost legendary status on the Mourne in Northern Ireland, and on the Moy in the west of Ireland where they have caught incredible numbers of fish. These are the Red and Gold Shadow Shrimp, the Orange and Gold Shadow Shrimp and the Silver Shadow Shrimp. Shadow Shrimps have also taken salmon on the Spey up to 24lb, on the Tyne up to 22lb and were used with exceptional success in Iceland in small sizes, particularly in low, clear water conditions.

These shrimp patterns are very important because they work well in fast, heavy water,

Finn Shadow Shrimp   Blue & Silver Shadow Shrimp

Orange & Gold Shadow Shrimp   Red & Gold Shadow Shrimp

Silver Shadow Shrimp   Blue & Gold Shadow Shrimp

PLATE 14: Bonner's Shadow Shrimps

exactly the conditions in which the traditional Irish shrimps are not at their best, whilst still being effective in slower water. This combination of strengths means that the Shadow Shrimps are one of those very rare patterns which can be fished right through a pool, from the fast neck right into the slower water of the main pool, with no loss of effectiveness.

Whilst it is, of course, possible to change flies to suit the different areas of a pool, for most anglers this is very inconvenient and rarely done, particu-

larly when the pool is both short and prolific.

The Shadow Shrimps combine elements of the traditional Irish Shrimps with the more modern hairwing types. A brief description shows a tail of silver fox body guard hair about one and a half times the body length, a body split into two halves with a centre hackle, a silver fox tail hair wing extending to the hook bend and a small collar hackle at the head. Additionally, a vee-shaped Golden Pheasant Tippet feather is tied over the rear body as a veiling. The tips of these feathers are

varnished together to represent the eyes of the shrimp. These are not the easiest of flies to tie, particularly in the smaller sizes. They are, however, well worth the effort. The wound hackle at head and mid-body still provide kick in the water, whilst the long tail and hair wing provide stability in heavy water flows and avoid skating. The correct choice of materials is critical to the success of the Shadow Shrimps. The use of substitute materials will substantially reduce their fishing effectiveness, as will changing the tying details. At the present time, there are six flies in the series.

Another effective series of modern shrimp flies developed by Paddy is the Living Shrimps (Plate 15). These are tied with a very slim profile using bright synthetic materials and are intended for use in fast water. They have a two tone body of Mylar and SLF with a long bucktail or polar bear hair tail, blended SLF hank wing, a soft genetic cock saddle head hackle and small jungle cock eyes.

As one of the very best professional flytyers in Ireland, Paddy is not a person to release new fly patterns onto the market until he is sure that they meet the highest standards of effectiveness. The

Shadow & Living Shrimps have already proved their worth in this respect.

Slimmer, slinky style flies such as the Living shrimps, Shadow shrimps, Arctic Fox shrimps and Ally's shrimps, that are longitudinally mobile are better suited to the fast flows, necks of pools and down and across fishing. These flies can be used on the floating line with little danger of skating. Flies in the traditional style that are more three dimensionally mobile are better suited to the Irish 'tipped' style of fishing. It should be borne in mind that these are general rules not to be interpreted rigidly, as both types of flies are sometimes used in both ways and flies like Shadow shrimps suit both styles.

About seven or eight years ago, Robert, together with Russell Whiteman, was gillying an angler from England on the Mount Falcon beat of the River Moy. The conditions were bad with the river carrying a lot of colour, so much so that Robert doubted that fly fishing was possible. Nevertheless they decided to give it a try. Over the next few days the visiting angler took six fish, Robert and Russell together took none. For a visiting angler to outfish two experienced gillies on

Flame Red

Sunset Orange

Fire Orange

Golden Glow

PLATE 15: Paddy Bonner's Living Shrimps

their home waters is somewhat more than unusual. The fisherman was certainly a highly competent angler but what gave him the edge was the fly that he was using. When he left, he gave Robert some samples of the fly in question. It was a pearl tinsel bodied hairwing, with a wing and tail of mixed orange and yellow fibres, with three strands of Krystal Hair over and a dyed red beard hackle. The look of this fly fairly asked to be tied in the style of an Ally's shrimp and this Robert did. Thus was born the Red Pearl Ally's Shrimp. Since then, this fly has proved itself over and over again when conditions are borderline. An absolute 'must have' pattern for the times when a dirty flood would make most fisherman reach for the spinning rod.

Red Pearl Ally's Shrimp

Wade's Arctic Shrimps

Wade's Arctic Shrimp was devised by the late Paul Wade when he was living in Co. Mayo. The fly is characterised by a tail and wing of arctic fox hair, hence the name. The original fly was tied with a silver ribbed old gold body and a tail and wing of hot orange. Three further variants were developed: a yellow version, a green and yellow version and another gold-bodied version. The yellow version is probably the most popular of the variants. It has a gold tinsel body and a rich yellow tail and wing. The front hackle is yellow dyed badger. The last fly has gold rather than silver ribbing and the head hackle is of orange dyed badger. The Arctic Shrimps are extremely effective due to the mobility of the fox fur combined with their long, slim profile. This combination makes them suitable for a variety of water conditions.

The Yellow Piglet, named with typical humour, is a fly devised by Garry Piggot, a popular character who owns the Ridge Pool Tackle Shop in

Ballina. It is basically a hybrid between a traditional Irish shrimp and an Ally's Shrimp. The long hair tail, hair wing and collar hackle are typical of an Ally's Shrimp, whereas the split body and centre hackle come from the Irish shrimp style of fly. As might be expected, the Yellow Piglet is very effective on the Moy on the beats around Ballina.

Yellow Piglet (Piggot)

The Owenmore Shrimp, named after the Owenmore river in County Mayo, is an interesting fly. This is a hybrid pattern that combines elements of the Ally's Shrimp with aspects of an Irish shrimp. It has a long tail in the Ally's style but the wing, rather than being tied in at the head, is tied in at the joint between the rear and front body.

Tolan's Owenmore Shrimp was devised by the late Michael Tolan, who was the manager of the Moy Fishery, for use on the Owenmore and Owenduff Rivers in County Mayo. The centre hackle may also be hot orange, rather than red as shown. Tied in this form the fly is, in fact, a different pattern which originated on the river Roe. The jungle cock eyes are usual but the pattern is sometimes tied without them.

Lemon & Purple Shrimp

The next two patterns also come from the River Moy. Both of these are quite simple patterns, without veilings or jungle cock wings. They are derived from Curry's Red Shrimp and, on their day, can be quite effective. They are named for the town of Ballina and are often used on the beats in this area. The Ballina Blue has proved to be particularly effective on the estuary beats.

Owenmore Shrimp

Ballina Red Shrimp

Ballina Blue Shrimp

Tolan's Owenmore Shrimp

The Lemon & Purple Shrimp is a fly that is quite popular on the Moy around Foxford. Russell Whiteman has taken this fly to Scotland with success. On one occasion, it outfished the local patterns on the Aberdeenshire Dee. A good fly for a wide range of conditions.

Another blue hackled fly from the Moy is the Silver Blue Shrimp. This is also often used on the estuary beats for fresh fish in bright weather.

Peter O'Reilly, author of many books including *Trout & Salmon Flies of Ireland* and *Flyfishing in Ireland* has also provided us with some interesting patterns.

Silver Blue Shrimp

Green Peter Shrimp (O'Reilly)

The first of these is the Slaney Badger, devised by Bernard Byrne. This fly returns to the theme of badger hair and colouration which has been popular throughout Irish salmon angling. An interesting variation to the standard construction has a sparse wing of badger hair with the addition of pearl mobile as an underwing to add a bit of sparkle to the fly.

O'Reilly Shrimp

Slaney Badger

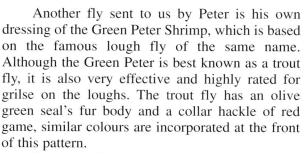

Another fly sent to us by Peter is his own dressing of the Green Peter Shrimp, which is based on the famous lough fly of the same name. Although the Green Peter is best known as a trout fly, it is also very effective and highly rated for grilse on the loughs. The trout fly has an olive green seal's fur body and a collar hackle of red game, similar colours are incorporated at the front of this pattern.

The next fly is again one of Peter's own patterns. Peter does not have a name for it so we have taken the liberty of calling it the O'Reilly Shrimp. It is primarily a clear water grilse fly for the smaller rivers of the west coast of Ireland. It has proved to be effective on the Erriff and also suits fisheries such as Delphi and Screebe. The colour

combination of red, black and orange has considerably more impact than might be imagined from a simple description of the fly.

The Mourne Rat is a pattern which was given to Peter by an unknown angler from the Mourne area of Northern Ireland. We are not absolutely certain but an alternative name may be the Campbell's Killer. We do not have any further details about this fly but the striking yellow, red and black colour combination certainly looks effective. This fly should not be confused with Joe McDonald's Rat Shrimp.

Mourne Rat

The Arctic Ally, which appeared around the River Moy area in recent times, is a combination of Wade's Arctic Shrimp with Ally's Shrimp. It is not known who developed them, but they are basically a fox winged Ally's Shrimp. The fly come in two colour variants, orange and yellow. Other variants based on the Ally's Shrimp design which use arctic fox fur can be found in the section on Scotland, where the Ally's Shrimp and its myriad variants are discussed. These flies may also be tied retaining the natural grey squirrel hair veilings top and bottom, as in the original Ally's Shrimp.

Pearl & Magenta Shrimp

Pearl & Orange Shrimp

Christmas Tree Shrimp

Orange Arctic Ally

Yellow Arctic Ally

The next group of flies, tied by Stephen Bailie of County Down, is typical of the small, modern shrimp patterns that have been developed for the grilse fisheries and smaller rivers of the west coast of Ireland. They are generally characterised by the liberal use of sparkling materials and the lack of jungle cock wings or eyes. The tails are normally of hair combined with a flashy material such as Krystal Flash. These flies present the fish with a flickering, brilliant spot of light in the water and are extremely effective. The flies are almost always tied on small trebles in the size range 10 to 14, although doubles may also be used. Typical examples of these flies are represented by the Pearl & Magenta and Pearl & Orange Shrimps.

The Christmas Tree Shrimp is another typical example of this hybrid style of fly. The tail consists of two hackles or bunches of hackle fibres together

with Krystal Flash. The split body is of pearl Mylar at the rear and magenta Mylar at the front. The fly presents a bright, glowing image which is very effective indeed.

The Cork Blackwater, in the southwest of Ireland, is a large salmon river, completely unlike the smaller spate streams and grilse rivers of the west of Ireland. There is, surprisingly, no great history of shrimp flies on the Blackwater but the following two local patterns were devised by Doug Lock.

The Kilbarry Summer Shrimp, which was devised in 1997, is a nice combination of orange, gold and red and has proved to be effective in the summer months in both clear and peat stained water. The Kilbarry Autumn Shrimp is a predominantly red fly for late running salmon. The downward pointing jungle cock eyes are very unusual, being elsewhere found only on a few of the classic Dee patterns.

Kilbarry Summer Shrimp (Lock)

Kilbarry Autumn Shrimp (Lock)

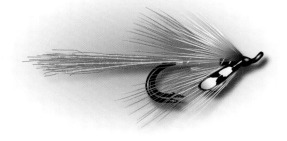

Golden Shrimp (Toohey)

Orange Shrimp (Toohey)

Lady Ethna

Brendan Begley is a well known fly caster and this is one of his patterns. The Ginger Shrimp has a good reputation on the Cork Blackwater and works extremely well for dour fish.

Ginger Shrimp (Begley)

The next two patterns also originate from the Cork Blackwater and were devised by the late Mossey Toohe in the modern hybrid style with long hair tails and wings.

The Lady Ethna was developed on the Screebe fishery where it is considered an essential early season pattern for fresh run fish. It later became very popular on the Bundrowes river in Donegal and since then has spread widely throughout Ireland.

So far in the discussion of Irish flies, no mention has been made of Spey flies. We found only one case of a Spey fly being used in recent times, oddly enough by Robert.

Robert's own use of Spey patterns for salmon angling began when he first started serious salmon fly fishing on the River Roe in Northern Ireland in the early 1970s. The fishing was mainly with larger singles on sinking lines for fresh run autumn salmon. The Roe, in common with other rivers of the Foyle system, was a stronghold for the old traditions as it was very much a single hook fly and sinking line river. It had prolific runs of large autumn salmon, a proper salmon river rather than a grilse river.

Had a visitor looked at a selection of the flies that were used for those autumn fish, among the many colourful Irish shrimp and full dressed patterns he would also have found a solitary Spey pattern, the Lady Caroline, which was a popular

and widely used fly. There was rarely a strict adherence to the original specification and the fly used would most likely be a variant. The body would often be plain dark olive green or dark brown seal's fur rather than the spiral strands of green and brown Berlin wool. Ribbing would usually be simplified and the hooks would be standard shank, standard wire, rather than Spey or Dee types. Depending on the size of fly the hackling would be real heron or heron substitute.

Around this time, Robert managed to purchase a copy of Pryce-Tannatt's book *How to Dress Salmon Flies*. Other Spey patterns were illustrated within it and there seemed no reason why the similar looking Grey Heron should not be tried. What a deadly fly this turned out to be, becoming one of Robert's absolute favourites.

The Gillespie version of the Grey Heron is dressed on a standard length single hook, normally a size eight. The body is tied in two sections, the rear being of yellow seal's fur, the front of black seal's fur. The hackling is of long soft blue dun chinese cock hackle, which is stripped on one side. The correct hackles may be found at the very rear of the cape. The hackle is tied in by the stalk, given two turns and then palmered forward. The ribbing is brought forward in the opposite spiral so as to secure the hackle. A throat hackle of natural guinea fowl is added and the fly is completed by a wing of bronze mallard.

Grey Heron (Gillespie)

SCOTLAND

ne of the problems with locating and describing Scottish salmon fly patterns lies in the historical system of salmon fishing lets in Scotland. Most beats on most of the rivers (particularly the best fly beats) are private lets on a weekly or seasonal basis with no day tickets. Almost every beat has its own gillie and many gillies have their own personal variants of standard flies, devised to meet local conditions. Only rarely are these patterns publicised and made available to a wider audience. The fact that there must be some real gems around that would be useful in other waters, is proved by the effectiveness of the patterns that have been released by gillies such as Wattie Burns, Sam Bremner, Davie McPhail and others.

We are indebted to Stan Headley for his reference work, *Trout & Salmon Flies of Scotland* which has proved to be an invaluable source of information and the starting point for many further inquiries.

There are two main types of shrimp flies used in Scotland. Firstly, there are the hairwing shrimps which can be characterised by the extremely successful Ally's Shrimp developed around 1985 by Alastair Gowans and first used on the Tay system. Secondly, there are the Irish style patterns and their derivatives and variations.

The main feature of the hairwing shrimp flies is that the tail of wound golden pheasant breast feather, as commonly used for the Irish flies, is replaced by long natural hair fibres such as bucktail or squirrel tail on the smaller sizes. In later variants, flashy artificial fibres such as Krystal Hair were used to give added impact in the water. The wing of jungle cock has also been largely replaced by golden pheasant tippet fibres, although small jungle cock eyes or cheeks may be found on many patterns.

One of the noteworthy features of these hair-tailed flies is that the style of dressing causes few constraints in terms of size. The hair tail can be extended almost indefinitely simply by changing the type of hair used. The bucktail fibres used for the tail can he up to 150mm (6") long. Conversely, the size of an Irish style of shrimp with its tail of golden pheasant breast feather is constrained by the maximum length of this feather. The Ally's style of dressing, with its more streamlined shape, is therefore ideally suited to tying large flies for fishing in heavy flows. The original Ally's Shrimp has now been tied in many variations, most of which maintain the construction method but change the colouration. In view of its importance in the spread of shrimp patterns throughout the world, we have devoted a separate section to the Ally's Shrimp later in this chapter (see page 69). Over the course of time there has been a degree of hybridization between the two types of shrimps and there are now many examples of flies which show features of both styles.

Davie McPhail is a noted fly tyer and gillie from Ayrshire who has evolved many new shrimp patterns which come into this category. Davie's flies are featured regularly in *Trout & Salmon* in his own flytying column.

The Ayrshire Red Shrimp is known to be a killing pattern for Ayrshire rivers. Davie McPhail considers this to be a fly which no angler on these rivers should be without. This fly is also popular in Ireland, as is a variant that uses badger hackles at the centre and front. The fly illustrated is shown as a tube dressing but it can be tied on all hook types.

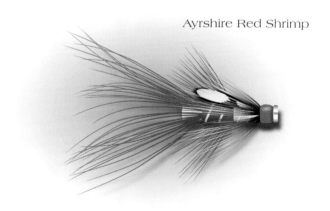

Ayrshire Red Shrimp

The McClure shrimp has proved very effective in the south west of Scotland in both summer and autumn. The black squirrel was added to the fly because Davie had no jungle cock available at the time. The yellow hair was added later in order to achieve a Willie Gunn colouration. With the Willie Gunn hairwing being so popular, it is surprising that not more shrimp flies use the yellow-orange-black colour combination.

McClure Shrimp (McPhail)

Also of note are the McPhail tube shrimps illustrated below. Although technically these flies may be tube flies called shrimps rather than shrimp patterns tied on tubes, they are nevertheless intended as shrimps by the tyer. These flies use dyed jungle cock wings and colour matched sleeving to produce a fly which really has impact in the water. With the seven colour variants shown above, a wide range of weather and water conditions are covered. They are tied on tubes varying from lightweight plastic, through to heavy brass to suit all kinds of water conditions. These flies can, of course, be dressed on normal hooks. In this case, the sleeving can be replaced by a tag of the appropriate colour. The winging of all these flies is a combination of sparse bucktail, together with a new glitter material called Rainbow which is available in a wide range of colours.

Davie has also devised a series of totally new shrimp patterns based on the use of new, metallic dubbing fibres for the bodies. These 'Lite-Brite' shrimps, although still young in terms of their development, are showing much promise in Scotland and are particularly good in low water and bright, drought conditions. With the tendency over the last few years for summers to be drier and water flows to be lower, any patterns that can attract fish in these conditions are sure to find lasting use. The Lite-Brite shrimps come in a wide range of colour variants, including an unusual blue-black combination called the Ocean Blue Shrimp. With this range to choose from, it should always be possible to find one that the fish appreciate.

Lime Shrimp   Copper Sunset Shrimp   Black Rainbow Shrimp

Highland Shrimp

O'Hara Shrimp   Blue & Magenta Shrimp   Red Devil Shrimp

PLATE 16: Davie McPhail Tube Shrimps

Orange & Gold Shrimp

Ocean Blue Shrimp

Ross Shrimp

Hot Gunn Shrimp

Blue Pearl Shrimp

Burgundy Shrimp

Sunburst Shrimp

PLATE 17: Davie McPhail Lite Brite Shrimps

The Blue Shrimp was developed by Davie specifically for Mediterranean type summer conditions after he saw an angler on the Ayrshire Doon succeed in catching fish with a blue shrimp pattern when conditions seemed nigh on impossible. This fly may pull a fish under blue skies and low water when little else will, but it has also proved to be equally effective when conditions are more favourable. As our summers in Europe seem to be getting ever more extreme, flies like this one, which are effective in extreme conditions, are becoming ever more necessary.

Blue Shrimp (McPhail)

Black and orange are known to be effective colours for salmon and the next fly, which is also from Davie McPhail, is a combination of these two colours. Note that Davie often ties these shrimps on small tubes as shown in this and the preceding illustration. Depending upon water conditions, the tube can be light plastic, through to heavy brass.

Black & Orange Shrimp (McPhail)

The Knockdolian Shrimp, which Davie received from Lord Richard of Knockdolian Estate, is a very effective pattern in Ayrshire waters but not well known outside this area. Reminiscent of the Irish shrimp patterns, this pretty orange and silver fly may well be worth a swim in other waters as an alternative when the fish have seen too many Ally's shrimps

Knockdolian Shrimp

Alexander Keachie of Kilmarnock has also developed some interesting patterns for the waters of south west Scotland. The Keachie Krill series was unusual amongst shrimp patterns at the time of its introduction because of the use of pearl tinsel for the body. This material, wound over a bed of black silk, was chosen to imitate the iridescent green flash of a shiny material reflecting light in salt water. To achieve the best effect a pearl tinsel with a green cast rather than a purple cast should be selected. The black underbody is essential. It is surprising that pearl tinsel bodies were not more often used for salmon flies, particularly when one considers how popular and effective they are for trout flies.

Keachie's Krill

Alexander is one of the few fishermen who has actually looked at the scientific studies of salmon vision as a basis for fly development and says that the iridescence produced by using this body material gives a new dimension to fly colour. The results speak for themselves: the flies taking fish in both high and low water conditions from the Spey to the Stinchar in both early and late season. This is a pattern that deserves wider use.

Claret is known to be a very killing colour for trout in Scotland and is well known as being effective for salmon in Ireland. It is surprising, therefore, that there are very few claret salmon patterns in Scotland.

A variant of the Claret Shrimp was devised by Stan Headley and the dressing was given in his book *Trout & Salmon Flies of Scotland*. According to Stan, he devised the fly for Sandy Leventon, editor of *Trout & Salmon*, to use during a visit to Ireland but it has subsequently found more widespread use and is highly rated.

Claret Shrimp (Headley)

The Tweed is the home of Burns's White Shrimp which was published in *Trout & Salmon* in 1992. Tied by gillie Wattie Burns to use in the last hours of daylight or in coloured falling water, this fly has since proved to be an excellent all-round pattern. White shrimp patterns are not found in great numbers, but the few that we know about are very effective fishing patterns indeed. Could this be due to the fact that white is somehow not seen as 'natural' for a shrimp fly whereas orange is? Perhaps a more general re-think in this area and a move away from the ubiquitous hot orange is overdue, following the Irish example where white hackles have long been successful.

White Shrimp (Burns)

Sam's Badger (Bremner)

Sam's Badger, which has become very popular locally, was devised by Sam Bremner,

gillie on the Wester Elchies beat of the Spey. The colours used are identical to a gold Willie Gunn, but the head is white varnish, which is very unusual. Tied full on a small treble, the fly is also recommended as a good 'dibbling' pattern for low water summer conditions.

The Findhorn Shrimp is a pattern which is widely used in Morayshire in the summer and autumn. It is clearly a derivative of Ally's Shrimp but is more sparsely dressed. The body is of red Lurex and the long tail consists of bucktail with filaments of orange Krystal Hair. The winging is of G.P. tippet and there is no hackle at the front.

Findhorn Shrimp

The Junction Shrimp was devised by boatman Gavin Brown and named after the famous Junction Pool on the River Tweed. This fly has similar colours to Burns' White Shrimp, but in this case the tail is of hot orange bucktail with orange Krystal Hair. The wing is again white. Can it be coincidence that both these flies originate on the Tweed, or is there something about this river that makes this colour especially effective? The example illustrated is tied on a Waddington shank which is very popular in Scotland.

Junction Shrimp - Waddington style

The General Practitioner, developed by Esmond Drury in England, still maintains it's popularity after many years and is much used in Scotland. A hybrid variant, which shows some

features of Ally's Shrimp, is the version of used on the River Oykel. The tail is of orange bucktail and the body is hackled. On the Oykel, this variant is considered to be more effective than the original tying although it is not widely used elsewhere.

Oykel G.P.

Another G.P. variant is commonly used on the River Helmsdale in Sutherland. This fly is much less like the standard G.P. in that it has a tail of long orange bucktail with a wing of golden pheasant tippet. The fly is finished off with a silver badger collar hackle and jungle cock eyes.

Helmsdale G.P.

The following version is dressed as the original GP except that orange has been replaced by purple throughout. The golden pheasant tippet and the breast feathers are dyed purple.

Purple G.P.

The Helmsdale Copper King is a shrimp style variant of the hairwing fly called the Copper King. Although called 'copper', there is actually no copper in the dressing. The copper colouration results from the mixture of a dark gold tinsel body, together with a tail of red golden pheasant breast feather, a centre hackle of yellow and a head hackle of red golden pheasant breast. This is a pretty fly which should be effective in peat stained water.

Helmsdale Copper King

There must be dozens of variations of the Black Shrimp. We have chosen three patterns to illustrate the variety that can exist and still be called a Black Shrimp. Surprisingly few salmon flies in Europe are really black, most having black notes combined with yellow and orange.

The first pattern is common all over Scotland and is also well used in Ireland. Peter O'Reilly thinks that it originated on the River Ness. It is an extremely effective pattern in both late spring and summer, particularly in clear water. Although called the Black Shrimp, the overall impression is very much like a Willie Gunn tied shrimp style.

Black Shrimp #1

The second of these black shrimps is a derivation from the Ally's Shrimp. Alastair Gowans considers this fly to be one of the very

best. Originally this fly had jungle cock wings, but these are no longer usual. It seems just as effective without them. The colours are the same as the pattern above, but are arranged in a different way and give a very different impression. Other black variants of Ally's Shrimp are shown on page 71.

Black Shrimp #2

The Helmsdale Black Shrimp is much more of a black Black Shrimp, the tail, centre and head hackles being of this colour. The split body is of silver tinsel and the fly is finished off with jungle cock eyes. This pattern makes a sombre impression, relieved by the jungle cock eyes and silver body which stand out exceedingly well against the dark hackle fibres. The fly should be dressed sparse and sleek and is an ideal clear water pattern for fast flows. This fly rather goes against the tendency noted by Stan Headley in *Trout & Salmon Flies of Scotland*, where he comments that flies tend to get brighter the further north one travels. This fly can also be tied in the Irish style, with a silver tag and a tail of golden pheasant red breast feather dyed black.

Helmsdale Black Shrimp

The first Black Shrimp illustrated is thought to come from the River Ness. It is possible that it is a variant of the next pattern which is called the Ness Shrimp. The colouration of this fly is also

similar to the long tailed Black Shrimp.

The fly illustrated above was tied by Gordon Mackenzie using hair fibres throughout, rather than feather hackles. Gordon applies this technique to a wide range of flies, including standard hairwing patterns as well as shrimps and Spey flies. A detailed discussion of these unusual and interesting flies can be found in the section on England & Wales later in this chapter (see page 74).

Hairy Ness Shrimp

The Kylie Shrimp is a shrimp style derivation from the very successful Kylie devised by Alan Donaldson. This fly is extremely effective on the tidal waters of the Kyle of Sutherland. Stan Headley reports that this fly hooked eight fish in two and a half hours for himself and Alan Donaldson one evening on the Amat beat of the Carron in 1996. Any fly that can perform like that, whatever the circumstances, is one well worth having in your box.

Kylie Shrimp (Donaldson)

The Lady Ewe Shrimp is a shrimp pattern devised by Dave Mateer for use on the River Ewe. This shrimp style dressing was derived from the Lady Ewe hairwing. Both flies were influenced by the Kerry Blue fly from Harry Davis, which is a standard pattern on the Ewe.

Lady Ewe Shrimp (Mateer)

The Brahan Shrimp is an older pattern dating back to before 1969 and was named after the Brahan beat of the River Conon. It was designed by John McKenzie, a gillie on the river, and is clearly based on the Black Brahan hairwing.

Brahan Shrimp

Sandy's Shrimp comes from Sandy Leventon, editor of *Trout & Salmon* for many years. It is unusual in that the tail is of marabou. This material, although very popular for reservoir lures, is rarely used in Europe for salmon flies. This is not the case in North America and in the North American chapter of this book you will find many patterns that use marabou for both hackling and winging. Stan Headley rates this as a good summer fly for both grilse and salmon and because of its mobility is particularly well suited to slack flows.

Jimmy and Gloria Younger are well known professional fly tyers who have been in business in Scotland for many years. The next pattern was devised in 1994 by Gloria Younger and named for Pat Somers, one of their customers, who wanted a claret based shrimp for fishing in Ireland. It certainly worked out, because he caught eight fish on this fly in three days. Since then it has been consistently successful. A later variation replaced the yellow top and bottom veilings with yellow Krystal Hair. The Krystal Hair variant also proved its worth with seven fish in one day to its credit. The jungle cock cheeks are optional. Somers' Claret Shrimp is very effective in peaty water. It still seems odd to us that claret is not more popular for Scottish salmon flies. Would Pat Somers have asked for this pattern if he had been fishing in Scotland, rather than in Ireland?

Sandy's Shrimp (Leventon)

Brown is not a commonly used colour for shrimp flies but the next pattern which originates from the east coast area between Bonar Bridge and Inverness is very popular and successful locally. It is also well favoured on the Kyle of Sutherland rivers such as the Oykel, Carron, Cassley and Shin.

Somers' Claret Shrimp

Brown Shrimp

The Megan Boyd Shrimp is named after the late Megan Boyd of Kintradwell, the famous salmon fly dresser. Details of Megan Boyd's life and her fly dressing career are to be found in *The*

Atlantic Salmon Fly, The Tyers and Their Art by Judith Dunham. The fly itself has a sleek, restrained look about it and being so sparsely dressed would be ideal for low water conditions.

Megan Boyd Shrimp

Hutchy Shrimp

The Hutchy Shrimp is a most unusual pattern. It was given to us by Peter O'Reilly who obtained it from a gillie from the River Tay, but unfortunately we have no other information about it. Unusual features include a palmered rear body, a double hackle, badger over hot orange, at the front and a single jungle cock eye both above and below the shank. Unusual it may be, but the fly certainly has a translucent, shimmering effect.

The Alistair Shrimp is a shrimp version of the Alistair hairwing, which was devised by a Mr. Chamberlain of Alness. This fly is very popular in Caithness and Sutherland but not well known outside the area. The subdued yellow and brown tones of this fly are not far away from the Golden Olive Shrimp from Ireland. In the summer it is often fished greased or with a riffling hitch. This is a nice looking fly which deserves to be tried more widely even though it is often held that flies from the far north of Scotland do not travel well.

Alistair Shrimp

The next pattern is called the Nameless Shrimp. It may not have a name but, in terms of its content, it has just about everything else! There is a tag of ribbed floss, a tail of G.P. crest, a two part split body, a centre wing consisting of three different feather elements, all finished off with two throat hackles and bronze mallard winging. One may wonder if such complications are really necessary but the fly is extremely effective. Where the fly comes from and how it got its complex form is a complete mystery. It is highly recommended for summer fishing.

Nameless Shrimp

The Yabbie is a very simple pattern with an unusual look and an odd name (Yabbie is an Australian term for a type of shrimp). The fly is not well known but is highly rated by those in the know, The Yabbie is effective on the Beauly, Carron, Conon and Spey.

Yabbie (Bett)

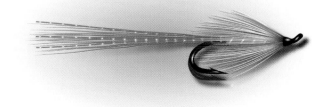

The Isle of Islay is the home of the following patterns. Islay is a small island approximately 32 km wide by 38 km long (20 x 24 miles) which lies off the west coast of Scotland. It is world renowned for its malt whisky, produced in seven distilleries, rather than for its fishing.

The islands of Scotland, both west and north, are better known for their fantastic wild brown trout fishing rather than for salmon, but they can have splendid runs of sea fresh grilse when the conditions are right. The Laggan is a short spate river which runs east to west through the middle of Islay, and it is here that Calum MacAffer has fished for over thirty years. He has developed a small range of effective, sparkling little flies which were described in an article in the July 1999 issue of *Fly Fishing & Flytying*.

Laggan Prawn (MacAffer)

Silver Roebuck (MacAffer)

Gold Roebuck (MacAffer)

The Laggan Prawn is a combination of brown and purple and is one of Calum's most successful flies. Tied on small trebles or doubles, this fly with

its purple tail could easily have come from the west coast grilse fisheries of Ireland.

The Silver Roebuck and the Gold Roebuck are very similar in construction to the Laggan Prawn, except that they have tinsel bodies and lack the long tail. Both flies are named for the roebuck hair used for the wing. These are bright little flies that look as if they are well suited to summer fishing in low water conditions.

An angler who has devised a range of shrimp patterns for clear, warm waters is Bill Currie who wrote about them in an article in *Trout & Salmon* in June 1996. His approach to shrimp type patterns is to use small doubles and trebles simple tied with sparse hair wings and long trailing tails. The flies themselves use combinations of black, orange, red and yellow hair, combined with silver and gold bodies. The important feature of these flies is the profile. The sparse winging is swept back to reach the tail and the tail itself is tied long - up to twice the body length, thus producing the slinky, mobile, shrimp-like appearance that has proved so effective. The fineness and mobility of the wings and tails is of prime importance and the choice of hair is therefore critical. Arctic fox guard hair is an obvious candidate if it can be found in the appropriate length. The following colour combinations are recommended:

#1 - gold body, black wing, orange tail
#2 - gold body, black wing, yellow tail
#3 - silver body, claret wing, yellow tail
#4 - silver body, black wing, yellow tail.

The flies have proved themselves to be extremely effective, fluttering and darting near the surface, especially 'on the dangle' i.e. after the fly has fished round on the swing and is hanging and hovering almost directly below the angler. There is an oft expressed fear that flies with long tails encourage 'short takes' - that is, pulls (often savage), that nevertheless do not convert into a firm hookhold. This fear is compounded if the fly is taken on the dangle, where presumably the fish takes the fly from behind, directly downstream. Whatever the theory, this does not seem to happen with these flies. Currie has noted that many fish, especially grilse, will follow some distance before taking and that the take, when it comes, is usually very definite and the hookhold is not in doubt. The same has been found in Ireland where again a long 'dangle' may be useful.

PLATE 18: Long Tail Shrimps (Bill Currie)

ALLY'S SHRIMPS

ecause of its significance in the spread of the use of shrimp patterns worldwide, we consider that it is worth looking at the Ally's Shrimp in some detail. The creation of the Ally's Shrimp is one the most significant developments in the history of shrimp flies, if for no other reason than that thousands of anglers worldwide have been introduced to shrimp flies by this pattern. According to Alastair Gowans, he first conceived the Ally's shrimp as an imitation of a particular type of prawn which was characterised by a long, slim body. By imitating this type of prawn rather than the shorter more compact variety he produced one of the most effective flies for fast water conditions that has ever been devised.

The second reason for taking a close look at the original is that although the Ally's Shrimp spread rapidly and gained a huge reputation since the tying first appeared in the August 1988 edition of *Trout & Salmon* magazine, it has since suffered from many inaccurate tyings which may have damaged its reputation. Many of these dressings bear little relationship to the original fly due to incorrect choice of materials or incorrect proportions of important elements such as the

veilings or tail length. With some patterns, tyings that are more or less incorrect can still be used with some success. The Ally's Shrimp however, relies upon various features being tied correctly in order for it to be fully effective. With a full blown reputation as one of the most generally effective patterns of all time, the Ally's Shrimp can prove to be a disappointment to many anglers who do not understand how it should be tied and when and where it should be used.

The rapid spread and proven effectiveness of the Ally's Shrimp can be attributed in large part to the fact that it is a super pattern for fast flowing waters. This vital attribute helped the fly to become popular with many anglers who had had no previous experience with shrimp patterns. It should also be noted that the Ally's Shrimp is also extremely effective in coloured water conditions. For those anglers who already used shrimp flies, the Ally's added a new dimension by extending the range of water speeds under which shrimp flies could be used successfully. Because the tail is made of hair, the Ally's Shrimp can be tied in a wide range of sizes. This has enabled anglers wanting to retain the shrimp fly qualities of mobility, glow and translucency, to evoke them in many different ways, with different colours and materials.

We are not aware if the Ally's Shrimp has been tried for steelhead on the west coast of North America, but it must certainly be worth a try. Ally's Shrimps tie well on single hooks. The fly is at its most effective in fast water and the slim form cuts through the flow to sink quickly when needed. We think that steelhead fishermen might be well advised to experiment with this pattern.

The length of the tail may vary considerably, the original tyings having tails of up to twice the hook length. The inclusion of several (usually 4) strands of Krystal Hair with the tail hair is optional and was not part of the original pattern. The tail material should ideally be fine, straight bucktail. One material that can dramatically increase the performance of the fly – particularly in bright conditions and evenings – is to tie the tail using polar bear hair dyed in the appropriate colours. Adding strands of polar bear hair to the veilings has also proved to be advantageous. Polar bear hair is a unique material in its translucency and inner glow. This material is absolutely deadly in the light conditions described: it transmits the light in a way that no other hair does and thus does not offer a dark silhouette against the light. This ability to transmit light is at a premium, both when the light is intense, as during a bright day, and when there is little light, as is the case with evening fishing. The only problem is availability. Good polar bear hair that is finely tapered and straight is very difficult to come by. There is absolutely no doubt in our minds, based on personal experience, that in the conditions outlined above, an Ally's Shrimp tied with a polar bear tail, will outfish the same fly tied with other materials by a substantial margin.

Occasionally when using Ally's Shrimps tied on trebles the tail fibres can have a tendency to wrap around the hook. In this case, it can help if the tail hair is divided up and tied in as separate bunches between the hooks, rather than one single bundle on top. If you wish to do this, we recommend tying in about 50% of the fibres at the top and about 25% in each of the other two gaps.

The Ally's Shrimp design has spawned a whole shoal of variants. Alastair Gowans devised several of these variants himself which are shown in Plate 19.

The Yellow Ally's Shrimp originally had a yellow floss body, but Robin McLeod altered this to silver tinsel. Alastair Gowans believes that this version is the better fly and recommends it for clear, bright conditions or coloured water. The Red Ally's Shrimp has been notably successful for resident fish as well as fresh run fish and is effective in the autumn. The Ally's Special Shrimp is Alastair Gowans' favourite fly from mid-season onwards. It is a little more complex to tie but it is worth it. The Cascade is newer than the other flies but has been proved to be very effective in high water. It has become a very popular fly in Ireland. The Tummel shrimp has been particularly successful in April and May on the rivers Tummel and Tay. The Copper Shrimp is a superb fly for clearing, peaty water but is good at any time and is highly recommended for spate rivers.

There are so many variants of the Ally's Shrimp that it would be impractical to list them all. We have, therefore, mentioned the following flies because they are successful, and in many cases are more effective than the original. Three variants which are quite popular have a one piece body of tinsel or Mylar in silver, gold and copper, respectively, but are otherwise identical to the original Ally's Shrimp. There are many variations of black Ally's Shrimps. The one we have chosen is from Jimmy Younger. Note that the tippet feather has been dyed red. A version of the Black Shrimp from the river Ness which is highly rated by Alastair Gowans is shown on page 65.

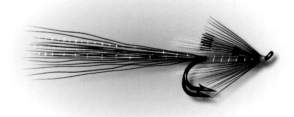

Black Ally's Shrimp

Purple Ally's Shrimp

Original Ally's Shrimp   Ally's Special Shrimp

Yellow Ally's Shrimp   Cascade

Red Ally's Shrimp   Copper Shrimp

Tummel Shrimp

PLATE 19: Ally's Shrimp Variants from Alastair Gowans

The Purple Ally's Shrimp is perhaps not as popular as some of the other versions but can be extremely effective at times. Purple is generally thought of as a colour for autumn but this is not necessarily so. The version shown is from Jimmy Younger and is effective at all times of the year..

The Silk Cut Shrimp from Andy Wren is another purple fly which has shown itself to be effective in the spring as well as later in the year. The unusual name comes from a well known brand of cigarettes that used purple as a theme throughout an advertising campaign.

Silk Cut Shrimp (Wren)

The Russian Ally's Shrimp is a yellow tailed fly with a white front hackle and a silver tinsel body. It has been signally effective on the rivers of the Kola peninsular in northern Russia.

Russian Ally's Shrimp

Two other variants of the Ally's shrimp are of special interest because the form has been altered rather than just the colours. These are known as the Beauly #1 and the Beauly #2. In both these flies, the bottom veilings have disappeared completely and the collar hackle has been replaced by a beard hackle. In this form the fly is even more streamlined than the normal Ally's shrimp and is ideally suited to fast water fishing. Both of these flies are from Jimmy Younger. These flies are ideally suited for use with the 'Beauly Belly' technique of fly presentation. This technique involves casting square across the current and allowing a downstream belly (sometimes augmented by handlining in the flyline) to bring the fly round very quickly across the flow.

Beauly #1

Beauly #2

The dressing for the Magenta Ally's Shrimp was devised by Alan Donaldson and was given by

Stan Headley in *Trout & Salmon Flies of Scotland*. It has a growing reputation.

Magenta Ally's (Donaldson)

The next variant is concerned with materials rather than colour or form. We have already seen in the Irish section that arctic fox fur is becoming increasingly popular for both wings and tails. Arctic fox is extremely fine and mobile, but is more robust than marabou. Since it has become more generally available it has been widely used in many patterns as a replacement for marabou and other furs. It was, therefore, only a matter of time before a batch of Ally style shrimps appeared which used this material. The Arctic Fox Shrimp was published by David Westwood in *Trout & Salmon* in June 1997. Apart from the floss body, all the elements of this fly are arctic fox of various colours. The general colouration is very similar in its overall impression to the Cascade shrimp from Alastair Gowans. It should be noted, however, that despite its mobility, arctic fox is not available with the fibre length of bucktail and thus the tails of Ally's style shrimps tied with this material are, by necessity, much shorter. The danger with such substitutions is that an essential element of the pattern design may be lost. This does not mean that the fly will necessarily be ineffective, it simply means that it will not *behave* like an Ally's Shrimp.

Arctic Fox Shrimp (Westwood)

Further flies of this type were published by Ewen Robertson of Inverness in the May 1997 issue of *Flyfishing & Flytying*. The flies were devised after a trip to a Game Fair in Ireland where he found some arctic fox tail patches. The flies can be tied in a variety of colours, orange, black, blue and yellow being preferred, but all of them have a flat silver tinsel body. The blue version is particularly interesting as there are not many shrimp flies of this colour around. This version of the fly would be a very sensible choice for fresh run fish or if seatrout are around. The other variant that we have illustrated is the yellow version, a fly that is highly recommended for fresh run grilse. The tying details generally follow the original Ally's Shrimp but the bottom veilings are discarded so as to allow the silver body to show up more clearly. A sparse wing of arctic fox fur is tied in above the grey squirrel veilings.

Arctic Fox Shrimps (Robertson)

The following two flies come from a well known Scottish fly tyer called Tam Wescott of Ayr. Apart from his flies, Tam is well known for fish carvings and produces excellent, highly accurate representations of salmon and salt-water game fish.

The Copper Shrimp is a simple pattern with a one piece body and a collar hackle of golden pheasant red breast feather. The jungle cock eyes are dyed fluorescent green, giving the fly a most unusual look.

Dyed jungle cock is fairly unusual throughout the fly-tying world but the effect produced can be highly effective. Other examples of this can be seen in the McPhail Tube Shrimps on page 60.

Copper Shrimp (Wescott)

The second fly is much more in the style of an Irish shrimp with a tail of wound golden pheasant red breast feather. A hen hackle is used at the front to aid mobility,

Orange Shrimp (Wescott)

The Lochdhu is a pattern from the river Thurso which was given by Buckland & Oglesby in *A Guide to Salmon Flies*. It is very much in the style of the early Grub patterns, but simple hackled flies like this can be very effective upon occasions.

Lochdhu

ENGLAND & WALES

here has been no great tradition of shrimp patterns in England and Wales to compare with that of Ireland. Nevertheless some of the forerunners of all shrimp patterns were devised in England and Wales (or on the borders between the two). Flies such as the Wye Grub, Usk Grub and the Tippet Grub had a great influence upon the development of the Irish shrimp patterns.

The Usk Grub is still a popular fly in Wales although the modern version, which was popularised by Lionel Sweet and dressed by his wife Molly, has become somewhat simplified in that the front collar hackle has disappeared. An earlier version used by Captain Coombe Richards was dressed in a much slimmer, semi low-water style. A range of Usk Grubs, from the earliest times up to the present day are shown in plate 4 on page 15. The version shown below has an orange centre hackle and no head hackle. Other versions may have two centre hackles of orange and white and a head hackle of red game or furnace cock.

Usk Grub

The Welsh Shrimp Fly was devised by J.O. Jones of Llanwrst, primarily for use on the Conway although its use later spread to many other rivers in western Wales. J. O. Jones used this fly dressed full on a size 6 hook in conjunction with a sinking line but other anglers later found that it was a good low water fly when tied in much smaller sizes. It is probably at its most successful for fresh run fish after a spate has thinned down.

Welsh Shrimp (Jones)

The Welsh Shrimp variant with a split body and centre hackle tied much more in the style of an Usk Grub is shown below. It is probably now more widely used than the original. According to Moc Morgan in *Trout & Salmon Flies Of Wales* it is popular on the river Dwyryd tied on double hooks.

Welsh Shrimp Variant

The Penybont has its home on the upper Dovey. Moc Morgan notes several variants of this fly. The version we have illustrated has a dirty yellow seal's fur body with a palmered brown hackle. In this guise, it is much more shrimpy than the standard version tied with a yellow floss body and no body hackle.

Penybont

European Shrimp & Spey Flies

The next two flies illustrated were developed by Davy Wotton, one of the best known anglers and fly tyers in Wales in modern times. He has now moved his business largely to the USA and is also well known there. The patterns are based on the Akroyd Dee fly. Davy has provided two versions, one with a yellow rear body, one with orange.

Akroyd Shrimp, Yellow (Wotton)

Akroyd Shrimp, Orange (Wotton)

There is some confusion as to the correct rear body colour of the original. Bates, in *Atlantic Salmon Flies & Fishing,* maintains that yellow is the correct dressing, basing this view on a fly that was sent to him by the Scottish fly dresser Megan Boyd. This fly was tied by Akroyd himself and was given to Megan Boyd's father by Akroyd.

Akroyd (white wing variant)

The General Practitioner was developed by Esmond Drury for use on the Broadlands water of

the River Test in Hampshire in 1953. It has been a very influential pattern, both at the time of it's development and in the broader development of shrimp patterns ever since. Many of its features have been adopted and incorporated into patterns from Ireland, Scotland and North America. The use of golden pheasant tippet feathers with their strong black barring to imitate the eyes of the natural prawn, has become one of the diagnostic features of shrimp and prawn patterns throughout the world, as has the use of golden pheasant red breast feathers for the carapace, rostrum, legs and hackling.

General Practitioner (Drury)

The pattern can be seen as a more naturalistic imitation than the Irish patterns. Nevertheless, it is not a slavish, lifeless copy but a fly which has life and which is still effective on its day. In the UK, the General Practitioner has a Jekyll and Hyde reputation - some people swear by it whilst others swear at it! This is in contrast to North America where the GP and its variants feature on pattern lists from the east coast, via the Great Lakes to the west coast.

It is reported that the GP won Esmond Drury several bets of whisky when it was first used on the Test in 1953, although he was said to have lost out on an 'accumulator' of four large scotches! The G.P. has become somewhat altered since its inception. The original tying had a pair of golden pheasant red breast feathers mounted concave to concave over the tail to represent the head of the prawn. This has largely disappeared and most modern tyings have only one feather mounted concave side down. This is followed by another two red breast feathers, one tied in about halfway along the body, the second being tied in at the head. There is no doubt that multiple feathers mounted flat along the hook shank gave the fly a segmented

look to suggest the carapace of the prawn, a look which many modern tyings seem to have lost. Similarly, with the tippet eyes. The originals were formed from a vee cut from a golden pheasant tippet feather but this has been replaced by a whole feather. These alterations are probably the result of fly tyers wishing to simplify the pattern and it is hard to say if they result in any lack of effectiveness.

The Excaliber is a west of England pattern that was devised around 1958 on the River Exe and is therefore no newcomer. The fly has a brown squirrel hair wing and, in modern tyings, the feelers and legs are suggested by a light cree hackle, palmered over an orange body. The palmered hackle may not have been used in the original version. The more modern versions of this fly are often tied with a body of Glo-Brite yarn or floss. This bright and effective fly is useful when fishing for fresh fish, and according to Tom Saville who gave the dressing in *Trout & Salmon*, one that deserves to be more widely used.

Excaliber

One note about palmered hackles for shrimp patterns. In order to produce a more shrimp-like profile, would it not be better to wind the hackle in the reverse manner with the longer fibres at the butt end of the fly as was used on the traditional Spey patterns?

Malcolm Greenhalgh, a thoughtful English fisherman and flytyer, has developed a range of shrimp patterns since the early 1990s. These soft-hackled patterns. have proved their worth, particularly in hard conditions of low water and bright skies. In designing these flies, Malcolm's priorities were mobility and a hot spot of colour. The essence of these flies is translucency and life provided by long mobile hackles of mallard flank feathers. The most effective colour for peat stained

water is orange and the fly is named accordingly the Orange Mallard Shrimp.

Orange Mallard Shrimp

The Pink Mallard Shrimp in the same series has a body of fluorescent pink floss and the front hackle consists of three turns of silver mallard dyed pink with one turn of bronze mallard in front. The pink version seems more effective than the orange in bright, clear water conditions. The third fly in the Greenhalgh series is called the Capercaillie Shrimp because the original hackles were of cock capercaillie. As these are almost impossible to obtain, silver mallard flank dyed iron blue dun makes a good substitute. These three variants give a range of colours from dark, through medium to light which can be used to suit a wide variety of water conditions.

The Orange Hackle Shrimp is of a simple design with a long bucktail tail, an orange floss body, a short thorax and a head hackle. It has nevertheless proved to an absolute killer when there is some colour in the water. The effectiveness of this fly is not in doubt. It has taken fish in England, Scotland, Ireland, Iceland, Canada, Russia and Scandinavia.

Orange Hackle Shrimp

Two further flies from Malcolm complete a most interesting list. The first of these is not a salmon fly at all - it is a trout fly which just happens to be as effective on salmon as it is on trout! Called the Orange Partridge Shrimp, it is in fact a version of the traditional old north of England wet fly called the Partridge & Orange. Tied on treble hooks in sizes from 12 to 14 it is effective on small, shallow rivers such as the Ribble, Hodder, Upper Lune and Nith, particularly for summer grilse. A tiny wisp of a fly which consists of no more than a gold ribbed, orange floss body with a brown partridge hackle at the head, it confirms Malcolm's opinion that we often use flies for grilse that are too large.

Orange Partridge Shrimp

Another interesting fly which Malcolm finds effective is the Pink & Purple Prawn (otherwise known as the 3P). This pattern originated from Philip White and was basically an attempt to imitate a natural brown prawn bait and was first used on the Hampshire Avon one September where it was immediately successful.

Pink & Purple Prawn (White)

Originally designed to be fished deep and slow, it has proved to be very effective in clear water conditions not just in the Autumn but throughout the season. Oddly enough, Robert thinks this fly is excellent in coloured water conditions. Philip reports that this is the fly that he uses most often and that if the fish are there to see it, they will usually take it. Robert rates this pattern very highly and tells of an angler who arrived at his house, hands still shaking with excitement after taking three good grilse in short order and breaking off in a fourth. He had one remaining version of this fly in his hand which he had not dared to use before obtaining some more examples.

Michael Evans is an experienced angler and fishing guide who is in an ideal position to judge the value of a fly pattern. He is fortunate enough to fish in many locations of the world where there are such prolific runs of fish that enormous catches are possible. In such locations experimentation is really possible and therefore his observations are of great interest.

His most successful fly, on which he has caught more salmon than any other, is the Tail Fire. This fly combines a hairwing with a wound Golden Pheasant red breast feather tail. The colours are predominantly black with yellow and orange. Michael's observations in Iceland and Russia show that bright yellow, red and orange are the best colours for stained or peaty water and that black is better in clear water conditions. The Tail Fire combines several of these colours in one fly and it is therefore not surprising that it has proved effective in a wide range of conditions, although it is ideally suited to clearer water.

Tail Fire (Evans)

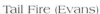

In the August 1991 issue of *Trout & Salmon*, Michael gave two other patterns which are of interest. The first of these is the Evans' Special which is unusual in that it uses lesser wing coverts from the jungle cock as an overwing. Although it is not called a shrimp the overall effect is quite shrimpy.

Evans' Special

The next flies are taken from an article that Dave wrote for the December 1991 issue of *Trout & Salmon*. Dave has always been a big fan of Spey flies and considers them to be among the most effective flies that one can set before a salmon. The flies in question were devised when heron hackles became unavailable. Having tried various substitutes, none of which were entirely suitable, Dave hit upon the idea of using barbs from a magpie tail feather which he had chanced upon whilst out walking the dog. Because the magpie tail feather has a very strong quill, the feather should be soaked in hot water and a sliver of the quill with the barbs attached should be peeled away. Alternatively, the hackles can be tied in as three of four separate bunches of fibres above and below the shank.

In this article, Michael also stated that he often used shrimp and prawn flies as a last resort in the Autumn when the water was extremely clear. His reasoning was that only this type of pattern would pass close scrutiny in very clear water, no matter how cold. The pattern given was a realistic prawn imitation, as illustrated here.

Shrimp Fly (Evans)

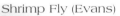

Magpie Spey (Riding)

The bodies of the Magpie Speys consist of either floss or Lurex in whichever colour you prefer, Dave normally uses black, red and blue. Note that these flies are normally tied on low water double hooks in sizes 4 to 6 rather than on single hooks as is usual for Spey flies.

Dave Riding has been a keen user of shrimp flies for many years and has devised several new patterns. The Latex Prawn has been around for a number of years and although the provenance is slightly obscure, we believe that the use of latex to represent the segmented body of a shrimp or prawn began with Dave. The following pattern is as given by Buckland & Oglesby in *A Guide to Salmon Flies*.

The last fly in this section is very unusual. It was found by Dave Riding in an old book and the pattern was detailed by him in an article published in *Trout & Salmon* in October 1991. The book (which unfortunately we are unable to trace) gave brief details of the fly and went on to say that it had risen and hooked fish in both high and low water at all times of the season, producing 16 salmon to one angler in ten days fishing on an exceedingly dour river. Inspired by this, Dave immediately set about tying some examples and first tried it in 1988. Success was immediate, Dave hooked a fish on his very first cast and over the next three years caught over 40 fish on this pattern. The construction of the fly is very unusual, the most interesting feature of

Latex Prawn

the dressing being two hackles with a vee cut in the end which are tied in at the middle joint of the fly, back to back, curving outwards. When fished with a sink and draw technique the butterfly motion of the hackles give this fly a unique action in the water. The original colours are shown in the dressing. The hackles are of ginger cock, the rear body is of pink wool ribbed with silver tinsel and the front body is of yellow wool. The middle joint has a pair of jungle cock feathers to represent the eyes, a sparse hackle of natural guinea fowl and a bunch of golden pheasant tippet fibres to represent the legs. The fly is completed with a throat hackle of guinea fowl and wings, tied flat and reversed, of silver or bronze mallard. Other colours could be tried (Dave has tried red bodies and hackles) but so far none have been as effective as the original tying. There is no name for this fly so, for the purposes of this book, we have taken the liberty of naming it Riding's Prawn.

Riding's Prawn

The Francis from Peter Deane has been a most influential pattern since its very conception. Many other prawn and shrimp flies have been devised which use the same basic form of a carrot shaped body and a palmered hackle. Although the Francis is no longer widely used in the UK, it remains one of the most popular and effective flies in Iceland. The pattern shown here is the original from Peter Deane, later versions have replaced the cock pheasant tail fibres, which represent the rostrum of the shrimp, with hair of various kinds.

The feelers are of stripped grizzle hackle stalks. Colour variations include black and a brownish olive green, known as the Black and Green Francis, respectively. Further variants can be seen in the section on Iceland on page 83.

Red Francis (Peter Deane)

The next fly is very much a generic type of prawn pattern, in this case tied as a tube. An orange seal's fur body palmered with an orange hackle, a golden pheasant red breast feather wound at the tail and golden pheasant tippets to represent the eyes are typical ingredients.

Prawn Fly Tube

The widespread use of hair probably started in North America with the hairwing versions of the classic salmon flies, but its application has developed considerably. The next pattern is based upon the General Practitioner style of fly but the body hackling has been replaced by bunches of hair tied in at intervals along the hook shank.

Hair Back Prawn

Gordon Mackenzie of Redcastle is a professional fly tyer of many years experience who has devised a series of flies based on the technique of hair hackles using a dubbing loop. This technique was not invented by Gordon – indeed the American flytyer George Grant has used it for over 60 years – but few other flytyers have developed it to the extent that Gordon has. The flies, known generically as 'Hairys' include a wide range of patterns: principally Shrimps, Practitioners and Speys. Gordon first announced these flies in an article in *Flyfishing & Flytying* in May 1998 and since then has extended the range of patterns considerably. These flies are very popular in North America and have proved to be very effective for steelhead as well as Atlantic salmon. They are perhaps not the easiest flies to tie, but the effort is well worthwhile because the flies are mobile, durable and have enormous potential.

The three flies illustrated above are all General Practitioner derivatives. The colour schemes for the first fly is taken from a classic North American steelhead fly from the great Syd Glasso. Further details about Sydney Glasso and his flies can be found in the chapter on North America. Mac's Purple Practitioner is one of Gordon's own patterns based on the colours of a Purple Ally's Shrimp, and has proved to be absolutely deadly on the river Findhorn, in Scotland, as well as being successful in North America. The colours of the last fly illustrated are derived from the classic Durham Ranger.

Hairy Deep Purple Spey

Hairy Mac's Purple Spey

Hairy Sol Duc Spey

Hairy Sol Duc Practitioner

Hairy Mac's Purple Practitioner

Hairy Durham Range Practitioner

One of the most obvious advantages of this style of tying is the degree of control that can be

exercised over the bulk of the fly. For low water conditions, the flies can be dressed small and sparse simply by putting less hair in the loop. For larger flies, with a denser profile, the amount of hair is increased. The overall profile can be also be adjusted by careful selection of the length of hair.

The Hairys represent more a method of tying rather than a particular range of patterns. The technique can be applied to flies ranging from small hackled flies for trout, through the shrimps illustrated up to Spey style flies. Gordon ties three basic types of fly for salmon and steelhead. These are the Practitioner style, Hairy Speys and finally a range of shrimp patterns based on a combination of features from Irish shrimp flies and the Ally's Shrimp.

The group of flies illustrated above are Spey patterns tied using the hair technique. These flies have found favour in North America but are also very effective on European waters.

Hairy Mac's Purple Spey is the Spey style brother of the Hairy Practitioner and is just as effective. The Sol Duc Spey is the hairy version of Glasso's classic steelhead pattern and the Deep Purple Spey is Gordon's version of the Deep Purple Spey from Walt Johnson. Details of these two steelhead flies can be found in the chapter on North America.

The illustrations also show some hairy shrimps. Any Irish or Scottish shrimp fly can be tied in this way, substituting hair for hackles and tails. The examples shown are the shrimp version of Mac's Purple and a version based on the Sol Duc. A further example of a shrimp fly from Gordon, the Hairy Ness Shrimp can be found in the Scottish section on page 65.

The last fly from Gordon that we have illustrated is an experimental development that is showing a lot of promise. The fly is similar to the general tying style of the Hairy Practitioners but the front body is replaced by a spun deer hair head. At the front, the deer hair is clipped and varnished or glued to produce a diving vane or lip, similar to that found on floating lures such as the Rapala. The idea is to produce a fly which floats but which will dive, flutter and wriggle in the water as it comes under more or less tension due to the water flow or the amount of pull on the line. The flies are normally fished on sink tip or sinking lines.

The only other salmon or steelhead fly which we know about which is tied in a similar manner is called the Dahlberg Diver. This is surprising when one considers the number of fly tyers in North America who are wizards with spun deer hair and that shaped deer hair is used for several surface skaters and many bass flies. It should be noted that on single hooks, 3 to 5 turns of lead wire are super-glued to the shank at the tag position, in order that the fly swims correctly. The pattern shown again uses the Sol Duc colour scheme, but other colours could of course be used.

Hairy Mac's Purple Shrimp

Hairy Sol Duc Shrimp

Hairy Wiggle Practitioner

The use of polythene for the bodies of prawn or shrimp flies has been around for a long time now, although it has generally been superseded by other, more modern, body materials. Nevertheless,

polythene does have some points in its favour. It is nearly transparent thus producing a translucent body effect which is very effective when wound over a brightly coloured underbody. Polythene is easily come by in all kinds of modern packaging and costs nothing. Lastly, Polythene is actually quite heavy although we tend not to notice this because we always experience it as a film. A body made of many wraps of polythene may provide sufficient weight to a fly that added lead is not necessary. The fly illustrated is given in *A Guide to Salmon Flies* by Buckland & Oglesby.

The Red Prawn is another pattern much in the same quasi-realistic style. The body is carrot shaped of fluorescent red wool. The body is palmered with red game hackles and a shell back of polythene runs along the spine. The eyes are of black plastic beads threaded onto monofilament. This particular tying was supplied to us by Fulling Mill Flies but there are literally hundreds of variations on this basic theme.

Red Prawn

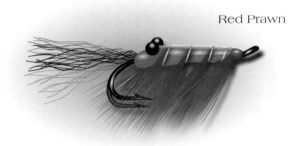

Polythene Prawn

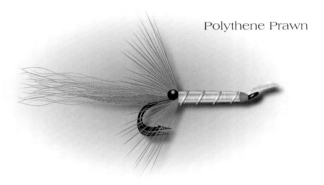

The next two flies are noted by John Buckland in A *Pocket Guide to Trout & Salmon Flies.* The origin of these patterns is France but we have included them here because they are quite closely related in style to the Polythene Prawn.

In the Scottish section we saw the Junction Shrimp as an example of a fly that uses white hackling to good effect. The following fly from Mark Purvis is a variant of that fly which has had some success, accounting for salmon on both the rivers Wye and Usk.

Junction Shrimp Variant (Purvis)

Crevette Rose

Crevette Gris

ICELAND & SCANDINAVIA

celand is one of the premier salmon fly fishing destinations of the world. There are at least 20 salmon rivers in Iceland with good reputations and large catches. Among the best known of these are the Midfjardara, the Ranga, the Laxa I Dolum, the Vididalsa, the Laxa I Asum, the Sela and the Hofsa. All of these rivers have an annual catch of over a thousand fish each, with the East Ranga reaching around 2,500 in 2000. If these figures do not seem very impressive, bear in mind that the season does not start until the last week in June and finishes in October at the latest - a short season indeed. The number of anglers is also very restricted, the Laxa I Asum fishing only two rods! There are some other notable features about Icelandic rivers, they are totally uncontaminated and run extremely clear and, at their best, they offer the ultimate in fly fishing water. The fish are also unusually fresh, often retaining their saltwater teeth after they have entered the rivers. This is quite unusual in other countries and for many fishermen who may never see this may tend to forget that in its marine environment the Atlantic salmon is an efficient predator. A salmon with a mouthful of teeth like a barracuda can be quite a sobering sight.

Until recent times, the recommended patterns for Iceland included all the British classics but this has now changed and more streamlined modern flies are now the norm. Popular shrimp flies from Iceland include the Francis series, the Krafla and the Raeken. The Francis was actually devised by the well known English flytyer Peter Deane but it has become so widespread that its name is now synonymous with Iceland. The Francis comes in five main colour variants - the Red, Black, Orange, Yellow and the Green (Olive) Francis. Of these, the Red is the most popular followed by the Black and Green variations. The Francis has a tapered body of wool in the given colour which is lightly palmered, and feelers (or legs) of bushy brown hair together with stripped hackle stalks as antennae. The tying as used in Iceland varies slightly from the Deane original in that the rostrum originally consisted of pheasant tail fibres. Ironically, the second version described below and known locally as the Icelandic Francis does retain the original material for the rostrum.

Black Francis Tube

Red Icelandic Francis (treble)

It should be noted that there are, in fact, two different versions of the Francis. The first is the Francis tube with a carrot shaped body and a spirally wound hackle which is the form most of us know. The second form is tied on small trebles. The body is too small to bother with palmering and the hackle is tied as a collar only at the thick end of the body. The body is ribbed with fine silver or gold wire. The tail of brown calf tail fibres is replaced with brown feather fibres taken from a pheasant tail. The hackle stalks representing the feelers of the shrimp are tied very long. Tied in this form, the Francis is a most impressive fly. The sample flies for this book were tied by Sküli Kristinsson, one of the most able professional flytyers in Iceland, on silver and gold hooks, which add to the jewel-like qualities of these super little flies.

The Francis series are probably the most widely used salmon flies in Iceland although Skuli assures us that the Francis is also effective in other countries. This is confirmed by the fact that Skuli keeps very busy tying hundreds of these flies for export. In Iceland, the Francis is considered to be at its most effective when it is fished very slowly over the fish. In order to achieve this the line may be mended several times whilst the cast is being

PLATE 20: Colour variants of Krafla

fished out. It is not unusual for the tube version of the Francis to be fished upstream, rather than cast downstream.

Both of the next two patterns were devised by the doyen of Icelandic flytyers, Kristjan Gislason, and we were fortunate enough to obtain sample patterns tied by the master himself.

The Raeken is predominantly orange with an unusual tail formed from saddle hackles tied in a vertical vee-form. It is noteworthy that the colour is a pale pinkish orange rather than hot orange. Can it be coincidence that one of Paddy Bonner's most effective new flies from Ireland also uses this lighter orange shade? This pattern impresses us with its lightness, mobility and general 'fishiness'. It is also simple in construction and easy to tie.

In his book *The Art of the Atlantic Salmon*

Fly, Bates features a fly called the Raekja which is very similar to this, with a wing of orange hackle tips and the rear tippet veilings mounted both under and over the shank. This is obviously a slightly different version of the same fly.

Raeken (Gislasson)

The Krafla (pronounced 'Krabla') has feelers of stripped grizzle hackle stalks, although some of the samples were tied with peccary bristles. The body is most unusual in being made of tightly palmered hackles which are then clipped to a carrot shape. The fly comes in a whole range of colours, most of which are a combination of two hackles as shown in the illustration above, although the white/red combination is the original tying. With no heavy body tying, this fly again looks impressive and has the necessary features of profile and translucence to be effective in many kinds of water.

Scottish shrimp patterns such as the Ally's Shrimp and Irish patterns such as Curry's Red Shrimp and the Black and Silver Shrimp are also often used in Iceland with success, mostly by visiting anglers, but we are told they are becoming more popular amongst the local anglers as well. It has been well documented over the years, by people such as Ashley-Cooper, Renie and Bates, that patterns with a bit of blue about them have been consistently successful in Iceland waters. Indeed, the Blue Rat was devised by Poul Jorgensen for a fishing trip to Iceland, specifically at Bates' request. On this basis we would venture to suggest that Irish shrimp flies such as the Swinford Blue, the Ballina Blue or the Light Wilkinson might well be worth a try as well.

Incidentally, before we leave the subject of Iceland, one of the best kept secrets in fly tying is Icelandic horse hair. Forget anything you think you know about horse hair: this hair is as fine as arctic fox, soft and mobile, but with a superb lustre which fox hair does not have. It has an underhair, generally between 20mm and 40mm (3/4" to 11/2") long with longer guard hairs which can be 75mm (3") or longer depending upon where it is taken from the skin. This is a fantastic material for the ultimate in mobile yet durable wings and tails and is only now becoming generally available. Ideal candidates for this material include Ally's Shrimps, Arctic Fox Shrimps and Fatback tubes, as well as the standard range of hairwings.

Norway is the home of big rivers and big fish, specimens over 40lb being taken each year. The quality of fishing on some of these rivers is absolutely astounding and, whilst the number of large fish caught today may not be quite as many as in the past, there is absolutely no doubt where a salmon fisherman should head if he wishes to catch the specimen of a lifetime.

Some published statistics may give the reader a flavour of some of the astounding catches made in Norway. Cyril Wells fished the river Vosso for nearly 25 years, up until 1950. During this period he caught fish of every pound weight from twenty to fifty-eight pounds, with the exception of 55 lbs. So many large fish were captured that he did not document fish under 20lbs and in total he caught over eighty fish in excess of forty pounds! Catches for the river Alta, as recorded by Charles Ritz, also make interesting reading. In 1954, out of 277 fish caught, 37 (including almost all the fish over 40lb) were taken on a General Practitioner prawn fly. All these catches were achieved with the fly. Whilst access to some of these rivers is difficult to come by, rivers such as the Gaula which share these huge salmon, do offer opportunities to visiting anglers.

The modern trend is to fish with large 'fatback' tube flies. The hairwing on these tubes is tied in facing forwards, over the head of the tube, and then doubled back to form the wing. This technique gives the wing a hump backed look, thus the name 'fatback'. Flies tied in this manner can be very large indeed, we have examples in front of us where the overall length is over 150mm (6"). Despite this, more traditional patterns continue to be used and a small band of dedicated enthusiasts have maintained the tradition of the classic Spey and prawn flies

Grey Palmer Grub

In Sweden, there is an ongoing tradition of using Spey and Dee flies, which continues to the present day. Our contributors have noted that the Grey and Black Heron are regularly used, as is the

Lady Caroline. Professional fly tyers, such as Ismo Saastamoinen, continue to offer a complete range of these traditional patterns, including Grubs such as the Usk and Wye Grubs as well as less well known patterns like the Grey Palmer Grub. The pattern illustrated is as given by Pryce-Tannatt in *How to Dress Salmon Flies*.

More modern flies that are much in the Grub tradition and which continue to be used include the Ullsock (Wool Sock). The Ullsock is quite simple, retaining a two piece body and hackles at the rear, centre and head of the fly. The tail of the Ullsock is golden pheasant tippet in the illustration but this is very often replaced by a tuft of bright red wool.

Ullsock

The following grub style patterns were tied by Nestor Dupo, a professional fly tyer from Sweden who specialises in tube flies and who sells not only to the Scandinavian market but also widely in North America. Although a tube fly specialist, Nestor also ties flies in the traditional Grub and Spey styles.

The Horstsocken is somewhat in the style of an Usk Grub. There is a hackle fibre wing and the front body is palmered, rather than there being a centre hackle.

Horstsocken

The M. Socken has a tail of wound golden pheasant red breast feather and is thus very much in the style of an Irish shrimp with the addition of a feather wing. The relatively subdued colours are relieved by silver badger hackles, so well loved in Ireland, used for the centre hackle and throat, giving a shimmering, translucent effect. An attractive pattern and one that could well be effective in other areas.

M. Socken

A further pattern with an unusual name is the 94 An. This is even more like an Irish shrimp but the addition of a third, short rear body or butt and a secondary, hot orange marabou tail, give this fly a slightly different look. The colours are again subdued, but the veiled effect of the marabou tail is most attractive and gives the fly a splash of strong colour as an aiming point. The idea of a strongly coloured, mobile inner tail is one that may well be of interest to tyers in Ireland.

94An

Apart from the traditional patterns, new Spey type flies continue to be devised and used. The Silver Wilkinson has been around since the early 19th century and has been successful in many reincarnations, from classic fully dressed fly, through Irish shrimp versions and now to Spey style. The dressing of this fly has varied in detail over the years but the basic design retains the common features of a silver tinsel body combined with magenta and blue hackles, The following dressing avoids complex winging and is very simple but effective.

Silver Wilkinson Spey

The next fly comes from Ole Andreassen and is of interest because the body hackling is of coot wing fibres rather than heron. In his comments on this pattern Andreassen notes almost any feather fibres that are soft and long enough can serve as Spey hackle provided that they do not marry too well. They need to separate out when wound, not clump together.

Silver Coot Spey (Andreassen)

In the section on England and Wales we have already remarked on the use of magpie tail feathers

for this purpose by Dave Riding (see page 78). The technique used by Martin Jørgensen for the Cheapskate Heron, illustrated on page 92, is also of interest in this respect.

Standard Swedish patterns may also be adapted to the Spey style. The next fly is the famous Mörrum, named after the river of the same name. In the illustration, it is tied by Nestor Dupo in the Spey style. This is an extremely handsome fly in this configuration.

Mörrum Spey

The Thunder Spey is another new Spey pattern from Sweden. The example illustrated was also tied by Nestor Dupo. The body hackling, restricted to the black dubbing part of the body, is golden pheasant red breast feather. The collar hackle is of blue dyed guinea fowl. The wings are long jungle cock.

Thunder Spey

Some of the Swedish Spey derivations can be quite extreme in form, as the two examples illustrated in Plate 21 show. These patterns were given by John Buckland in *A pocket Guide to Trout*

No. 1 Spey

No. 2 Spey

PLATE 21: Swedish Spey derivatives

& *Salmon Flies* and are characterised by an extremely long hairwing rather than the traditional bronze mallard. They may be tied as large as a size 9/0 single hook and, if the proportions were maintained, would produce a fly with an overall length in excess of 180mm (7"). In form, they are the precursors to the large hairwing tubes which are now so common in both Sweden and Norway.

As mentioned above, Nestor specialises in tube flies. The next one is simply known as Shrimp #1. In terms of its elements, it is very similar to an Usk Grub. The body is in two parts: orange dubbing at the rear and black dubbing at the front. The tail is of wound golden pheasant red breast feather. The centre hackle is white under orange and the front hackle is black. Long pairs of back-to-back jungle cock wings are tied in above and below the shank underneath the front hackle. A very similar tube fly, with a weighted cone head, is known as the Pardo Shrimp.

Cone heads are becoming increasingly popular in Scandinavia as a means of weighting a fly. The effect produced is different from that obtained by using heavyweight brass tubes as the weight is concentrated at the front of the fly. The advantage of this configuration is that the fly does

not tend to sink tail first when slacker water is encountered. The effectiveness of nose heavy flies that can be made to dive and climb as the water flow and tension on the line changes is well known to all stillwater trout fishermen with flies such as the Dog Nobbler. This motion, combined with a long mobile tail or wing, produces a darting, fluttering lure that is extremely attractive to all predatory fish.

Shrimp #1

The Shrimp #2 is very similar in style but has a green rear body and centre hackle and lacks the jungle cock wings.

Shrimp #2

Jurij Shumakov is the originator of the Flag Wing Shrimp which was first used in 1996. Since then it has been consistently successful on Kola rivers such as the Belousiha and the Titovka. This is a simple pattern but looks effective for all that.

Flag Wing Shrimp

Chapoma Spey

The Chapoma Spey was also devised by Jurij Shumakov. It was first tried on the River Mörrum in 1998 and proved to be very effective right from the start. A trip in 1999 to the Southern Kola brought success on the rivers Chapoma, Strelna and Chavanga. The fly works very well on both floating and intermediate lines and is especially

effective when the water is stained tea colour. The silver rear body and the flash of colour of the red tag are extremely effective when contrasted against the dark front body and wing.

Ismo Saastamoinen is one of best known professional fly tyers in Sweden. His flies are known for the superb quality of their workmanship and he has built up a dedicated customer base all over the world, including North America where his work is well known.

The first fly is called the I.Q. Shrimp. The I.Q. part of the name is used by Ismo to designate his own original patterns which are tied with attention to detail that one rarely sees. The I.Q. Shrimp comes in two colour variants, brown and burnt orange and orange.

I.Q. Shrimp

I.Q. Orange Shrimp

The Glow Butt Spey is a derivation from the Red Butt Spey from North America. The winging is a pair of burnt orange hackles tied back to back with a black fox tail wing over. The body is a mixture of black and burnt orange Crystal Seal dubbing.

Glow Butt Spey

The following two flies by Nestor Dupo are special tube versions of the General Practitioner. The body is of dubbed seal's fur, palmered with a hackle of the appropriate colour. The shellback is represented by a series of six golden pheasant tippet feathers getting progressively smaller towards the head of the fly. There are two normal colour variants, red and yellow. In both cases, the tippet feathers are dyed to match the body colour.

Yellow G.P. Special Tube

Red G.P. Special Tube

Denmark is not one of the major salmon fishing countries but nevertheless does have some good runs of autumn salmon and is also interesting because of its high quality seatrout fishing both in fresh and salt water. Denmark is unique in having a first class stocking and preservation system in place for seatrout and is one of the few places in the world where seatrout runs are actually improving. Uniquely, much of the Danish seatrout fishing is done in saltwater around the coast, rather than in the rivers.

Paul Kohler, from Denmark, who is a friend of Robert's, has had success with both salmon and seatrout in the rivers using an Irish Bann Special shrimp on a fast sinking leader. He has also fished very successfully in Norway for grilse, using the same fly and method.

The majority of the following flies were found on the web site *Globalflyfisher.com* which is jointly run by Steve Schweitzer from the U.S.A. and Martin Jørgensen from Denmark. This on-line magazine is one of the best fishing sites on the web

and has a wealth of information about all kinds of fly fishing, with expert contributors from both Europe and North America. It is highly recommended. The following patterns were primarily designed for seatrout fishing but they have all the features necessary to make them effective for salmon as well. The Omø Brush has already been used for salmon and the Umbrella was originally intended for both seatrout and salmon. Martin was kind enough to provide us with the samples of the flies that we have illustrated.

The first three patterns are hackle flies which continue a long tradition of grub style patterns and which are also popular in Sweden.

The Mia fly was devised by Mark Hansen and is named after his dog, Mia, from which he obtained the body dubbing.

Mia Fly (Hansen)

The Dalby Dribbler is also from Mark Hansen and is named after a town in Western Sealand where he often fishes. The Dribble part of the name has nothing to do with the way that the fly is fished, it is the nickname of a friend's dog!

Dalby Dribbler (Hansen)

The Umbrella from Martin Jørgensen also has two hackles, but in this case they are tied in quite close together towards the front of the fly, separated by a short dubbed body. The rear body is of silver tinsel. The colours of this fly may be varied: either red or yellow body feathers from the golden pheasant are used for the tail and wing. The hackle colour can be chosen to complement or contrast with these elements – chestnut, furnace or badger being the main choices. The top fly illustrated shows the hackles as tied by Martin, the bottom illustration shows the same fly with the hackle proportions reversed in order to produce a more shrimp-like profile.

Opossum Shrimp (Jørgensen)

Omoe Brush (Bonde)

Umbrella (Jørgensen)

The Opossum Shrimp is an attempt to capture the transparency, segmentation and extremely visible black eyes of the natural shrimp. The name comes from opossum fur body dubbing. Barred wood duck hackle fibres are used for the legs. The colours used in this fly are all pale natural colours which match the very subdued colouring of the natural shrimp.

The Omø Brush has nothing to do with washing powder but is named after an island in the Danish Storebælt. The fly was designed by Ken Bonde for seatrout but Martin has already tied it for salmon fishing. It is, in essence, a combination of a hackle fly with a General Practitioner. The fly is normally tied with red breast feathers from the golden pheasant but the yellow body feathers can also be used as an effective alternative. The illustration above shows two versions of the fly. The top one is tied in the original manner, the

bottom one in a slightly adapted version which uses much longer hackling of golden pheasant red breast feathers.

The next fly described is called the Cheapskate Heron because Martin devised a method of utilising the otherwise useless butt ends of scarce heron hackles as a quasi Spey hackle. The idea can be applied, not only to heron hackle, but to any other feather hackles which have the right type of barbs but cannot be wound because the stem is too thick. In the following example the hackles are tied in at the throat of the fly but it is also possible to spread the hackling over the body by tying segments of hackle in three or four positions along the body, before continuing with the body wraps. The Magpie Speys from Dave Riding (page 81) are an example of where this technique might be applied.

Cheapskate Heron (Jørgensen)

In this method, a small vee-shaped section is cut from the feather. This is then held under the shank in wishbone fashion whilst several turns of thread are taken around the hackle barbs, but behind the short stem. When the hackle barbs are secure, the stem is cut away.

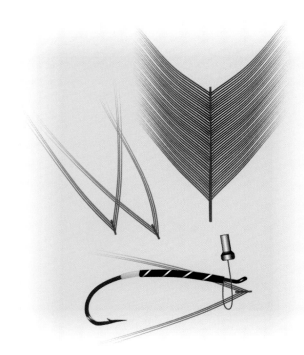

North American Shrimp & Spey Flies

he range of shrimp patterns used throughout the North American continent is very extensive indeed, reflecting the vast size of the continent and the very great differences in geography and fishing traditions. The spectrum ranges from the rivers of eastern Canada such as the Mirimichi with their runs of Atlantic salmon, through the steelhead fisheries of the Great Lakes, to the Pacific salmon and steelhead fisheries of Oregon and Washington states in the U.S.A. and British Columbia in Canada. So great are the distances and geographical differences between these locations that it is impossible to speak about them as one unit. For the purposes of this book we have arbitrarily split them up into smaller sections on a geographical basis. One of the almost inevitable consequences of setting such boundaries is that the impression is given that there are hard and fast divisions between these areas. This is certainly not meant to be the case and, as with many other aspects of fishing, it should not be thought that the various areas have developed fly patterns without reference to each other. One of the most revealing aspects from writing this book has been to discover the extent of the exchange of information between fly tiers and anglers from countries throughout the world. It was not unusual to discover, for instance. a keen fisherman in Newfoundland who gave us his favourite pattern for use on his local rivers. This pattern turned out to be a modification of a very old Scottish pattern which had been tied by a Finn to use in Sweden.

One of the most interesting and surprising aspects of the research in North America turned out to be the continuing influence of older flies, the use of which has declined in their home waters. There is a popular misconception in Europe that all flies from the new world are garish creations of flashy tinsel, held together with epoxy resin. Nothing is further from the truth. It is certainly true that fishermen and flytyers from North America seem more willing to experiment with new materials than their European cousins, but the other side of the coin seems to be that they don't throw away patterns that work simply because they are a few years old.

To a European eye the most noticeable amongst the patterns that we found in everyday use

were the Spey flies. Spey flies are seldom used today in Scotland, but have found favour throughout North America from the east coast to the west. Far from being 'old' patterns, these flies are as modern as they come and are constantly being developed as the following paragraphs will show. It should be noted that the use of the word 'Spey' in the North American context is used rather loosely. The ultra long heron hackles are in fact as much a feature of the strip wing Dee flies as the Spey flies, which were as often hackled with Spey cock hackles (a type of fowl which was bred in the Spey valley specially for their long hackles), as they were with heron. The heron hackles used on the Spey flies were in fact very often not the normal hackles as may be imagined, but the crest feathers found on the head of various heron and crane species - some of the larger flies had a hackle length of up to 150mm (6")! In the 19th century enormous quantities of feathers and skins were imported into Great Britain from the India, Asia and South America, primarily for the millinery trade. It is thus far from certain that the 'heron' was always from the European grey heron. A noticeable feature of the modern Spey patterns is that the body hackling is often restricted to the front third of the body. This may be due partly to the fact that feathers long enough to hackle the complete body are hard to find but possibly more important is the fact that many, if not most, of the new Spey patterns have a short body which is divided into a slim rear portion and a more heavily dressed front portion. The rear body is normally of floss or tinsel, the front body of dubbed fur. This configuration gives the fly a humped shoulder look and the hackling, being restricted to the front body tends to stand out from and veil the rear body, giving a most attractive effect, particularly when the rear body is of tinsel. The fact that the Spey hackle is embedded in the dubbing also helps to make the fly more durable.

The patterns in use are in fact a mixture of Spey and Dee types and characteristics of both traditions are to be found in the modern tyings, particularly with respect to winging. The wings of the modern Speys are often simple strip wings, tied flat in typical Dee style, matched pairs of hackles Glasso style, or even hairwings.

Another of the most noticeable features of flies from North America, particularly those which

Moonshine
a classic Dee fly

Lady Caroline
a classic Spey fly

are primarily designed for steelhead fishing, is the common use of very bright colours. This has three primary reasons. Firstly there is a perception that steelhead are more susceptible to bright colours than Atlantic salmon. Whether this is in fact true is a moot point. Many anglers in Europe would need to fish with these colourful patterns for several seasons before any firm conclusions could be drawn. The second reason is that on many rivers in North America there is a fly only rule. This means that in flood conditions or when the rivers are carrying a lot of colour, the option of using a spinner is not open to fishermen. Many of the extremely colourful patterns from North America can therefore be considered as spinner replacements. For fishermen who do not live close by a good river, and who cannot therefore be choosy about when they fish, effective patterns of this type are absolutely essential, and can make the difference between success and failure.

The third reason is the fishermen themselves - many European anglers are simply more conservative in the colour choices that they are prepared to use. This is rather ironic when one

considers that Europe, and Great Britain in particular, was the home of the fully dressed classic salmon fly. You don't have to look far in these flies to find brilliant patterns dressed in light blue, purple, grass green, bright yellow, bright red and so on. The restriction of salmon flies to being predominantly black, yellow, orange and red is comparatively recent. It may fairly be said that the fishermen of North America changed nothing, they simply continued to use the colours that were in common use and simply extended these to include fluorescent chartreuse, lime green and pink. There is no doubt that the few salmon fishermen in Europe who have used flashy stillwater trout lures (the Cat's Whisker, etc.) for salmon fishing in adverse conditions have found that they can and do catch salmon.

Silver Heron (Glasso)

The widespread use of Spey patterns for steelhead fishing in North America was encouraged and developed in the North West of the United States by a well known angler and flytyer named Sydney Glasso whom lived on the Olympic Peninsular in Washington State. It was he who first used Spey type flies for steelhead fishing and a large part of their present day popularity can be attributed to his inventiveness and success in adapting this style of tying. Many of the well known modern tiers such as Bob Veverka were strongly influenced by the flowing lines and elegance of these flies, and the Glasso influence is still strong amongst the modern Spey patterns being developed today.

The innovative use of hackle wings is typical of the Glasso Speys and give these flies added mobility and translucency over their Scottish forbears. The look of these flies in the hand is somewhat different to the humpbacked appearance of the traditional Scottish Spey patterns. It should,

however be remembered that once the fly is wetted and fishing in the current, the hackles will lie back on to the body and present a much more streamlined appearance. More details about Sydney Glasso and his flies are to be found in the books *Steelhead Fly Fishing & Flies* and *Steelhead Fly Fishing*, both by Trey Combs. Plate 22 shows a range of Glasso Spey flies, it is clear to see why they caused such a stir and why they have been an inspiration to other flytyers.

For the European angler we should make a comment about the sizes of the flies that appear on the following pages. Steelhead flies, particularly the Spey flies can be very large indeed to our eyes, particularly the flies used for winter fishing in extreme cold water conditions. Most of the Spey patterns shown vary from a hook size 4 up to hook size 5/0, i.e. from $1\frac{1}{2}$ to $2\frac{1}{2}$ inches (38 to 64mm) long overall.

The General Practitioner, in various forms and variants is another 'old' fly that occurs again and again when one looks at favourite pattern lists for waters as geographically spread as the Fraser and the Mirimichi. Maybe the old world has forgotten some of its own hard learned lessons in these cases and it may be time for us in Europe to reinvent a part of our salmon fishing history. Shrimp patterns certainly have their place here and there are many patterns that could and should make the return journey across the Atlantic. The General Practitioner, in various forms, is one of the most successful North American flies, both for steelhead in the West and for Atlantic salmon in the East

The use of the Ally's Shrimp is sporadic throughout North America. It is popular in pockets such as the Mirimichi where it was introduced by Alastair Gowan, but in other areas it is little used. In fact, due to its form and style, it is ideally suited to fishing in fast flowing water and would therefore be very suitable for steelhead fishing in some of the big, brawling waters so typical of much of North America. Considering the Ally's Shrimp as a style of tying rather than a single fly pattern, the Ally's Shrimp can be dressed in any colour combination and thus could easily be adapted to take on the hues that have proved successful for steelhead. The style of construction of the Ally's Shrimp means that it can be tied in almost any size and it is also well suited to tying on single hooks, a most important factor in North America.

Brown Heron

Orange Heron

Gold Heron

Sol Duc Spey

Courtesan

PLATE 22: Sydney Glasso Spey Flies

An interesting sideline for European readers of magazine articles and other material from North America is the use of the words 'Spey rods' and 'Spey casting'. We have found that these expressions often refer simply to the use of long (by North American standards) double handed rods, such as would normally be used on the Spey and other large European rivers. It should not be assumed that 'Spey rod' necessarily means a rod designed for Spey casting or that 'Spey casting' necessarily means casting using the Spey casting technique. Often these terms are used loosely to mean using and casting a double handed rod, even with the overhead technique. It is also noteworthy that the exchange of ideas about rods and techniques goes in both directions over the north Atlantic. Many European anglers are increasingly turning to single handed rods for grilse fishing in the smaller rivers and conversely many North American anglers now appreciate that the major advantage of the long double-handed rod lies in the vastly increased degree of line control that it offers. The argument about casting distance is largely irrelevant and although the long rod may offer advantages in a strong wind, a competent caster with either rod can cast far enough. The question is, even if a small single handed rod will cast over 30 meters (100ft), what happens to all the line between the angler and the fly? The degree of control that can be excercised over this line, both in terms of mending or lifting the line from the water is fairly minimal.

THE EAST COAST

 One of the most interesting things about the patterns used in this area is the love affair many anglers have with the Spey patterns which originated on the river Spey in Scotland in the early part of the 19th.. century. This is despite the fact that the eastern coast of Canada has been the home of the development of modern hairwing salmon flies

True the tyings have been somewhat modernised and substitutes have been found for the difficult to obtain heron hackles, nevertheless these flies retain all the main characteristics of their origins and in many cases the original patterns are still used. The users of these flies maintain, rightly in our opinion, that the long flowing hackles and slim wings produce a fly that is full of movement and life in the water.

Although the Spey patterns may not be called shrimps, they certainly have all the elements necessary to be classed as shrimps. even in the original Scottish dressings. Tied as they are in the modern way, where the hackle length is even more exaggerated, these flies are shrimp patterns in all but name. There is one further aspect of these flies that may have something to do with their continued popularity, and that is to do with hooks. The Spey style of dressing is ideally suited to large single hooks. Because of the almost universal introduction of catch limits and catch-and-release throughout North America, flies are rarely tied on the double and treble hooks so common in European waters. Large single hooks, either barbless or de-barbed are a legal requirement on many fly rivers in North America so as to reduce damage and improve the survival chances of released fish. Conversely one of the reasons why these patterns have been so out of favour in European waters in recent times may be due to the fact that Spey and Dee flies are always tied on long single hooks which are held to be bad hookers of fish by European fishermen who almost always use treble hooks. Whether this is in fact true is open to doubt, there are few anglers in Europe with any great experience of fishing large single hooks. It is also true that hooking (penetration) and holding are not the same thing, but that's another argument!

Fly fishers in the eastern U.S.A. and Canada have certainly been aware of the allure of shrimp

flies for some considerable time, Wells (author together with Nobbs of *Salmon Tactics*, 1934) noted that he had hooked six salmon, of which he landed four, in 1887 on a Moisie Grub. This fly is a wingless grub which was developed on the Moisie river in north-eastern Canada and as can be seen from the date is of considerable antiquity.

Moisie Grub

Another early shrimp pattern that is noted by Bates in *Atlantic Salmon Flies and Fishing* is the Lapointe Shrimp. This Canadian fly is a hairwing pattern devised by a well known fly dresser L. A. Lapointe in 1949 and was primarily used in New Brunswick and on the Gaspé. Lapointe later opened his own tackle shop in Matepedia from 1956 to 1966.

Lapointe Shrimp

A modern fly that has had a great influence here, as in many other areas. is the Ally's Shrimp. Many versions of this are used, some variations are certainly to do with bad communication of the correct tying, others being purposeful as a response to local needs and conditions. The popularity of

this fly is spreading widely and Paul Marriner in *Modern Atlantic Salmon Flies* writes as follows:

'... this is the 'miracle' fly of the last few years on several Nova Scotia and New Brunswick rivers. Several of my friends who tie professionally told me it was impossible to keep up with the demand as tales of the pattern's prowess spread like the flu'

As previously noted, the construction of the Ally's Shrimp lends itself to single hooks, there are no practical limits to the sizes in which it may be tied, the colours may be varied to meet different local conditions and it is an excellent fly in a wide range of water conditions. All in all, any angler who does not have this fly is depriving himself of one of the most potent weapons yet invented. Full details of Ally's Shrimp are given on page 70 in the Scottish section.

Ally's Shrimp

The venerable Usk Grub is also a fly that has found success here. Tied in a slightly more modern way, with a slimmer body and longer hackles. it is very similar to the modern Irish shrimp patterns, particularly the Agivey Wye Bug, with a touch of a Spey fly thrown in. An extremely interesting fly, documented in *Modern Atlantic Salmon Flies* by Paul Marriner, is Ray's Spey from Raymond Plourde. Although the name suggests a Spey fly, it is in fact a typical Usk Grub or Irish shrimp. The tail and head hackle are of golden pheasant red breast feather, the centre hackle being of a yellow golden pheasant body feather. The rear body is of peach floss, the front body is of deep purple floss.

Among the best known of the many Atlantic salmon rivers in the New Brunswick area are the Mirimichi, Cains and Restigouche. These rivers frequently run with a dark, peaty colour and in answer to this problem one of the regular visitors, Bill Hunter of New Boston, has devised some

Usk Grub

Ray's Spey (Plourde)

Looking at the dressing, this is a son of Ally out of the Irish tippet shrimp. With this parentage it should be good, and it is.

Flies recommended by local guide Bryant Freeman for use on the Mirimichi include not only the Ally's Shrimp but also the Tippet Shrimp (Irish pattern - see page 20) and a locally developed fly called Barnett's Shrimp which is generally used in the autumn. This fly has an unusual colour combination of blue and pink, but the flowing hackles and long tail are absolutely typical of an effective shrimp fly.

Barnett's Shrimp

shrimp patterns that have proved to be extremely effective. These patterns have also exported well and have been used with success in Norway, Russia and other countries.

Hunter's Tippet Shrimp uses golden pheasant tippet feathers as an all round veiling under a long hackle of golden pheasant red breast feathers. The rear body is of golden orange chenille and the long tail consists of fibres of orange bucktail mixed with pearl Krystal flash. Bill actually named the fly simply the Tippet Shrimp, but we have taken the liberty of preceding this with his name, to distinguish his fly from the Irish pattern of the same name.

Hunter's Tippet Shrimp

Amongst the classic Spey flies that have continued to be used with some success by local anglers, our contributors have noted the Lady Caroline and both the Grey and Black Herons. In *Modern Atlantic Salmon Flies*, Paul Marriner gives examples of hairwing conversions of the Lady Caroline and the Grey Heron tied by Rob Solo, both using winging of grey squirrel tail dyed dark brown. An interesting alternative which was suggested to us was the use of bassarisk tail hair dyed brown. The tips of this hair are black with white barring along the length and thus when dyed the original colouring of the bronze mallard, dark tipped getting lighter towards the tying in point, could be recreated. Bassarisk hair has much the same texture as grey squirrel tail. The body hackling in both these examples is large white Chinese cock dyed grey. The effect is somewhat lighter and sparser than that which is obtained using heron and the fibres are not as long. Nevertheless these conversions look extremely good and should be very effective. Robert Gillespie uses the same hackle material for his version of the Grey Heron which is shown on page 58 in the Irish section.

Grey Heron (Solo)

Lady Caroline (Solo)

A less typical example of a Spey fly that has also had some success is the classic Spey called the Glen Grant. This fly was devised by Major Grant of Castle Grant, a recognised authority on the River Spey, at about the middle of the 19th century. The fly is not the most difficult to tie but has one major disadvantage - one fly requires six jungle cock feathers - it is still cheaper than the cost of a salmon, but not by much! The fly is beautiful to look at but it is doubtful if so many jungle cock feathers are really necessary.

Glen Grant (Whorwood)

We have illustrated an example of this fly beautifully tied by Rick Whorwood of Ontario, a recognised expert on classic salmon flies. The hackling in this example is of grey heron but long black Spey cock hackle was often used.

New Spey flies have also been developed on the east coast. Many of these flies are more correctly called a 'modified' Spey because the long hackling is generally confined to the front of the body rather than being palmered over the whole length. They nevertheless retain all the essential qualities of the original Spey flies.

An interesting example of a modified Spey pattern is one called Out-to-Lunch by Marc LeBlanc. First tied in 1994 this fly proved immediately effective on the Petite Cascapedia in high, dirty water conditions. The jungle cock eyes give the fly a bit of 'life'.

Out-to-Lunch (LeBlanc)

Bonne-Aventure LeBlanc)

Another Marc LeBlanc fly called the Bonne-Aventure is also of interest because of the unusual

construction of the front body. This consists of a series of four clumps of rabbit fur tied on the top and bottom of the hook shank. The colours of the rabbit are, from back to front, green, blue, red and then black. Between the clumps of fur is a rib of flat embossed silver tinsel and silver twist followed by a body hackle of grey heron. Unusual and harks back to the idea of the old 'maned' flies from Ireland, such as the Owenmore.

Another Marc LeBlanc fly that we like is the Rallye. The original fly was conceived as a classic salmon fly in honour of the Club Rallye Baie-de-Chaleurs in 1995 using the orange and black club colours. This fly is a Dee style conversion which has been successful in practical fishing applications.

Rallaye (LeBlanc)

Jones' Special is another Marc LeBlanc fly tied in a modified Spey style. It is based upon a successful sea-trout pattern named after a guide on Quebec's North Shore. The adaption has proved effective for salmon. With its muted colours, this fly is reminiscent of a silver smelt.

Jones' Special (LeBlanc)

Until we read *Modern Atlantic Salmon Flies* by Paul Marriner we were unaware of Marc LeBlanc's work. These flies really impress us with their inventiveness and overall balance. There are many skilled fly dressers around but being able to develop new patterns that combine elegance and beauty with practical fishing success demands higher skills.

A fly which we find has an immediate appeal because of its construction is the MacKenzie from Bob Boudreau. This is a modern Spey with the addition of a tail of wound golden pheasant red breast feather in the Irish style. He notes that the fly has a unique movement in the water due to the combination of tail hackle and long body hackle and has been successful in both high and low-water conditions. We have not seen the combination of Spey hackling with an Irish style tail on any other fly, but both are effective and putting them together shows a real touch of imagination.

MacKenzie (Boudreau)

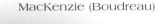

We have noted previously in this book that there is a dearth of green salmon flies. There is however, always an exception and the exception here is the eastern seaboard of Canada. Many successful flies here have a green colouration, ranging from the fluorescent green butt used on the myriad variants of the Black Bear flies, through to the bright yellow and green body of the Green Highlander. The next three flies all have a large element of green in their make-up (see also the Pompier Shrimp on page 105).

The Gaby from Michel Boivin is a typical, wide shouldered 'pseudo-Spey' with a long rear body of tinsel and the black Spey hackling restricted to the front body of ostrich herl. A sparse wing of black squirrel or bear and a long chartreuse dyed collar hackle of mallard flank feather

complete the fly. A tail and rear body veiling of lime green Krystal Flash give added sparkle.

Gaby (Boivin)

The Matepedia Spey, from Brian Sturrock, is a Spey fly which shows the signature chartreuse butt, so common on flies from the eastern provinces. It is named after the river on which it has been successful.

Matapedia Spey (Sturrock)

The Gaspey Highlander, also from Brian Sturrock is a Spey style conversion of the classic Green Highlander which works well on the Gaspé and St.-Marguerite. Given the success of the Green Highlander in the eastern provinces, the Green Highlander Shrimp from Ireland would also seem to be a promising candidate.

The Sea Lice from Roddy MacLeod is a combination of Spey and shrimp fly. Because golden pheasant red breast feathers are short, the hackling is tied in at mid-shank rather than being palmered over the whole body. This makes the fly easy to tie and, in combination with the red/orange colour, gives the fly a really 'shrimpy' look. Simple and effective, we like this fly.

Gaspey Highlander

Green Highlander Shrimp

Sea Lice (MacLeod)

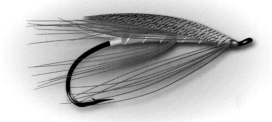

Logan's Silver Tip Spey is a fly from Roddy MacLeod which is named after the Silver Tip, a popular Newfoundland fly, and an angler from Nova Scotia who first used this fly successfully. It has proved to be particularly effective for stale autumn fish.

Logan's Silver Tip Spey (MacLeod)

Irish style shrimp flies have certainly been known on the east coast of Canada for some time. There is anecdotal evidence at least, that Curry's Red Shrimp was introduced to anglers in Canada when the crews of submarines operating out of Northern Ireland in World War II brought examples with them when visiting ports in Nova Scotia. It is quite clear however, that they never became well known or widespread and there are almost no references to them in North American literature apart from a brief mention of two of Curry's patterns in Bates' *Atlantic Salmon Flies & Fishing*.

More recently things have begun to change and with the publication of more information they will certainly become more popular. Paul Marriner gives several examples of Irish shrimp flies in his book *Modern Atlantic Salmon Flies* published in 1998. He also shows one new local pattern called Danny's Shrimp, developed by Jack Ripley in 1996. This fly is closely resembles Curry's Red Shrimp but substitutes a hair wing for the more usual jungle cock winging. This fly has proved to be very effective on the River Philip and during the 1997 season ran neck and neck with Lester the Lobster (see page 105) as the top fly.

Danny's Shrimp (Ripley)

The Irish shrimp flies in Paul Mariner's book also include two original patterns from Peter Dunne who comes from County Lewis in Eire. The first of these, the Dunmore Shrimp is a combination of features from the typical Irish shrimp style with influences from the General Practitioner. In typical Irish style the tail of the fly is a wound golden pheasant red breast feather. The body is split into two with collar hackles at both the mid-point and the head, again in the normal Irish

style. The shell back is represented by golden pheasant red breast feathers tied flat in typical G.P. manner. Burnt monofilament eyes are also specified as an optional extra. The colours of this fly are typically Irish, combining as they do, fiery brown, black and the natural brick red of the golden pheasant feathers. A measured amount of Krystal Flash and the front hackle of yellow give the fly an element of additional sparkle. The fly is designed for heavy water conditions, particularly for spring salmon.

Dunmore Shrimp (Dunne)

The second pattern given is called the F.P. Shrimp. This is a modified style of Irish shrimp, the body being divided into three, rather than two segments. The tail is a combination of golden pheasant red breast feather and fluorescent orange squirrel tail. The rear two body segments are of fluorescent orange fur, the front segment being red.

F. P. Shrimp (Dunne)

The hackles between the body segments are of golden pheasant red breast feathers and are doubled and wound as backward sloping collars, each overlaying the last towards the head. Again, red breast feathers are tied in at each position as a

shell back. The end effect is similar to a General practitioner but with a bit more mobility. The colours are well chosen for fishing in summer floods and peat stained water, the orange body glowing from within. Peter Dunne notes this pattern as being his first choice for large resident salmon in the summer months.

Other flies that have had a very great influence include the General Practitioner. This fly is generally thought to have been in use for from the early 1950s (it was first devised in 1953) but it really seems to have first found favour with North American anglers after the publication of *Atlantic Salmon Flies & Fishing* by Joe Bates in 1970.

There are hundreds of variants, most of which are simplifications of the original, in order to make tying easier. Of the many variants, four are listed in Paul Marriner's book. Two of these are of interest because they use hair rather than feather, the other two are unusual because of their colour.

The first of these flies is Ed's Black G.P. from Edwin Taylor. This is a much simplified version of the G.P., so much so that it bears little relationship to the original. Nevertheless, it is of interest because of its extraordinary track record - in over four years of successful use on the Cape Breton rivers it has never taken a fish under twelve pounds! The fly is at its best in high, heavily coloured water. Noteworthy is the use of jungle cock to represent the eyes, but tied in a rearward position rather than at the head.

The second fly, called the General Practitioner Hairwing, is tied by Louis Melanson. This is a slightly misleading name because the wing is not in fact of hair but of separated fibres of golden pheasant red breast feather. The tail is golden pheasant tippet with long red breast feather fibres over. The body is of gold-ribbed orange

seal's fur and the fly is completed with a throat hackle of orange cock or hen hackle.

G. P. Hairwing (Melanson)

The last two G.P. variants were developed by Bryant Freeman who has already been mentioned. These two flies are much more like the original G.P. but are of interest because of their unusual colours - green and blue. First used in the fall of 1997 the green version was intended to be a change of pace for jaded salmon that had seen enough of the ubiquitous red and orange flies. The blue version is tied in an identical fashion and is for use in low light conditions.

Green G. P. (Freeman)

Amongst other variants that have proved effective on rivers such as the Humber is the Purple Practitioner which is tied with a tail of purple Kristal Flash strands. The rest of the fly is black apart from the golden pheasant tippet feathers which retain their natural colouration.

Lester the Lobster is noted by Paul Marriner as the Atlantic salmon version of the Squamish Poacher, a British Columbia steelhead fly. Apart from the shell back which is of surveyor's tape, it also bears a marked resemblance to Peter Deane's

Ed's Black G. P. (Taylor)

Purple Practitioner

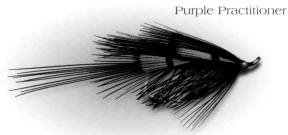

Black Eyed Prawn, perhaps better known as the Red Francis and an extremely popular fly in Iceland. The body is of wool rather than the chenille used in the original fly.

Lester The Lobster (Ripley)

The Shrimp Fly from John Clarke is another pattern much in the same vein, presenting as it does, a realistic imitation of a shrimp (although it should be said that the colour is more representative of a boiled or cooked prawn rather than the natural). If experience in Europe of fishing real prawns as bait is anything to go by, these flies should also be effective in purple and dark red. The use of marabou feathers to represent the shrimp's rostrum gives added mobility.

Shrimp Fly (Clarke)

Dileas is another Roddy MacLeod pattern which is a striking combination of red, orange and black with a touch of fluorescent chartreuse thrown in. The eyes of the shrimp are suggested by a vee-shaped segment of golden pheasant tippet feather which is, unusually, tied in under the hook shank.

Dileas (MacLeod)

The Pompier Shrimp from Brian Sturrock is based on the very successful Pompier fly devised by Michel Beaudin of Gaspé. It is yet another indication of how much the green and yellow colouring is favoured in the eastern provinces of Canada. The Pompier Shrimp has proved itself effective on both the York and Patapedia rivers.

The pattern for this fly as given in Paul Marriner's *Modern Atlantic Salmon Flies* makes no mention of the top and bottom veilings under the collar hackle. In the illustration provided they are however quite clear and seem to be a white tipped hair, possibly grey squirrel.

Pompier Shrimp (Sturrock)

The River Shrimp series of flies from Marc Madore shown on Plate 23 (overleaf) are a simple but effective range of shrimp patterns, tied in a variety of colours to take advantage of a wide range of water conditions. There are five colours: orange, light blue, yellow, green and black. The yellow version differs slightly from the rest

River Shrimp - Blue

River Shrimp - Orange

River Shrimp - Yellow

River Shrimp - Black

River Shrimp - Green

PLATE 23: River Shrimp Series - Marc Madore

because it has a standard yellow feather strip wing and jungle cock eyes. All the other flies have feathers which are tied flat and overlapping and then laquered to represent the shrimp's shell back.

are the most effective fishing colours for Newfoundland and Labrador and thus both of them are incorporated in this pattern. The fly has proved to be an effective spring pattern on the Codroy, Robinson and Fischells rivers.

St. Georges Spey (Burry)

Derek's Summer Spey (Tay)

The St Georges Spey was created by Daryl Burry and is named after the Bay St. George region of Newfoundland. After twenty years of angling experience Daryl believes that green and red they

Derek's Summer Spey is the creation of Derek Tay who is a fly fishing instructor from Halifax, Nova Scotia. The colours of this fly are

subdued but grey bodied flies do have a proven record of success over many years. The wing, which is a single golden pheasant red breast feather, is tied flat in the horizontal plane, a style that is not uncommon amongst trout flies but which is unusual for salmon flies. A variant also exists with an orange body. Both flies are recommended for Nova Scotia rivers in the autumn.

An alternative to this fly which shares the subdued colouring and which might also be useful is the Lemon Grey Spey shown below. This is a modern Spey conversion of the old classic Lemon Grey fully dressed salmon fly which was very popular in Ireland in times gone by and which still sees occasional use. In this case, the grey is combined with lemon yellow but a further option which might suit the maritime provinces of Canada extremely well would be to use a green (possibly fluorescent) front body and throat hackle. The fly shown has a wing of dark brown bucktail over red-brown bucktail as a substitute for the classic bronze mallard winging.

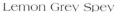

Lemon Grey Spey

A version of the Lemon Grey from Joe McDonald, tied as an Irish shrimp, is shown on page 35 in the Irish section of the chapter on European Shrimp & Spey Flies.

STEELHEAD FLIES

hat is a steelhead? If asked to explain to a European angler you might answer that the steelhead is the Pacific equivalent of the European seatrout. Both are trout species that have a residential population and a sea run population that exist side by side in rivers, yet do not mix or interbreed. The steelhead is the sea run form of the rainbow trout, native to the Pacific coast of North America.

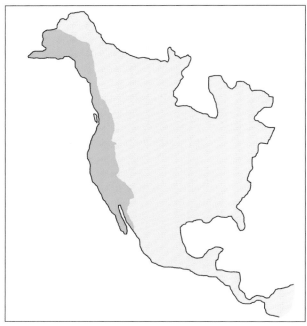

Natural range of the rainbow trout

As can be seen from the distribution map above, the natural range of the rainbow trout was restricted to the west coast of North America, steelhead being found only in rivers that flowed west, disgorging into the Pacific Ocean. The famous rainbow trout fisheries of the Rocky Mountains together with those of the mid-western and eastern states were based on stocking with trout transported from the west. Incidentally the name 'rainbow', so called because of the iridescent colours on the flanks, originated with the first importers in the east.

The above explanation, whilst factually true, misses the most important truths about steelhead. For a start it gives the impression that fishing for

steelhead is akin to fishing for European seatrout, and that the habits of steelhead are similar to seatrout. Neither of these assumptions are true. In fact the steelhead is more accurately described as the Pacific equivalent of the Atlantic salmon, at least as far as anglers are concerned.

The taxonomy of the steelhead is a different matter. Until 1989 the rainbow trout was known to scientists as *Salmo gairdneri* - Gairdner's salmon. The sea-run and residential forms simply being two races of the same species. As one of the Salmo species it was a first cousin to *Salmo salar*, the Atlantic salmon. This all changed in 1989. The trout of western North America and the northern Pacific Ocean were reclassified as belonging to the genus *Oncorhynchus*, the Pacific salmon, and the rainbow trout was duly assigned the species name *mykiss*. This re-classification put the steelhead in the same genus as the Pacific salmon, fish such as the Chinook which dies after spawning and which is largely managed as a food resource. To fishermen of the American west coast this news was disconcerting to say the least. Whilst the taxonomists were undoubtedly correct scientifically, it seemed to fly in the face of reason when any fly fisherman knew that the steelhead shared far more characteristics with the Atlantic salmon than it did with Chinook or Sockeye salmon. What are the factors that led to this perception?

For a start the steelhead and the Atlantic salmon share a very similar life history. The steelhead starts life as a parr, spending between one and four years in fresh water before migrating to the ocean as a smolt. The length of residence in fresh water varies from river to river but generally speaking the length of stay increases the more northerly the home river is.

The four-year freshwater residence is a feature of the northerly cold water systems of British Columbia where growth rates are slow. On the other hand steelhead from the more southerly rivers usually spend only one year in saltwater, remaining in coastal waters. However, most steelhead are known to range great distances to reach rich marine feeding grounds and may live in saltwater up to four years. It is no surprise therefore, that returning steelhead can be very large indeed, fish over 50 lbs have been recorded and fish in the 20-30 lb range are not uncommon.

Steelhead, similar to the Atlantic salmon and unlike the other Pacific salmon species do not die after spawning. As kelts they can recover condition and once more return to the marine environment. Multiple spawning is quite common and cases have been recorded of fish on their fourth return to the spawning grounds. It is impossible to say what percentage of fish would naturally return to spawn a second, third or even fourth time because, in common with the Atlantic salmon, life histories have only been recorded in recent years when the returning fish have had to negotiate a barrage of high seas netting on the feeding grounds, inshore netting, coastal netting and estuarial netting, not to mention netting in the rivers as an accidental by-product of the commercial netting for food species.

The most important feature of the steelhead is the fact that, like the Atlantic salmon, and again unlike the other Pacific salmon species, it can be taken regularly on a well presented fly. The similarities extend to the fact that many of the fishing techniques used for both species are similar. Atlantic salmon anglers will be quite at home with the casting and line mending techniques described by our steelhead angling contributors in order to present a fly at the correct speed and depth.

Fly fishing for steelhead also shares a common history and heritage with the Atlantic salmon. The first flies used for steelhead were Atlantic salmon flies and the development of flies for steelhead share many of the most important features of salmon fly development. There are certainly differences of emphasis but nevertheless, most flies that are effective for steelhead would almost certainly be effective for Atlantic salmon, we know that the reverse is true because many of the most effective steelhead flies are in fact Atlantic salmon flies. The flies shown on the following pages may give food for thought to Atlantic salmon anglers, the Spey flies used for steelhead being perhaps the best example.

In comparison with Atlantic salmon fishing, the history of fly fishing for steelhead is comparatively short. The first steelhead rivers such as the Eel were discovered in the 1890s and further discoveries continued northwards into the wilderness of British Columbia only slowly. The first fly fishermen to sample the wonders of systems such as the Skeena did so in the early 1950s. On most watersheds steelhead return in two

main runs, one in the spring or early summer and one much later into the winter. Almost all the early steelhead fishing was primarily a summer sport, similar to that for resident rainbow trout. The introduction of lead core shooting heads in the 1950s led to the first experimentation with fly fishing rivers much later in the season for winter run steelhead. These first experiments with winter steelhead fishing were very important in terms of fly development. In order to make an impact and to attract fish in cold water conditions, flies were required that had presence and movement but not bulk and that could cut through and sink to the depths required to find fish. The use of Spey and Dee type flies for steelhead fishing dates back to the first experimentation with flies using traditional Atlantic salmon patterns. Some of the most successful of the early patterns were standard flies such as the Lady Caroline, the Carron Fly and the Akroyd but new flies by Sydney Glasso in a modified style had a very far reaching influence which has extended to the present day.

Carron Fly

The Spey flies, tied mainly as large singles on Alec Jackson Spey hooks have come to represent one of five important groups of steelhead flies, the second group being the more realistic shrimp and prawn imitations as represented by the General Practitioner and its variants, the third important group being that which contains the many variants of waking and surface effect flies such as the Bombers, the fourth group contains realistic imitations of various nymphs and the last group contains the marabou flies typically represented by patterns such as the Alaskabou series.

Among the earliest shrimp patterns were the Orange Shrimp and Horner's Silver Shrimp both

dating from the late 1930s and thought to have originated on the Eel River. The Silver Shrimp is no longer used to any extent but the Orange Shrimp lives on in the guise of the Polar Shrimp which is simply a variant of the Orange Shrimp tied with a polar bear hair wing rather than with bucktail.

Most of these early shrimp patterns were comparatively simple and fall into two main groups, those with a tinsel body and a shellback normally formed from bucktail and chenille or wool bodied flies, combined with a palmered hackle and a hair wing. Horner's Silver Shrimp, together with the Brown and Orange Legged Shrimps are typical of the first group, whilst the Orange and Polar Shrimps are typical of the second group.

The Polar Shrimp has proved to be a lasting pattern and is still in use today. The materials used and the tying style has however changed over the years. Chenille which is fairly lifeless in the water has largely been replaced by dubbed fur (usually seal's fur) and the throat hackle has been replaced by longer flowing hackles often wound over the whole front part of the body in Spey fashion. Tied in this way the fly has mobility and translucence as well as colours that are known to appeal to steelhead. Polar Shrimp variants using more mobile materials include that devised by Mike Brooks, both a light and a dark variant from Steve Gobin, one from Trey Combs and another, Spey style version, from Bob Blumreich illustrated below.

Polar Spey (Blumreich)

A further variant, which is given in *Fly Patterns of British Columbia* by Art Lingren is Tolley's Polar Shrimp. His version of the fly was devised in the early 1960s and by 1965 was landing over 30 fish per season from the Squamish. The emphasis is clearly on the combination of gold tinsel and orange dubbing.

Polar Shrimp (Tolley)

Bob Blumreich has developed a very distinctive method of using marabou for Spey hackling. The fibres, particularly towards the tips are coloured with a spirit based fibre tip pen. This has two effects, firstly the colour of the fibres can be changed or enhanced and secondly the spirit based ink has the effect of burning the fine flue off the fibres, leaving the tips very fine and producing a very good substitute for the largely unobtainable natural heron feathers. When the ink is applied the feather becomes matted, it is then allowed to dry out and finally it is brushed out using a piece of Velcro.

A Walt Johnson fly which was one of his favourite winter patterns is the Red Shrimp, dating back to 1963. Tied on a long shank hook this fly has a body of fluorescent orange floss which is overlaid with red seal's fur and ribbed with flat silver tinsel. The body hackle is dark brown tied Spey-style. A red dyed collar hackle is followed by red hackle-tip or turkey strip wings that are set low over the body. The fly may be completed with a topping of golden pheasant crest. The retention of such a traditional topping material is not unusual, even to the present day, many modern anglers believing that the glow of these feathers is an important factor in attracting fish. The Red Shrimp has proved its effectiveness and is still used today.

Stylistically, the Prawn Fly (see page 112) which was devised in 1966 by Walt Johnson and Craig Shreeve is also much in the same vein. The hackling is of heron which gives added mobility.

Orange Legged Shrimp

Brown Legged Shrimp

Orange Shrimp

Horner's Silver Shrimp

Bucktail Shrimp

Pete's Shrimp

Red Shrimp
(Schweitzer)

Pink Shrimp

PLATE 24: Early Steelhead Shrimps

Red Shrimp (Johnson)

Prawn Fly (Johnson/Shreeve)

The Great Lakes

he area around Lake Michigan is the home of steelhead which run from Lake Michigan and the other Great Lakes in the same way that the west coast steelhead run from the Pacific Ocean. Spawning runs are made up the rivers connected to the lakes and form the basis of an extended fishery that extends north into Canada. This area is the home of many Spey type patterns, generally referred to as 'Steelhead Speys'. The flies are a mixture of classic Spey patterns and newer tyings in the same general style, but with a modern touch. Worthy of mention among these are the flies tied by Bob Blumreich of Chicago and Steve Schweitzer of Geneva, Illinois.

Amongst these patterns are tyings that use brilliant oranges, reds, purples, pinks and greens, the 'hot' colours being particularly effective for steelhead. Generally, these flies have even longer hackling, often consisting of long fibred marabou, than their Scottish forebears and represent a mobile, translucent and lifelike appearance in the water. Although designed mainly for steelhead, there is no reason why they should not be equally successful for salmon in other waters.

The Purple Spey from Steve Schweitzer is a more slimly tied variant of the Purple Spey from Phil Strobel. Extra flash is gained by the use of a gold Alec Jackson Spey hook. The standard tying uses a rear boy of flat gold tinsel but holographic Mylar may also be used. The collar hackle is guinea fowl dyed to match the body dubbing and

Purple Spey (Schweitzer)

the whole fly should be tied sparse and slim.

Amongst the many patterns which are loosely based on the General Practitioner is a fly called Joe's Shrimp. This is an eyed pattern which has a

Joe's Shrimp

SSSS (Soule)

Milwaukee Spey
(Blumreich)

Winter's Hope Spey
(Blumreich)

Orange CDC Shrimp
(Schweitzer)

CDC Spey Shrimp
(Schweitzer)

PLATE 25: Great Lakes Patterns

long tail of a mixture of bucktail, red golden pheasant body feather fibres and Krystal flash. The seal's fur dubbed body is divided into two parts with golden pheasant red breast feathers as hackles. Simpler to tie than the original General Practitioner, this fly looks as if it could be very effective for Atlantic salmon as well as steelhead.

The Milwaukee Spey from Bob Blumreich, which has been very successful for the winter run steelhead in the Wisconsin tributaries of Lake Michigan, uses this technique to combine the pink and black colouration which has proved to be so effective for steelhead. Other flies of a similar type and colouration include the Spawning Purple Spey (McNeese), the Purple Spey (Gobin), the Car Body (Kinney) and the Purple Heart Spey (Veverka). Most of these flies were developed for the west coast steelhead fisheries but their effectiveness should not limited to one area or river and they would certainly be successful in other locations.

The Winter's Hope Spey is an adaption by Bob of one of Bill McMillan's classic steelhead patterns which was originally designed for floating line fishing in cold water winter conditions.

Christopher Soule has developed a series of flies which are a combination of traditional steelhead patterns together with features of Spey flies. These flies were developed specifically for salmon and steelhead on the Great Lakes and in particular for the rivers in Michigan. The fly is known as the Secret Salmon Steelhead Seducer, thankfully normally shortened to the SSSS! The main features of these flies are a body tied of Lite-Brite, weighted eyes, an optional wing of Krystalhair or Flashabou and flowing hackles at the head. The fly is tied in a variety of colour combinations including blue, copper and Peacock. It should be noted that Firefox Peacock Lite-Bright is a superb imitation of peacock herl but with more flash and sparkle than the original material. The flies have been in use now for about four years and to date have taken king salmon to 30lbs, steelhead to 15lbs, coho to 12lbs and brown trout to 10lbs.

A development which we find very interesting is the use of CDC feathers as body veilings. This technique originated by John Alevras of Colorado but was picked up by Marvin Nolte and later by Steve Schweitzer and applied to Spey style flies. Four CDC feathers are mounted at the top, bottom and both sides of the hook shank at the front of the body, reaching back to the tag position and cloaking the body. The effect is most interesting, being translucent and giving colour and impact without bulk. Being stemmed whole feathers, the CDC does not collapse around the body as would marabou. Examples of this technique are shown in the flies from Steve which we have illustrated, including two versions of a shrimp fly. The Orange CDC Spey is an example of the superb effect that can be obtained, in this case producing a shrimp imitation which has all the right credentials to be successful in many different areas. Further examples of this technique from Marvin Nolte are also shown in Plate 28 on page 120.

CDC feathers may also be used as winging material as is shown in the following pattern, also from Steve Schweitzer. This fly is intended for use as an attractor pattern on the larger mid-western rivers, inducing the strike out of curiosity or anger. The rear two thirds of the body is of fluorescent chartreuse floss, tied very slimly.

CDC Wing Spey (Schweitzer)

The West Coast

The fishing on the north west coast of America is for a whole mixture of species and covers a vast area, stretching as is does from northern California up to the north of British Columbia in Canada. This area includes some of the most famous rivers in the world, renowned for their enormous runs of the Pacific salmon species such as the king, silver and chinook as well as steelhead. The names of rivers such as the Oxbow, Deschutes, Klamath, Skagit, Dean, Squamish, Fraser, and Skeena are synonymous with huge Pacific salmon and anadromous steelhead which can run to over 30lbs.

In British Columbia few flies are as popular for winter steelhead fishing as the prawn and shrimp imitations. The General Practitioner is again a favourite on these waters. In his book *Steelhead Fly Fishing* published in 1991, Trey Combs makes the comment that he knows of no other fly that has had such an influence on steelhead fishing over the previous ten years.

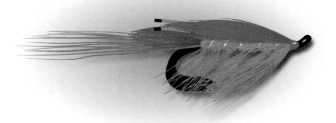

General Practitioner (Drury)

In his book *Fly Patterns of British Columbia* published in 1996, Art Lingren gives a great deal of detail about the spread of the G.P. in north America. Although is was invented in 1953 and publicized in Joe Bates's book *Atlantic Salmon Flies & Fishing* in 1970, Art Lingren gives credit to Bob Taylor for the original introduction of the G.P. into north America in 1960. The spread of the fly was not immediate however and it was not until 1984 that the fly gained the reputation that it has today. Art Lingren writes as follows:

'That is the General Practitioner's story. Introduced by and first fish caught on a Pacific coast river by Bob Taylor, first fish hooked in British Columbia by Bruce Gerhart, first British Columbian fish landed by Bill Yonge, first big fish by Peter Broomhall, and polarised locally by Jack Vincent........ The General Practitioner became well known in the Pacific Northwest as 'the Fly' after my group returned home from our 1984 Dean River trip. With 175 hookups, most of them on General Practitioners, word spread of this amazing fly and it has become one of the Pacific Northwest's most productive steelhead patterns'.

Art Lingren's personal favourite among the many GP variants is the black version illustrated below. To say that this fly is successful is an understatement - just look at the statistics that he quotes:

- Used successfully on 27 different British Columbian rivers.
- 10 different types of fish caught: steelhead to 20lbs cutthroat to 18 inches, rainbows to 16 inches, browns to 23 inches, dolly varden to 23 inches, pink salmon to 5lbs coho salmon to 10lbs chum salmon to 15lbs and chinook to 35lbs.

Black General Practitioner (Lingren)

- Best day's fishing: 16 steelhead hooked, 15 salmon hooked.

One of the disadvantages that has emerged from tying the G.P. on single hooks is the fact that the fly is not as quick sinking and stable as the original which was tied on a double hook. If tied on a single hook with lead wire weighting along the hook shank the fly is likely to turn over and fish upside down. Trey Combs notes that this may be more disconcerting to the angler than to the fish but nevertheless recommends that the fly is tied unweighted on heavyweight hooks and used on a sinking line in softer water and tailouts.

The Black Marabou Practitioner from Sean

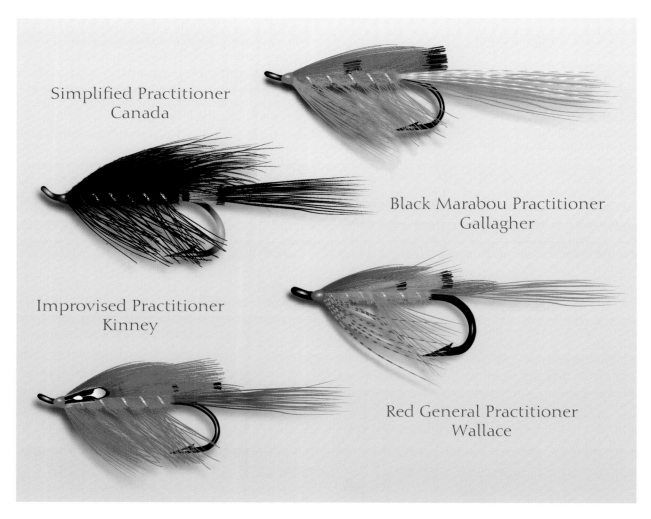

Simplified Practitioner
Canada

Black Marabou Practitioner
Gallagher

Improvised Practitioner
Kinney

Red General Practitioner
Wallace

PLATE 26: General Practitioners

Gallagher is rated by Trey Combs as one of the very best all-season flies. It combines high visibility with a superb action and works in all water conditions. Taken together with the comments of Art Lingren there is no doubt that the various black variants of the G.P. are some of the most successful flies ever used on the west coast fisheries.

There are many other variants of the G.P. such as the Improvised Practitioner from Mike Kinney, a slightly simplified version from Trey Combs together with a whole range of shrimp patterns that have been based on the G.P. but which are nevertheless sufficiently different to justify a new name. Many of these variants such as Sean's Prawn

Sean's Prawn (Gallagher)

(also from Sean Gallagher) illustrated below are more popular locally than the original G.P.

Amongst the best known of the flies that take a realistic approach to shrimp imitation is the Squamish Poacher, which was developed by Joe Kambeitz in 1974 and is still effective today. Brian Silvey supplied us with a stunning variant of the Poacher which combines a translucent body and feelers of pearl blue Lite-Brite with a sparkling carapace of orange Edge-Bright. Leaded weights are added to the fly next to the eye of the hook to enable the fly to be fished right side up and to achieve depth in deeper waters. This fly has proved

Squamish Poacher Variant (Silvey)

effective for both spring and winter steelhead in a variety of water colours and conditions.

An effective winter shrimp fly which has been around for some time is the Sauk River Shrimp from Alec Jackson of Spey hook fame.

This pattern occurs in two forms, one with a

tail which is called the Shrimp and a tailless version simply known as the Sauk River Grub. This is very similar in construction to the traditional grub patterns which were first originated on the River Wye in the early 1800s.

The form of the fly is very simple. The tail which consists of bucktail is at least as long as the hook. The body is formed of a twisted rope of dyed red ostrich herl which is divided into segments by four orange hackles, each larger than the previous, as the eye of the hook is neared. At the head position the fly is finished with an orange collar hackle.

Another early series of shrimp patterns called the Estuary Shrimps was designed by Les Johnson for use on California rivers such as the Russian and the Navarro. The flies were originally intended for spawned out winter steelhead from January through to May but later also proved effective for fresh fish entering the estuaries. The flies come in a range of colours and the general preference for steelhead is black, orange, pink, green and finally tan.

The construction of all these flies is very similar and consists of a tail which is a mixture of hair (calf or squirrel) and Flashabou. The body is is dubbed and ribbed with pearl tinsel. A sparse hackle is tied at the head. Over this lies a long wing of calf tail mixed with Flashabou. A few strands of polar bear hair are tied in over the wing as a topping. Despite their relative simplicity these flies have been used with success for steelhead on rivers in Oregon, Washington and British Columbia. All of the flies are fished near the surface using slow

Sauk River Shrimp (Alec Jackson)

Estuary Shrimp (Johnson)

Polar Shrimp
Mike Brooks

Dark Polar Shrimp
Steve Gobin

Light Polar Shrimp
Steve Gobin

Orange Shrimp
Dave McNeese

PLATE 27: Polar Shrimp Variants

sinking or 'slime' lines, often being sight cast to cruising steelhead.

The Polar Shrimp has maintained its popularity, primarily because it has a colour combination of bright orange/red and white which has lasting appeal to steelhead. Its effectiveness has been improved because of the new styles of tying and the new materials which have been used in its construction. To the colour scheme, which was always effective has been added mobility and translucence, properties which were not present in the original tying. The elements which have been subject to change are the body, which is no longer of chenille but usually of sparsely dubbed seal's fur or slimly tied floss, the winging which often uses a more flexible hair than polar bear and the collar hackling which is normally tied much longer than previously in a semi-Spey fashion. The use of polar bear hair for the winging is an interesting point.

Polar bear hair possesses translucence and light transmission like no other hair and would normally be considered to be an ideal choice. The problem is the stiffness. It is becoming increasingly difficult to find the really fine polar bear hair which is necessary to give the winging on smaller patterns the required mobility. Certainly we have obtained samples of polar bear hair which would suit the smallest patterns that would normally be required, we have also received hair which was so coarse that it was suitable only for for large streamer flies. Steve Gobin overcomes this problem entirely by tying the Polar Shrimp as a Spey fly. In this case the movement and mobility is provided by the long fibred body hackling, the wing consisting of feather slips tied in typical Spey style.

One of the most interesting flies that we found on the west coast is the Gibb's Shrimp from Mike Brooks which is documented in Trey Combs

Steelhead Fly Fishing. It is certainly derived from an Irish shrimp pattern but we were unable to trace any references to it in the Irish literature and it is the only fly in this style which we have found in the U.S.A. Where Mike Brooks found it we were unable to ascertain. Suffice it to say that if this fly is as effective as Mike Brooks maintains then steelhead anglers have a rich vein of fly patterns to

Gibb's Shrimp (Brooks)

explore, there being at least eighty flies of this type in the Irish catalogue.

The Horney Shrimp from Joe Butorac is another imitative pattern which again is based on the theory that steelhead are susceptible to flies which resemble the last item in their saltwater diet.

Horney Shrimp (Butorac)

This looks a more realistic imitation, largely due to the very noticeable black eyes.

The Reiff's Shrimp is a similar type of fly. It is slimly dressed and was developed as an alternative to the General Practitioner. Reiff's Shrimp is less complicated to tie, sinks more quickly and remains upright when under tension. The fly is used in sizes as small as an 8 for summer fishing and up to a size 2 for winter fishing. One of the largest fly caught winter run steelhead of all

Reiff's Shrimp (Dan Reiff)

time, a buck from the Skagit weighing over 25lbs. was taken on this fly.

Bob Borden, the man behind Hareline Dubbin, is the creator of Borden's Prawn. This fly is an alternative to the General Practitioner with a much improved action. The fly is notable for the innovative use of wrapped rabbit fur as a body/hackle material. The rabbit fur consists of a strip of pelt cut crossways so that the fur will lie backwards when wound. The fly is tied in a variety of colours including red, orange, yellow/pink and black/purple.

The antennae consist of vee-shaped golden pheasant tippets and strands of Krystal Flash. The

Borden's Prawn - orange

carapace is formed from two or three (depending upon hook size) golden pheasant rump feathers.

Bob Veverka is very well known for his Spey flies as well as being one of the world's best tiers of classic fully dressed Atlantic salmon flies. Although he lives Vermont many of his Spey patterns are very well known on the west coast and are extremely effective for steelhead.

Two of his shrimp type flies are shown in Plate 28. Both are called Tiger prawns but we have found two variants of the dressing. The first has a

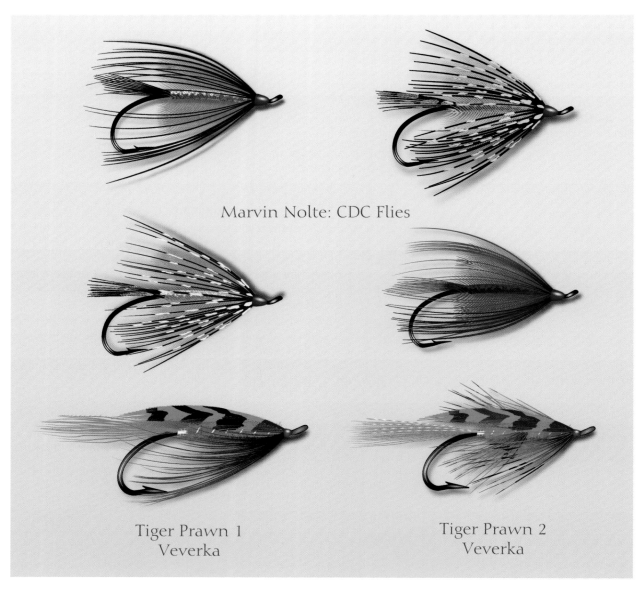

Marvin Nolte: CDC Flies

Tiger Prawn 1
Veverka

Tiger Prawn 2
Veverka

PLATE 28: CDC Flies & Tiger Prawns

purple throat hackle whilst the second has a split body with a centre hackle and throat hackle of orange dyed grizzle. Both share a body of orange crystal seal and a wing of red-orange dyed grizzle hackle tips which gives the flies a most striking appearance..

The Kispiox Shrimp originates from the Bighorne River in Montana and was devised by Mike Craig, one of the major outfitters in the area. Being heavily weighted with a lot of hackle and no

wing, the fly tends to turn over in use. but this may help to avoid fouling the bottom as it is fished and does not seem to reduce the effectiveness of the fly at all. The fly is normally fished very deep using a High Speed Hi-D head or a Deep Water Express sink tip. Scud patterns of this type are very popular on the Bighorne.

Among the newer shrimp flies from the west coast are some very interesting patterns developed by Brian Silvey. Brian is a full time steelhead guide

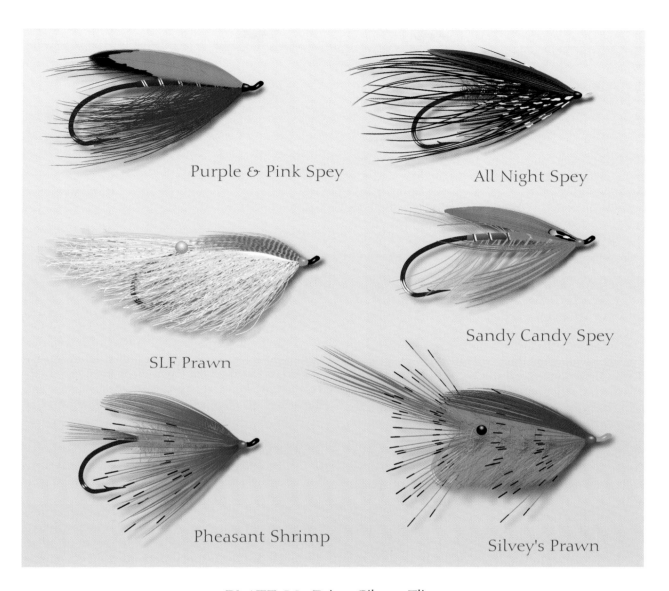

Purple & Pink Spey

All Night Spey

SLF Prawn

Sandy Candy Spey

Pheasant Shrimp

Silvey's Prawn

PLATE 29: Brian Silvey Flies

Kispiox Shrimp (Craig)

and is perhaps best known for the fly that bears his name - the Silvey Prawn, but he is also an innovator who has devised many stunning new Spey patterns. Brian operates from the base of Mount Hood in Welches, Oregon and guides mainly on the Deschutes and Sandy rivers. Apart from the Squamish Poacher variant already mentioned, Brian has supplied us with three superb shrimp patterns, three Spey patterns and an absolutely lovely example of a Dee fly - all of them practical fishing flies which are used every day. The Silvey's Prawn, which was first tied in 1994, is

characterised by a body which consists of a wound rabbit strip. This technique was first used by Bob Borden in 1989 for Borden's Prawn, gives a body profile which is extremely soft and mobile. At the rear of the fly are large black mono eyes. The feelers are represented by red Super Hair followed by a collar of long golden pheasant tippets. At the front there is again a collar hackle of golden pheasant tippets and the the carapace is represented by a golden pheasant red breast feather tied low over the back. Silvey's Prawn can be tied in a variety of colours, the most commonly used are orange - red - black - purple - pink and finally white. The fly is usually fished on the swing on a sink tip line down deep. It has proved to be effective at all times of the year, depending upon the colours used.

The SLF Prawn is a variation of a fly first tied by Davy Wotton using SLF hanks. The SLF Prawn has proved its effectiveness for winter steelhead in low water. The fly is used on a sink-tip line in soft currents where the fine SLF fibres give a lot of action. This pattern can also be tied in a wide range of colours: red, orange, black and purple.

The Sandy Candy Spey (named after the Sandy River) was first tied in 1996 for winter steelhead but has since proved to effective for spring fishing as well. It is normally used on a floating line using a standard wet fly swing technique and is effective in both high, off-colour water as well as low, cold water conditions.

The Eye Opener Dee is an absolutely stunning descendant of the original Dee flies and remains true to its lineage. First tied in 1997 it has proved its worth for early summer steelhead, fished on a floating line. It is really inspiring to see 'new' Dee flies tied to this standard of artistry which are also effective every day fishing flies.

It is generally believed that the modern use of marabou as a substitute for heron hackles on Spey flies was pioneered in the early 1980s by tiers such as John Farrar and Bob Aid. We say modern use because if we define marabou as a type of feather rather than coming from a specific species of bird, then marabou plumes, taken from from the thighs of the golden eagle, were in use as body hackles in the mid 19th century for the Eagle series of Dee flies. Whether these flies were known to the tiers when they started to develop the modern patterns is not known but in terms of their form the Eagles are

Eye Opener Dee (Silvey)

the direct forerunners of the modern marabou Spey flies, so much so that a Grey or Yellow Eagle would not be out of place for example, if it were to be found amongst John Farrar's Skagit Spey series.

The Eagle series of flies fell out of favour due mainly to the difficulty of obtaining the necessary feathers as well as the vagaries of fashion. It may be thought ironic that probably the cheapest and most easily obtainable feather of modern fly dressing, the turkey marabou, is an almost perfect substitute for a feather which was exotic and difficult to obtain, even in the less enlightened days of the the 19th. century. Examples of the Eagles are illustrated in the chapter on the *History and Development of Shrimp Flies* on page 5.

Several different techniques were developed for the use of marabou. Apart from simply winding the plume around the hook using the stem, these also included the use of a dubbing loop containing fine marabou blood plumes which was then palmered forward around the body. This technique enables plumes of different colours to be mounted in sequence in the loop thus producing blends unobtainable in any other way. The resulting flies are beautiful to look at and are unmatched in underwater mobility. The only disadvantage of this style of fly is the undoubted fact that the marabou hackles are not very robust.

It may well be thought that with both Atlantic salmon and steelhead becoming scarcer and more difficult to catch, the investment in a few more flies than might otherwise have been the case is a small price to pay for their extra effectiveness in bringing fish to the bank.

Black Skagit Spey

Orange Skagit Spey

White Skagit Spey

Yellow Skagit Spey

PLATE 30: Skagit Speys - John Farrar

We have illustrated some classic and elegant examples of flies tied in this style. The Marabou Spey and the Skagit Spey series from John Farrar were evolved during the years that he guided fishermen on the Skagit River during the months of March and April. We would be happy to use these flies anywhere in the world.

The use of marabou for salmon flies in Europe and especially in England has been heavily influenced by its use as a material for lures for stillwater fishing for large rainbow trout. It has suffered from this connection and is somehow seen as a 'down-market' material which is unworthy for the king of game fish. It should however be noted that the reasons why it has proved to be so effective for trout lures such as the Cat's Whisker are exactly the same reasons why it can be effective for salmon. Bill Pennington ran an experiment in conjunction with the readers of *Trout & Salmon* magazine in England to test the effectiveness of marabou flies, particularly those tied in small sizes.

The results were most encouraging, particularly as the top fly proved to be a Red Shrimp. Nevertheless the prejudice remains and marabou winged or hackled patterns still stubbornly refuse to enter the lists of standard salmon flies in Europe.

Marabou Spey (Farrar)

The legacy of Sydney Glasso is maintained and continued on the west coast by a group of anglers and master flytyers who combine classic elements with new features to produce flies that are superbly effective, beautiful to look at and which are worthy of the attention of salmon anglers throughout the world.

A typical example of these flies is the Harlequin Spey from Steve Brocco. This fly which combines standard elements of the Spey fly with a hair wing was primarily developed for the Snoqualmie River in Washington.

Harlequin Spey (Brocco)

Two flies from Scott Noble which are given in *Steelhead Fly Fishing* by Trey Combs caught our eye immediately, the Prismatic Spey and the Midnight Spey. These flies are unusual in that they both have wings of married fibres, something that is very rare in a new pattern in the last twenty years. It should not be thought however that these flies are for exhibition, they are every day flies that produce highly visible images in both clear and coloured water conditions. The Prismatic Spey is considered strictly a winter fly whereas the Midnight Spey is effective throughout the year.

The idea of prismatic mixing of colours in flies is not new. Certainly in North America flies such as the Lord Iris and Lady Iris from Preston Jennings have had a lasting influence and it may not be coincidence that many flytyers over the years have come to the conclusion that colours produced by the conjunction of different shades are more effective than a solid colour. In the world of painting it has been well understood for years that the juxtaposition of complementary colours brings added brightness and impact to each colour

separately and that the resulting mixing by the eye produces a richness of colour unobtainable by simply mixing the pigments together. This may have the added advantage that the colour produced will alter according to the prevailing light and water colour, in effect a natural adaption which may make the fly visible in a much wider range of conditions than would be the case with a single pre-mixed colour.

Prismatic Spey (Noble)

Midnight Spey (Noble)

Patrick's Fly Shop in Seattle was an institution for north west anglers in the late 40s and 1950s. The owner Roy Patrick wrote a book in 1948 called *Pacific Northwest Fly Patterns* which was amended and re-issued up until 1958 and was the bible for a generation of fly tiers. Hand typed and copied, this book wouldn't win any prizes for elegance and beauty, it does however contain the tying details for hundreds of patterns for rainbow trout, cutthroat and special sections on flies for British Columbia and steelhead, together with brief comments on the use of each fly. For the student of steelhead fly history who wishes to see what flies were really being sold and used at that time it is indispensable.

Jimmy LeMert was later the manager of

Patrick's and one of his patterns, the Amethyst Spey is an extremely beautiful fly. The body is of wound peacock herl which makes an interesting colour change change from seal's fur or floss, This is combined with a purple dyed wing and a combination of purple and red hackling. There is also a hairwing version which substitutes purple dyed squirrel tail for the wing.

Following the widespread success of Spey

Amethyst Spey (LeMert)

patterns an obvious and interesting development both on the west coast and in the Great Lakes area is the idea of re-tying other proven steelhead patterns in the Spey style. Typical flies to which this technique has been applied include the Winter's Hope and Polar Shrimp as well as the Green Butt Skunk and the Purple Peril.

The Green Butt Skunk is a close relative of the Black Bear series of hairwing flies that were first developed on the east coast Atlantic salmon fisheries of Canada. The basic pattern of a silver ribbed black body, black wing and black hackle was given added impact by green butt section. This butt section was later changed to a fluorescent wool or floss and the patterns have proved effective up to the present time for both Atlantic salmon and steelhead. With a simple and successful pattern like this there are of course a wide range of variants as you might expect. The butt colour can be changed and common colours include fluorescent red, orange and yellow. The winging material has also been varied to include skunk and, more recently, fox hair of various kinds which offer added mobility. Examples of the Green Butt and Ken McLeod's Purple Peril tied Spey style are shown

below but it is obvious that this idea can be extended to encompass almost any successful pattern. The Green Butt shown has a white hair wing but versions are also tied using black hair of various kinds.

Green Butt Spey

Purple Peril Spey

The name of Walt Johnson has already been mentioned in connection with his Red Shrimp pattern first developed in the 1960s. More recent Spey patterns include the Golden Spey, Royal Spey and the Deep Purple Spey.

The Deep Purple Spey is also based on Ken McLeod's Purple Peril and combines the purple body with a wing of red golden pheasant body feathers which provides a remarkable degree of underwater visibility. The fly is simply tied with no tail and no tag, following the example of the original Spey flies.

The Golden Spey is a harmonious blend of gold, yellow and orange. As has been remarked earlier the use of golden pheasant topping adds extra flash and sparkle to the wing. Whilst there is no doubt that many of the extravagances of the classic, fully dressed salmon fly were totally irrelevant and unnecessary to their success in

Spring Spey - Stetzer

October Spey - Stetzer

Golden Spey - Johnson

Royal Spey - Johnson

Deep Purple Spey - Johnson

PLATE 31: Walt Johnson & Randy Stetzer

persuading fish to take, the use of a leading edge topping does seem to have a practical effect and may well be worth retaining. Even a hairwing enthusiast such as Lee Wulff used toppings over some of his salmon hairwings. The dubbed body of a rich yellow seal's fur is laid over a base of fluorescent light yellow floss. You will find that many experienced fly tiers and anglers insist on an underbody, very often tinsel, before dubbing. This is very important in retaining brightness and translucence when the dubbing is wet and should on no account be ignored if the effectiveness of the fly is to be retained.

The last fly of this trio, the Royal Spey is a startling combination of colours, combining as it does, bright light blue, peacock herl and fluorescent pink. The fly is also unusual in that it has cheeks consisting of Lady Amherst pheasant tippet, dyed light blue. It is surprising that these tippets are not more often used. The feathers are readily obtainable at reasonable cost and being white tipped with black in their natural state are ideal candidates for dying in a whole range of colours. Note that the larger feathers of the neck have a double black band, whereas the smaller feathers, as shown in the illustration above, have only black tips.

We have also illustrated two flies from Randy

Stetzer. These two Spey flies were inspired by Sydney Glasso's patterns and retain all the simplicity and elegance that is the mark of the best Spey flies. They have no frills and are effective because of the movement inherent in the flowing hackles and the mobile way in which they swim.

We have already seen the Polar Shrimp and the Gibb's Shrimp from Mike Brooks, two of his Spey patterns are also of interest, the Red Dog and the RVI. The Red Dog is a classically styled Spey fly, retaining the traditional bronze mallard wing. The RVI, which was named after Ron Van Iderstein a steelhead guide from Oregon, has proved extremely effective for summer steelhead, particularly in the evenings, once rising ten and landing seven fish in one evening. The fly can be tied in a variety of colours, recommended are orange (as illustrated), light orange, green and purple.

and the Purple King as well as flies of his own devising. His love of tradition goes as far as dressing his flies with braided gut eyes. It should be noted that he does this to gain a practical advantage, rather than as an affectation, as he considers that the flies have a much superior fishing action to those tied on normal eyed hooks. The Gobin version of the Purple King varies slightly from the pattern as given by Francis Francis which is shown above. He uses a deep purple floss for the body rather than light purple mohair. The ribbing on his pattern is oval gold tinsel paralleled by a single strand of deep purple floss. The palmered black schlappen is then counter-wound with gold thread. The throat hackle on his fly is of guinea fowl rather than teal. It should be noted however that variations such as these are perfectly legitimate and simply match those of the original flies. Alternative dressings for the Purple King are given by Knox, Francis Francis, Kelson and Hale, all of them slightly different.

Red Dog Spey (Brooks)

RVI Orange (Brooks)

Tartan Dee (Gobin)

Purple King (Gobin)

Steve Gobin is a Tulalip Indian who is a traditionalist, both in the rods he uses and in the flies that he fishes with them. His normal flies for every day use are traditional Spey patterns including classics such as the Tartan, the Carron

The Purple Spey is a simple pattern which uses the deep purple colour so favoured by many steelhead anglers. In this case it it relieved by a splash of hot pink at the rear of the body.

Purple Spey (Gobin)

The Skykomish Light and the Skykomish Dark are based generally on the classic steelhead hairwing fly the Skykomish Sunrise. This has a red chenille body and a tail and and hackle of mixed red and yellow fibres. The bodies on the two new flies retain these colours with a combination of orange and red with yellow Spey hackling. The wing on the original was white bucktail but has been replaced here by a traditional Spey wing of bronze mallard.

Skykomish Dark (Gobin)

Skykomish Light (Gobin)

The next fly that we have illustrated is the Purple Heart Spey from Bob Veverka. This fly continues the purple/red/black combination that has proved to be so consistently successful for steelhead. In this case the rear body is of fluorescent red floss with a front body of purple seal's fur. The throat is a black hackle and the winging consists of red hackles flanked by purple hackles. This wing combination gives an intensity of colour which would be unobtainable by using just a single colour. This type of mixed colour winging is also used on the Rusty Heron and the Black & Orange Heron. The dressing that we have illustrated is taken from, *Steelhead Fly Fishing* by Trey Combs.

Purple Heart Spey #1 (Veverka)

We have also found another dressing for the Purple Heart where the body is a combination of red silk floss and blue dubbing. The wing is purple dyed goose quill and the throat hackle is of red golden pheasant flank. Apart from sharing the colour purple, these two dressings are quite different. It is possible that some confusion has arisen in the naming and that they are in fact two different flies.

Purple Heart Spey #2 (Veverka)

<table>
<tr><td>Car Body</td><td>Turkey Tracker</td></tr>
<tr><td>Dragon's Tooth</td><td>Boulder Creek</td></tr>
</table>

PLATE 32: Mike Kinney Spey Flies

Mike Kinney has spent most of his life guiding fishermen on the Olympic Peninsular and has gained an encyclopedic knowledge of the Stillaguamish and Skagit Rivers. His Spey flies are practical fishing flies, mostly dark in hue which combine a striking silhouette with vivid splashes of colour. Four of his flies are illustrated in Plate 32 (above). The Turkey Tracker is unusual in that it has wings of Highlander Green, a colour rarely seen other than on the classic salmon fly of that name. This is all the more surprising when one considers that the Green Highlander in various guises, mainly hairwings in recent times, has been consistently a successful fly over the years, not only in Scotland but also in Scandinavia, Ireland and the eastern provinces of Canada.

Joe Howell is another angler who has continued the legacy of Syd Glasso in his flies. His Spey flies are used on the North Umpqua throughout the season. The Silver Streak is his favourite fly and it is effective at all times of the year. This pattern, which apart from the tinsel body, is very much in the traditional style is shown

below, together with the Gold Streak. It is tied in sizes from 2 to 4/0. In both these patterns the heron body hackling should be as long as possible.

Silver Streak (Howell)

Gold Streak (Howell)

Grey Heron - Gobin

Green Heron - Veverka

Orange Heron #1 - Howell

Orange Heron #2 - Howell

Blue Heron - Veverka

Orange Heron - Gobin

PLATE 33: Heron Series Spey Flies - 1

Golden Heron - McNeese

Brown Heron - McNeese

Black & Orange Heron - Veverka

Rusty Heron - Veverka

PLATE 34: Heron Series Spey Flies - 2

The Heron series of flies consisting of the Grey Heron, the Black Heron and the Gold Heron belong to the original early Spey flies dating back to the first quarter of the 19th. century, indeed there is reason to believe that the Grey Heron may be the oldest of them all. These flies have been a source of inspiration to fly tiers up to the present day and the next series of flies that we have illustrated from Sydney Glasso, Steve Gobin, Joe Howell, Dave McNeese and Bob Veverka are new patterns that all belong to this group. Both the Orange Heron and the Brown Heron are originals attributed to Syd Glasso.

As far as we can ascertain the Black & Orange Heron, the Green Heron and the Blue Heron are all Veverka originals. As you will see from the illustration there are a wide range of variants, particularly of the Orange Heron. The Grey Heron from Steve Gobin is very similar to the original tying, the body is simply changed to floss

rather than Berlin wool. We have shown three versions of the Orange Heron, one from steve Gobin and two from Joe Howell. Of these flies the version from Steve Gobin is nearest to the original Spey patterns such as the Grey and Black Herons in as much as the traditional bronze mallard wing is retained and there are no added features such as tags or cheeks. The two Orange Heron patterns from Joe Howell vary considerably from both from the original style of tying and also the Glasso pattern. The Orange Heron 1 has a tag as well as jungle cock cheeks, the rear floss half of the body being of fluorescent floss. Orange Heron 2 is much nearer the original Spey patterns apart from the wings which are of peacock secondary wing quills. This heavily marked feather gives the fly a completely different look from the far more subdued patterns tied with the traditional bronze mallard wing. Both of these patterns have considerably more visual impact than the

traditional flies but still retain the elegance and simplicity of form which is the hallmark of a good Spey pattern.

The Green and Blue Herons from Bob Veverka retain the Glasso style of hackle tip winging, the difference being only in the colours of the body and wing. As has been noted earlier these are not the most popular of colours for steelhead flies, but nevertheless they offer a useful 'change of pace' from the more common orange, red, purple and black and should do well early in the spring. The Rusty Heron is similar in construction but combines wing colours of both yellow and orange or red. The throat hackle is of red golden pheasant body feather. The Black & Orange Heron, also from Bob Veverka, combines the two most popular colours for steelhead flies, black and orange, in a pattern which should work well in almost all water conditions. The ribbing on this fly combines a double spiral of oval silver tinsel with a central strand of fluorescent orange floss. Multiple ribbing is one of the features of the original Spey flies and is very effective against the black floss of the rear body. Other flies in the Heron series from Syd Glasso are illustrated on pages 95 and 96.

Two fly tiers from Canada, Kyle Whyet and Ken Chandler are believers in the use of Spey patterns for practical fishing and both of them have devised patterns that could find wider application outside the areas in which they were developed.

The fly from Kyle Whyet, called the Mickey Mouse Spey (so called because of its appearance from head-on!) has proved very successful for steelhead on a range of rivers. The use of green floss together with silver oval as ribbing gives this fly a special touch and is typical of the close multi-strand ribbing used on the original Spey patterns.

Jungle cock wings, although not normal on Spey flies give the fly 'lift' and give an aiming point for the fish. Because they are tied over the hackle, these wings lie in a vee-shape, reminiscent of the Dee winging style. When used on the traditional Dee flies, jungle cock cheeks were usually mounted sloping downwards pointing towards the hook point. Whether this configuration has any practical effect when the fly is fished is difficult to say. We presume that the idea of tying the cheeks in this way was to avoid masking the action of the wings.

K.C.'s Steelhead Spey from Ken Chandler is a black fly with a slim body and an elegant shape

which looks as if it could be effective for Atlantic salmon as well as steelhead. The KC has proved to successful in both clear and coloured waters.

The style of both these flies is similar - both having a thorax of black dyed ostrich herl. This helps to give a dense shoulder profile at the head of the fly which nicely balances the slim body and flowing hackles. The basic design is very simple but elegant, hallmarks of the original Scottish Spey and Dee flies. The purity of line and the lack of complication are features that should be preserved when designing new flies of this type and the two flies shown above do this extremely well.

Mickey Mouse Spey (Whyet)

K.C's Steelhead Spey (Chandler)

Phil Strobel from Colorado is the originator of two Spey patterns that we like a lot. The Purple Spey is a simple but elegant pattern. The tail is unusual in that it is made of rabbit fur which gives additional mobility and the long rear body of silver tinsel adds sparkle to the fly. The long Spey hackles are of blue-eared pheasant fibres. When they can be obtained in large enough sizes the flank feathers from the blue-eared pheasant make an ideal substitute for heron hackle. The natural colour, being a light smokey grey graduating to a dark steel grey nearer the stem, is superb, the only problem is that there are very few large feathers on each skin.

The Orange Spey combines a rear body of gold tinsel with dubbed orange seal's fur for the front half. The hackling of grey marabou should be extremely long. On both of these patterns the Spey hackling is restricted to the front half of the body which produces a wispy veiling over the sparkling tinsel of the rear body.

Purple Spey (Strobel)

Orange Spey (Strobel)

Originally designed as a bass fly, the Fatal Attraction from Dan Blanton has proved to be a really killing autumn pattern for chinook, Atlantic salmon and steelhead on rivers as varied as the Salmon River (NY) as well as the west coast and Nova Scotia. The fly can be tied in a whole range of colour combinations. Among the recommended colours are orange/black, white/silver and Fire Tiger which has a copper coloured tail and body with an orange wing. An important part of this fly is the body which consists of Diamond Braid, a flashy glitter material. This, combined with the Krystal Flash used in the tail and wing produces a fly which can be considered as the equivalent of a Mepps spinner. It is, not surprisingly, highly effective in coloured water.

Fatal Attraction
black/orange

Fatal Attraction
white/silver

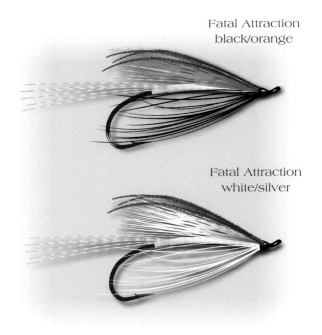

When we saw this pattern, our first reaction was that it would lend itself very well to being dressed in the style of an Ally's shrimp.

Fatal Attraction - Fire Tiger
tied Ally's style

The next flies that we have illustrated are all variations on the same colour theme - purple. There is no doubt that purple, usually combined with either black or red, has proved extraordinarily successful for steelhead although it is a colour that is little used for Atlantic salmon apart from in Ireland. The use of various colours and which of them are effective is an extremely interesting subject which has come up for discussion very often during the writing of this book. We have

Purple Prince

Purple Spey

Spawning Spey

Purple Brat

PLATE 35: Variations on a Purple Theme - Dave McNeese

already mentioned the dearth of green salmon and steelhead flies, despite the fact that in the right conditions the few green patterns around are very effective. Much the same applies to the the dark red wine colour generally known as claret. There are a range of shrimp patterns from Ireland that use claret but apart from these there are very few salmon flies from other areas that use this colour. This is all the more extraordinary when one considers how often salmon are taken on claret coloured trout flies. The arguments that are used to explain why purple flies are so effective would equally well justify the use of claret and indeed in the fading light conditions of evening a dark claret fly may be even more effective. As evening fades towards darkness the red light rays are the last to disappear and it is well known that claret coloured trout flie collect and intensify the dying rays causing a glowing image that is extremely visible from underwater. On a clear summer evening,

when the sun has set and all that remains is an afterglow, it could well be worthwhile for some enterprising angler to try one of the following patterns using a dark claret instead of purple, particularly when fishing near the surface. There is also some historical precedence for the use of claret. Bryan Williams, in his book *Rod and Creel in British Columbia,* published in 1919, stated that the Claret & Grouse was better for steelhead than either the Jock Scott or the Silver Doctor. The flies illustrated were all designed by Dave McNeese and combine a richness of colour with mobility and elegance.

The Purple Prince is a combination of old and new. The old is represented by the use of indian crow substitute in the tail, the use of golden pheasant toppings over the wing and the addition of jungle cock cheeks. Nevertheless, this pattern is by no means overdressed and each of these features fulfils a practical rather than a decorative role. The

fly has mobility and colour and is effective in both summer and winter.

The Purple Spey dates from 1978 and was first used on the South Santiam where it proved to be immediately successful, taking ten steelhead for two anglers in one evening.

The Spawning Spey is a more recent development of a fly known as the Spawning Purple which dates from 1977. It is tied slimly but has a lot of mobility to entice the winter steelhead.

The Purple Brat is a Spey style variant of Brad's Brat one of the most enduring classic steelhead patterns, devised by Enos Bradner on the North Fork of the Stillaguamish River over 60 years ago. The Purple Brat has been used with success throughout the year.

Gerald Bartsch is a professional fly tier from British Columbia. Apart from recreating the classic Spey flies of yesteryear he has also designed his own series of patterns that combine the elegance and simplicity of the traditional flies with startling new colour combinations and an innovative use of materials to produce flies that are not only beautiful but eminently 'fishable'. Gerald ties his flies to the highest standards and is insistent that the time and care spent makes a real difference to the fishing performance. Almost all his flies are tied with an underbody of tinsel to ensure that the translucence and sparkle of the dubbing or the floss is not lost when the fly is wet. There is no doubt that touches like this make the difference between a usable fly and one that has 'that special something extra'.

Ice Blue Spey (Bartsch)

The Ice Blue Spey is an unusual fly in that it has a rear body of ice blue tinsel. We have not seen another fly that uses this colour material. The effect of the sparkling blue tinsel veiled by the long black Spey hackle together with the fore-body of black dubbing and a traditional wing of bronze mallard produces a fly which has a dark silhouette combined with mobility and an extra bit of 'flash' that has proved to be extremely effective in clear water conditions. Blue is a seldom used colour for steelhead flies (or for Atlantic salmon flies for that matter) but can be surprisingly effective at times and the success of this pattern shows that further experimentation may well be worthwhile.

The Golden Spey combines traditional materials with an unusual tying style. The body is a combination of yellow and black which has been a favourite combination since the 19th century and remains effective today. The use of tippet feathers as a kind of tail (or rear body veiling) is unusual but looks very good. Two black dyed, blue eared pheasant feathers provide lots of mobility and the fly is completed with a golden pheasant topping to give added sparkle. The fly has proved to be effective in murkey water conditions on dark days, early mornings and evenings.

Golden Spey (Bartsch)

'As Specified #1' is the name of a fly first developed by Arthur Lingren in 1982 which has been consistently successful for steelhead on rivers as varied as the Thompson, Dean, Morice and Campbell. Tied sparsely with a black Spey hackle, slim body of purple floss and dubbing and a traditional bronze mallard wing, this fly is one that should always be in your fly box.

As Specified #1 (Lingren)

The H.D. Purple Spey uses the same colour combination but in this case the fly is tied in traditional Spey style with a bronze mallard wing. The red floss is again undertied with flat silver tinsel in order to maintain a true red when the fly is wet. Gerald recommends this as an effective pattern at all times of year.

H.D. Purple Spey (Bartsch)

The Deuce is a variant of the very well known Sol Duc from Syd Glasso. The yellow, black and orange colours of the original fly have been maintained but the ribbing is slightly different and the hackle tip wings have been replaced by the traditional bronze mallard. For the first casts of the day when the mood and preferences of the fish have yet to be established, any fly with this combination of colours has got to be a pretty good starting bet.

The Deuce is a really good looking fly that has proved to be extremely effective on sunny days and when the water has some colour. In his notes to us, Gerald said he hoped that Syd would have been pleased with this fly. We are sure he would, the

Deuce retains all the elegance and grace which is the hallmark of a Glasso original.

The Deuce Spey (Bartsch)

The Orange Spey is a traditional style pattern which is well suited to the phrase 'bright day, bright fly'. This homily, like many others in flyfishing, seems to be true about half the time! The effectiveness of this pattern is however, not is doubt. The extremely long hackle of blue eared pheasant is very webby and provides a great deal of movement in the water.

Orange Spey (Bartsch)

The Blue Knight Spey has a two part blue body, floss at the rear, seal's fur at the front. This is combined with blue body hackles and a purple throat hackle. The Blue Knight joins a very small group of salmon and steelhead flies which have a blue body although the use of blue throat hackling is much more widespread. Gerald created this pattern about two years ago and it has become one

of his personal favourites which he fishes at any time, anywhere. The Blue Knight is also effective when tied in smaller sizes.

Blue Knight Spey (Bartsch)

The Red & Purple Spey returns to two recurring themes in modern steelhead Spey flies - marabou combined with purple. In this case these two elements are brought together with a red floss body and a black collar hackle to produce a very effective combination. The silver rib stands out well against the red body providing an extra sparkle to the fly. The marabou has great mobility and gives a dense silhouette without having bulk. The Red & Purple Spey has proved itself effective in a wide range of water conditions.

Red & Purple Spey (Bartsch)

Troy Bachmann is the man behind the Frontier Fly Company, familiar to anglers throughout the Pacific Northwest. His company

has a reputation for producing flies that combine excellent quality tying, together with innovative modern designs - patterns on the cutting edge as they are described.

The Winter Punch Spey is one of Troy's own designs and is quite startling, combining as it does pink and fluorescent chartreuse.

Winter Punch Spey (Bachmann)

Catalogue of Dressings

 he following pages contain a full catalogue of all the flies which are illustrated within the main text. Dressing details for each fly are given, together with an illustration. The flies are organised in alphabetical order and are split into two groups - Europe and North America. Certain flies are contained within both groups - the General Practitioner for example. The page numbers may be found within the index.

We have not given hook details for these dressings, this is not an oversight but simply because hook types vary so widely and the rules governing what is and is not allowable in each area and country vary equally as much. The typical hook sizes are also vary according to the geographical area and the type of fish For example, shrimp flies in the west of Ireland may be tied as small as a size 14 or as large as size 4, steelhead flies may be as large as a size 11/2.

Dressings have also been shown on a variety of hook types - singles, doubles, trebles, Waddington shanks and tubes. Most of the dressings given here will translate quite easily from one type of hook to another.

Always be aware that the stiffness of the tying material, particularly for the long tails on so many shrimp dressings, is critical to the performance of the fly. Small flies need flexible fibres.

Another important point concerns materials from rare or protected species. Some of the dressings given in the following pages mention feathers from birds such as macaws, toucans etc. in order to maintain historical accuracy. On no account do we wish to encourage the illegal use of plumage from protected species, particularly when perfectly acceptable subsitutes are readily available. Even if the use of such plumage is not illegal we can see no reason why rare species should be further endangered by flytyers. The fish certainly can't tell the difference when a substitute is used!

94AN

TAG: Oval gold tinsel
TAIL: Hot orange marabou plus orange flash
BODY JOINTS: Black dubbing
REAR JOINT HACKLE: Golden pheasant red breast feather
FRONT JOINT HACKLES: Brown cock
CHEEKS: Jungle cock
HEAD: Black

AKROYD

TAG: Silver tinsel
BUTT: Black ostrich
TAIL: a topping and tippet in strands
REAR BODY: Light orange seal's fur
RIB: Oval silver tinsel
BODY HACKLE: Lemon cock
CENTRE BUTT: Black ostrich herl
FRONT BODY: Black floss
RIB: Flat silver tinsel
BODY HACKLE: Black heron
THROAT: One turn of teal
WING: Cinnamon turkey tail strips
CHEEKS: Jungle cock, drooping
HEAD: Black

AKROYD, WHITE WING

TAG: Silver tinsel
BUTT: Black ostrich
TAIL: a topping and tippet in strands
REAR BODY: Yellow seal's fur
RIB: Oval silver tinsel
BODY HACKLE: Lemon cock
CENTRE BUTT: Black ostrich herl
FRONT BODY: Black floss
RIB: Flat silver tinsel
BODY HACKLE: Black heron
THROAT: One turn of teal
WING: White turkey tail strips
CHEEKS: Jungle cock, drooping
HEAD: Black

AKROYD SHRIMP, ORANGE - Wotton

TAG: Gold tinsel
TAIL: Black hackle, wound
BODY: Rear half orange seal's fur, front half black seal's fur
RIB: Oval gold tinsel
EYES: Jungle cock
HACKLE: Silver badger cock over yellow
HEAD: Black

AKROYD SHRIMP, YELLOW - Wotton

TAG: Gold tinsel
TAIL: Black hackle, wound
BODY: Rear half yellow seal's fur, front half black seal's fur
RIB: Oval gold tinsel
EYES: Jungle cock
HACKLE: Silver badger cock over orange
HEAD: Black

ALISTAIR SHRIMP

TAIL: Natural barred grey squirrel dyed yellow
BODY: Old gold Mylar
RIB: Oval silver tinsel
BODY HACKLE: Yellow cock, palmered
HACKLE: Sparse G.P. red breast feather, length 5mm past hook bend
CHEEKS: Jungle cock
HEAD: Black

ALLY'S SHRIMP, ORIGINAL

TAIL: Hot orange bucktail with four strands of pearl Crystal Hair optional
BODY: Rear half red floss, front half black floss
RIB: Oval gold
UNDERWING: Top & bottom, natural grey squirrel, tied flat extending to bend of hook
WING: Golden pheasant tippets, extending to hook barb
HACKLE: Hot orange, tied as collar and dressed back, length to match tippets
HEAD: Red

ALLY'S SHRIMP, BLACK - Donaldson

TAIL: Black bucktail with four strands of black Crystal Hair
BODY: Flat silver tinsel
RIB: Oval silver tinsel followed by Glo-Brite #14 fluorescent lime green floss
UNDERWING: Top & bottom, natural grey squirrel dyed yellow, extending to bend of hook
WING: Golden pheasant tippet to hook barb
HACKLE: Black cock, tied as collar and dressed back, length to hook barb
HEAD: Black

ALLY'S SHRIMP, BLACK - Younger

TAIL: Black bucktail with four strands of pearl Crystal Hair
BODY: Rear half orange Multi-yarn, front half black floss
RIB: Oval silver
UNDERWING: Top & bottom, natural grey squirrel, tied flat extending to bend of hook
WING: Golden pheasant tippets dyed red, extending to hook barb
HACKLE: Black cock, tied as collar and dressed back, length to hook barb
HEAD: Red

ALLY'S SHRIMP, CASCADE

TAIL: Mixed yellow and hot orange bucktail with four strands of silver Crystal Hair optional
BODY: Rear half silver Mylar, front half black floss
RIB: Oval silver
UNDERWING: Top & bottom, natural grey squirrel, tied flat extending to bend of hook
WING: Black bear, stoat or squirrel with four strands of pearl Crystal Hair
HACKLE: Hot orange over yellow cock, tied as collar and dressed back, length to hook barb
HEAD: Black

ALLY'S SHRIMP, COPPER

TAIL: Mixed black and hot orange bucktail with four strands of pearl Crystal Hair optional
BODY: Copper Mylar
RIB: Oval silver
WING: Golden pheasant tippets, extending to hook barb
HACKLE: Hot orange over black cock, tied as collar and dressed back, length to hook barb
HEAD: Black

ALLY'S SHRIMP, MAGENTA - Donaldson

TAIL: Magenta bucktail with strands of pink Twinkle
BODY: Rear half lilac Lurex, front half Glo-Brite #4 fluorescent floss
RIB: Oval silver
UNDERWING: Top & bottom, natural grey squirrel, tied flat extending to bend of hook
WING: Golden pheasant tippets, extending to hook barb
HACKLE: Magenta cock, tied as collar and dressed back, length to hook barb
HEAD: Red

94AN	AKROYD	AKROYD, WHITE WING

AKROYD SHRIMP, ORANGE	AKROYD SHRIMP, YELLOW	ALISTAIR SHRIMP

ALLY'S SHRIMP, ORIGINAL	ALLY'S SHRIMP, BLACK	ALLY'S SHRIMP, BLACK

ALLY'S SHRIMP, CASCADE	ALLY'S SHRIMP, COPPER	ALLY'S SHRIMP, MAGENTA

ALLY'S SHRIMP, PURPLE

TAIL: Purple bucktail with strands of purple Crystal Hair
BODY: Rear half purple Multi-yarn, front half black floss
RIB: Oval silver
WING: Top & bottom, natural grey squirrel dyed purple, tied flat
HACKLE: Purple cock, tied as collar and dressed back, length to hook barb
HEAD: Red

ALLY'S SHRIMP, RED

TAIL: Red bucktail with four strands of pearl Crystal Hair (optional)
BODY: Rear half red floss, front half black floss
RIB: Oval gold
UNDERWING: Top & bottom, natural grey squirrel, tied flat extending to bend of hook
WING: Golden pheasant tippets, extending to hook barb
HACKLE: Red cock, tied as collar and dressed back, length to hook barb
HEAD: Red

ALLY'S SHRIMP, RED PEARL

TAIL: Equal mix of yellow, red and orange bucktail with three strands of pearl Crystal Hair. 1 1/2 to 1 3/4 times overall hook length
BODY: Fluorescent red floss or wool overwrapped with pearl Mylar
RIB: Oval gold
WING: Equal mix of yellow, red and orange bucktail with three strands of pearl Crystal Hair, extending to halfway along tail
HACKLE: Red cock, tied as collar and dressed back, length to hook barb
HEAD: Black

ALLY'S SHRIMP, RUSSIAN

TAIL: Yellow bucktail with four strands of pearl Crystal Hair.
BODY: Gold Mylar
RIB: Oval gold
UNDERWING: Top & bottom, natural grey squirrel, tied flat extending to bend of hook
HACKLE: White or cream cock, tied as collar and dressed back, length to hook barb
HEAD: Black

ALLY'S SHRIMP, SPECIAL

TAIL: Red and hot orange bucktail with four strands of pearl Crystal Hair (optional)
BODY: Rear half red floss, front half black floss
RIB: Oval gold
UNDERWING: Top & bottom, natural grey squirrel, tied flat extending to bend of hook
WING: Golden pheasant tippets, extending to hook barb
HACKLE: Hot orange over red cock, tied as collar and dressed back, length to match tippets
HEAD: Red

ALLY'S SHRIMP, TUMMEL

TAIL: Yellow, black & and hot orange bucktail with four strands of pearl Crystal Hair (optional)
BODY: Black floss
RIB: Oval silver
UNDERWING: Top & bottom, natural grey squirrel, tied flat extending to bend of hook
WING: Black bear, stoat or squirrel with four strands of pearl Crystal Hair
HACKLE: Blue dyed guinea fowl over hot orange cock, tied as collar and dressed back, length to match tippets
HEAD: Black

ALLY'S SHRIMP, YELLOW

TAIL: Bright yellow bucktail with four strands of pearl Crystal Hair (optional)
BODY: Rear half silver Mylar, front half black floss
RIB: Oval silver
UNDERWING: Top & bottom, natural grey squirrel, tied flat extending to bend of hook
WING: Golden pheasant tippets, extending to hook barb
HACKLE: Bright yellow cock, tied as collar and dressed back, length to match tippets
HEAD: Black

APACHE SHADOW SHRIMP - Atkins

REAR BODY: Holographic gold Mylar
RIB: Silver wire
TAIL: Tied at centre joint, red bucktail plus four strands red Krystalflash
VEILINGS: G.P. tippet "V"
CENTRE HACKLE: Yellow
FRONT BODY: Red holographic Mylar
RIB: Silver wire
WING: Red arctic fox
COLLAR HACKLE: Scarlet cock
HEAD: Black

APACHE SHRIMP - Atkins

TAG: Flat or oval silver
TAIL: GP red breast feather, wound
REAR BODY: Golden yellow floss
RIB: Oval Silver
CENTRE HACKLE: Golden yellow hen or soft cock
FRONT BODY: Scarlet floss
RIB: Oval silver
FRONT HACKLE: Scarlet hen or soft cock
HEAD: Black

APACHE SHRIMP (Low water) - Atkins

REAR BODY: Golden yellow floss
RIB: Fine oval silver
TAIL: Tied at centre joint, GP red breast feather
FRONT BODY: Red Lite-Brite
RIB: Fine oval silver
FRONT HACKLES: 2 turns scarlet cock over 2 turns yellow
HEAD: Black

ARCTIC ALLY'S, ORANGE

TAIL: Orange bucktail with four strands of pearl Crystal Hair (optional)
BODY: Gold Mylar
RIB: Oval gold
WING: Hot orange arctic fox
HACKLE: Hot orange, tied as collar
HEAD: Red

ARCTIC ALLY'S, YELLOW

TAIL: Yellow bucktail with four strands of pearl Crystal Hair (optional)
BODY: Gold Mylar
RIB: Oval gold
WING: Hot orange arctic fox
HACKLE: Yellow, tied as collar
HEAD: Red

ALLY'S SHRIMP, PURPLE   ALLY'S SHRIMP, RED   ALLY'S SHRIMP, RED PEARL

ALLY'S SHRIMP, RUSSIAN   ALLY'S SHRIMP, SPECIAL   ALLY'S SHRIMP, TUMMEL

ALLY'S SHRIMP, YELLOW   APACHE SHADOW SHRIMP   APACHE SHRIMP

APACHE SHRIMP (Low water)   ARCTIC ALLY'S, ORANGE   ARCTIC ALLY'S, YELLOW

ARCTIC FOX SHRIMP, BLUE - Robertson

TAIL: Arctic fox dyed blue with two strands of silver Crystal Hair
BODY: Flat silver tinsel
RIB: Oval silver
UNDERWING: Top only, natural grey squirrel, tied flat extending to bend of hook, sparse arctic fox dyed blue over
WING: Golden pheasant tippets, extending to hook barb
HACKLE: Blue cock, tied as collar and dressed back, length to match tippets
HEAD: Black

AYRSHIRE RED SHRIMP - Robertson

TAG: Oval silver tinsel
TAIL: GP red breast feather, wound
REAR BODY: Red floss
RIB: Oval silver
CENTRE HACKLE: Red cock
FRONT BODY: Primrose yellow floss
RIB: Oval silver
CHEEKS/WING: Jungle cock
HACKLE: Badger cock
HEAD: Red

BADGER & RED SHRIMP

TAG: Oval silver tinsel
TAIL: GP red breast feather, wound
REAR BODY: Red seal's fur
RIB: Oval silver
CENTRE HACKLE: Creamy badger
FRONT BODY: Black seal's fur
RIB: Oval silver
FRONT HACKLE: Creamy badger cock
HEAD: Red

BALLINA GREY SHRIMP

TAG: Oval copper tinsel
TAIL: GP red breast feather, wound
REAR BODY: Pearsall's orange floss
RIB: Oval copper
CENTRE HACKLE: White or cream
FRONT BODY: Pearsall's blue floss
RIB: Oval copper
FRONT HACKLE: Silver badger or grizzle cock
HEAD: Black

ARCTIC FOX SHRIMP, YELLOW - Robertson

TAIL: Arctic fox dyed yellow with two strands of silver Crystal Hair
BODY: Flat silver tinsel
RIB: Oval silver
UNDERWING: Top only, natural grey squirrel, tied flat extending to bend of hook, sparse arctic fox dyed yellow over
WING: Golden pheasant tippets, extending to hook barb
HACKLE: Yellow cock, tied as collar and dressed back, length to match tippets
HEAD: Black

BADGER & GOLDEN OLIVE SHRIMP

TAG: Oval silver tinsel
TAIL: GP red breast feather, wound
REAR BODY: Golden olive seal's fur
RIB: Oval silver
CENTRE HACKLE: Creamy badger
FRONT BODY: Black seal's fur
RIB: Oval silver
FRONT HACKLE: Creamy badger cock
HEAD: Red

BADGER SHRIMP (Low water) - Atkins

REAR BODY: Golden yellow floss
RIB: Fine oval silver
TAIL: Tied at centre joint, GP red breast feather
FRONT BODY: Red Lite-Brite
RIB: Fine oval silver
FRONT HACKLE: Silver badger with large black centre
HEAD: Red

BANN SPECIAL SHRIMP

TAG: Oval silver tinsel
TAIL: GP red breast feather, wound
REAR BODY: Yellow floss or seal's fur
RIB: Oval silver
CENTRE HACKLE: Hot orange
FRONT BODY: Black floss or seal's fur
RIB: Oval silver
WINGS: Roofed jungle cock
FRONT HACKLE: Silver badger cock
HEAD: Black

ARCTIC FOX SHRIMP - Westwood

TAIL: Arctic fox dyed orange, twice shank length. Strands of pearl Crystal Hair (optional)
BODY: Rear half red floss, front half black floss
RIB: Oval silver
THROAT HACKLE: Arctic fox summer coat (black with white tips)
WING: Arctic fox summer coat (as above) with dyed yellow, black tipped arctic fox over (use Pantone marker for tips)
HEAD HACKLE: Arctic fox dyed orange
HEAD: Red

BADGER & ORANGE SHRIMP

TAG: Oval silver tinsel
TAIL: GP red breast feather, wound
REAR BODY: Orange seal's fur
RIB: Oval silver
CENTRE HACKLE: Creamy badger
FRONT BODY: Black seal's fur
RIB: Oval silver
FRONT HACKLE: Creamy badger cock
HEAD: Red

BALLINA BLUE SHRIMP

TAG: Oval silver tinsel
TAIL: GP red breast feather, wound
REAR BODY: Red floss
RIB: Oval silver
CENTRE HACKLE: Blue
FRONT BODY: Black floss
RIB: Oval silver
FRONT HACKLE: Silver badger cock
HEAD: Red

Note: BALLINA BLUE SHRIMP - identical but with a red centre hackle instead of blue

BANN SPECIAL SHRIMP (Low water)

REAR BODY: Golden yellow floss
RIB: Oval silver
TAIL: GP red breast feather, tied at centre joint
FRONT BODY: Red wool or seal's fur
RIB: Oval silver
FRONT HACKLES: Two turns of orange cock with silver badger cock over
HEAD: Red

ARCTIC FOX SHRIMP, BLUE   ARCTIC FOX SHRIMP, YELLOW   ARCTIC FOX SHRIMP

AYRSHIRE RED SHRIMP   BADGER & GOLDEN OLIVE SHRIMP   BADGER & ORANGE SHRIMP

BADGER & RED SHRIMP   BADGER SHRIMP (Low water)   BALLINA BLUE SHRIMP

BALLINA GREY SHRIMP   BANN SPECIAL SHRIMP   BANN SPECIAL SHRIMP (Low water)

BEAULY SHRIMP #1

TAIL: Yellow bucktail
BODY: Olive green floss
RIB: Oval silver
UNDERWING: Top only, natural grey squirrel, tied flat extending to bend of hook
WING: Golden pheasant tippets, extending to hook barb
THROAT HACKLE: Bunch of scarlet cock hackle fibres
HEAD: Red

BEAULY SHRIMP #2

TAIL: Orange bucktail
BODY: Orange Multi-yarn
RIB: Oval gold
UNDERWING: Top only, natural grey squirrel, tied flat extending to bend of hook
WING: Golden pheasant tippets, extending to hook barb
THROAT HACKLE: Bunch of scarlet cock hackle fibres
HEAD: Red

BESSIE BELL

TAG: Oval silver tinsel
TAIL: Long purple cock hackle, wound
REAR BODY: White floss
RIB: Oval silver
VEILINGS: Yellow toucan
CENTRE HACKLE: Short dark grizzle cock
FRONT BODY: Old gold floss
VEILINGS: Yellow toucan
RIB: Oval silver
WINGS: Roofed jungle cock
FRONT HACKLE: Long grey grizzle cock
HEAD: Black

BISHOP SHRIMP - McDonald

TAG: Oval gold tinsel
TAIL: GP red breast feather, wound
REAR BODY: Orange seal's fur
RIB: Oval gold
CENTRE HACKLE: Hot orange cock
FRONT BODY: Purple seal's fur
RIB: Oval gold
WINGS: Jungle cock - back to back
FRONT HACKLE: Long grey grizzle cock
HEAD: Black

BLACK & ORANGE SHRIMP - McPhail

TAG: Oval gold tinsel
TAIL: GP red breast feather, wound
REAR BODY: Orange seal's fur
RIB: Oval gold
CENTRE HACKLE: Hot orange cock
FRONT BODY: Black seal's fur
RIB: Oval gold
CHEEKS: Jungle cock
FRONT HACKLE: Badger cock
HEAD: Red

BLACK & SILVER SHRIMP

TAG: Oval silver tinsel
TAIL: GP red breast feather, wound
REAR BODY: Flat silver tinsel
RIB: Oval silver
CENTRE HACKLE: Black cock
FRONT BODY: Flat silver tinsel
RIB: Oval silver
WINGS: Roofed jungle cock
FRONT HACKLE: Black cock
THROAT: Blue jay or guinea fowl dyed blue
HEAD: Black

BLACK HERON - Knox

BODY: Black Berlin wool
RIB: Flat gold tinsel, between one strand gold and one strand silver thread
BODY HACKLE: Black heron (very long)
WINGS: Bronze mallard set low, keel fashion
HEAD: Black

BLACK RAINBOW SHRIMP - McPhail

TUBE: 1/2" to 2" copper slipstream
BODY: None, use black silicone tubing to hold hook in place
WING: Black bucktail and strands of Rainbow Reflections
CHEEKS: Jungle cock
HEAD: Red

BLACK SHRIMP #1

TAG: Oval silver tinsel
TAIL: Long black cock hackle, wound
REAR BODY: Fluorescent or plain yellow floss
RIB: Oval silver
CENTRE HACKLE: Hot orange
FRONT BODY: Black floss
RIB: Oval silver
FRONT HACKLE: Black cock
EYES (optional): Small jungle cock
HEAD: Black

BLACK SHRIMP #2

TAIL: Black bucktail with four strands of black Twinkle (optional)
BODY: Rear half orange floss, front half black floss
CENTRE HACKLE: Short orange hen
RIB: Oval silver
UNDERWING: Top & bottom, natural grey squirrel, tied flat extending to bend of hook
WING: Golden pheasant tippets, extending to hook barb
HACKLE: Black over bright yellow hen, tied as collar and dressed back, length to hook barb
HEAD: Black

BLACK SHRIMP, HELMSDALE

TAIL: Long black squirrel, 1/ times overall hook length
REAR BODY: Silver Mylar
RIB: Oval silver
CENTRE HACKLE: Black, to 1/8" (3mm) past hook bend
FRONT BODY: Silver Mylar
RIB: Oval silver
FRONT HACKLE: Black cock
CHEEKS: Jungle cock
HEAD: Black

BLACK SHRIMP (Low water) - Atkins

REAR BODY: Fluorescent green floss
RIB: Fine oval silver
TAIL: Tied at centre joint, GP red breast feather dyed claret
FRONT BODY: Red Lite-Brite
RIB: Fine oval silver
FRONT HACKLE: Black hen
HEAD: Red

BEAULY SHRIMP #1   BEAULY SHRIMP #2   BESSIE BELL

BISHOP SHRIMP   BLACK & ORANGE SHRIMP   BLACK & SILVER SHRIMP

BLACK HERON   BLACK RAINBOW SHRIMP   BLACK SHRIMP #1

BLACK SHRIMP #2   BLACK SHRIMP, HELMSDALE   BLACK SHRIMP (Low water)

BLUE & MAGENTA SHRIMP

TUBE: 1/2" to 2" copper slipstream
BODY: None, use blue silicone tubing to hold hook in place
WING: Blue & natural brown bucktail and strands of blue & magenta Reflections
CHEEKS: Jungle cock
HEAD: Red

BLUE HACKLE SHRIMP

TAG: Oval silver tinsel
TAIL: GP red breast feather, wound
REAR BODY: Pale orange floss
RIB: Oval silver
CENTRE HACKLE: Medium or light blue
FRONT BODY: Black floss
RIB: Oval silver
WINGS: Pair of roofed jungle cock
FRONT HACKLE: Silver badger
HEAD: Red

BLUE PEARL LITE-BRITE SHRIMP - McPhail

TAG: Minnow blue Lite-Brite
TAIL: GP red breast feather dyed red, wound
REAR BODY: Minnow blue Lite-Brite
FRONT BODY: Pearl Lite-Brite
WING: Natural grey squirrel dyed teal blue
FRONT HACKLE: Silver badger cock
HEAD: Red

BLUE SHRIMP (Low water) - Atkins

REAR BODY: Golden yellow floss
RIB: Fine oval silver
TAIL: Tied at centre joint. GP red breast feather dyed claret
FRONT BODY: Red seal's fur
RIB: Fine oval silver
FRONT HACKLE: Rich blue hen
HEAD: Black

BLUE SHRIMP - McPhail

TAG: Oval silver tinsel
TAIL: GP red breast feather, wound
REAR BODY: Glo-brite #14 fluorescent blue floss
RIB: Oval silver
CENTRE HACKLE: Dyed blue cock
FRONT BODY: Red floss
RIB: Oval silver
WINGS: Pair of roofed jungle cock
FRONT HACKLE: Badger cock
HEAD: Red

BRAHAN SHRIMP - MacKenzie

TAG: Copper tinsel
TAIL: GP red breast feather dyed black, wound
BODY: Red Lurex
RIB: Copper tinsel
THROAT: Small bunch of hot orange hackle fibres tied under hook
WINGS: Two small jungle cock feathers, back to back
HEAD: Black

BROWN SHRIMP - Pryce-Tannatt

TAG: Oval gold tinsel
TAIL: GP red breast feather fibres with a pair of small jungle cock feathers back to back
REAR HACKLE: Two turns red game cock with two turns brown partridge over
REAR BODY: Olive Berlin wool
CENTRE HACKLE: Two turns red game cock with two turns brown partridge over
FRONT BODY: Olive Berlin wool
WINGS: Pair of roofed jungle cock
FRONT HACKLE: Two turns red game cock with two turns brown partridge over
HEAD: Black

BROWN SHRIMP

TAG: Oval silver tinsel
TAIL: GP red breast feather, wound
REAR BODY: Yellow floss
RIB: Oval silver
CENTRE HACKLE: Orange cock
FRONT BODY: Black floss
RIB: Oval silver
WINGS: Pair of roofed jungle cock
FRONT HACKLE: Brown henny (soft) cock
HEAD: Red

BURGUNDY LITE-BRITE SHRIMP - McPhail

TAG: Gold Lite-Brite
TAIL: GP red breast feather dyed red, wound
BODY: Burgundy Lite-Brite
WING: Natural grey squirrel dyed red
FRONT HACKLE: Furnace cock
HEAD: Red

BUSH RED SHRIMP

TAG: Oval silver tinsel
TAIL: GP red breast feather, wound
REAR BODY: Red floss, seal's fur or wool
RIB: Oval silver
CENTRE HACKLES: Silver badger over red cock
FRONT BODY: Black floss, seal's fur or wool
RIB: Oval silver
FRONT HACKLES: Silver badger over red cock
HEAD: Red

BUSH SPECIAL SHRIMP - Atkins

TAG: Oval silver tinsel
TAIL: GP red breast feather, wound
REAR BODY: Red floss, seal's fur or wool
RIB: Oval silver
CENTRE HACKLE: Blue cock
FRONT BODY: Red floss, seal's fur or wool
RIB: Oval silver
FRONT HACKLE: Hot orange cock
HEAD: Red

CARRON FLY

BODY: Orange Berlin wool
RIB: Flat silver tinsel, scarlet floss & silver thread (last in reverse direction)
HACKLE: Black heron from fourth turn of tinsel
THROAT: Teal flank
WINGS: Bronze mallard tied flat, keel form
HEAD: Black

BLUE & MAGENTA SHRIMP   BLUE HACKLE SHRIMP   BLUE PEARL LITE-BRITE SHRIMP

BLUE SHRIMP (Low water)   BLUE SHRIMP   BRAHAN SHRIMP

BROWN SHRIMP   BROWN SHRIMP   BURGUNDY LITE-BRITE SHRIMP

BUSH RED SHRIMP   BUSH SPECIAL SHRIMP   CARRON FLY

CHAPOMA SPEY - Shumakov

TAG: 3 turns fine oval silver tinsel
BUTT: Glow-Brite red floss & black ostrich
TAIL: Red SLF hank
BODY: Rear 2/5ths flat silver tinsel, front 3/5ths black SLF dubbing, black ostrich butt between sections
RIB: Oval silver tinsel
BODY HACKLE: Long black cock over black dubbing
WING: Small bunch black tipped badger, black arctic fox over. Four or five strands brown ripple flash fibres
FRONT HACKLE: GP red breast feather
HEAD: Black

CHRISTMAS TREE SHRIMP

TAIL: Long yellow hackle with hot orange hackle over. Three strands pearl Krystal Flash
REAR BODY: Pearl Mylar
RIB: Oval silver
CENTRE HACKLE: Hot orange
FRONT BODY: Magenta Mylar
RIB: Oval silver
FRONT HACKLE: Red cock
CHEEKS: Jungle cock
HEAD: Red

CLARET SHRIMP - Somers

TAIL: A bunch of claret bucktail surrounded by a long claret hackle, wound
REAR BODY: Claret seal's fur
RIB: Oval gold
VEILING: Yellow hackle fibres, above and below
CENTRE HACKLE: Claret cock
FRONT BODY: Claret seal's fur
RIB: Oval gold
VEILING: Yellow hackle fibres, above and below
FRONT HACKLE: Claret cock
CHEEKS: Jungle cock
HEAD: Red

COLONEL CHRISTIE SHRIMP

TAG: Oval silver tinsel
TAIL: GP red breast feather, wound
REAR BODY: Yellow floss
RIB: Oval silver
VEILING: Yellow swan strips, above and below
CENTRE HACKLE: Badger cock
FRONT BODY: Black floss
RIB: Oval silver
VEILING: Yellow swan strips, above and below
WINGS: Jungle cock, back to back
FRONT HACKLE: Long badger cock
HEAD: Red

CHEAPSKATE HERON - Jørgensen

TAG: Flat silver Mylar tinsel
BUTT: Orange floss
TAIL: GP red breast feather fibres
BODY: Black wool or dubbing
RIB: Medium embossed silver tinsel
BODY HACKLE: Natural grey heron, tied as shown on page 92, natural guinea fowl over
WING: Bronze mallard tied low, keel fashion
HEAD: Black

CLARET SHRIMP - McHaffie

TAG: Oval gold tinsel
TAIL: GP red breast feather, wound
REAR BODY: Light or medium claret seal's fur
RIB: Oval gold
CENTRE HACKLE: Rich claret
FRONT BODY: Dark claret seal's fur
RIB: Oval gold
FRONT HACKLES: Hot orange cock or hen under two or three turns of badger cock
EYES: Small jungle cock
HEAD: Black

CLARET TAIL BANN SPECIAL SHRIMP

TAG: Oval silver tinsel
TAIL: GP red breast feather dyed claret, wound
REAR BODY: Yellow floss
RIB: Oval silver
CENTRE HACKLE: Hot orange
FRONT BODY: Black floss
RIB: Oval silver
WINGS: Roofed jungle cock
FRONT HACKLE: Badger cock
HEAD: Black

COOLRAW KILLER

TAIL: Yellow bucktail with 3 or 4 strands of pearl Crystal Hair
REAR BODY: Yellow floss
RIB: Oval silver
FRONT HACKLE: Yellow
CHEEKS: Jungle cock
HEAD: Black

CHILLIMPS - Jørgensen

TAIL: Two orange hackle points tied back to back
BODY: Red-orange wool
RIB: Oval gold tinsel crossing body hackle
BODY HACKLE: Hot orange cock, two extra turns at head
HEAD: Black

CLARET SHRIMP - Headley

TAG: Two turns flat silver tinsel
TAIL: A slim bunch of red bucktail with a few strands of red Crystal Hair, twice body length
BODY: Dark claret seal's fur
RIB: Oval silver
UNDERWING: Natural unbleached squirrel dyed red, extending past hook bend
THROAT: Natural unbleached squirrel dyed red, NOT extending past hook bend
WING: Red dyed GP tippet feather, extending to hook bend
HACKLE: Dark claret hen, to hook bend
HEAD: Black

CLARET TAIL BANN SPECIAL SHRIMP - DROPPER STYLE

HOOK: Low water double
TAIL: Slim bunch of GP red breast hackle fibres dyed claret
REAR BODY: Yellow floss
RIB: Oval silver
FRONT BODY: Black floss
RIB: Oval silver
FRONT HACKLE: Hot orange under badger, swept well back
CHEEKS: Small jungle cock
HEAD: Black

COOLRAW KILLER, ORANGE

TAIL: Yellow bucktail with 3 or 4 strands of pearl Crystal Hair
REAR BODY: Yellow floss
RIB: Oval silver
FRONT HACKLE: Orange over yellow
CHEEKS: Jungle cock
HEAD: Black

CHAPOMA SPEY   CHEAPSKATE HERON   CHILLIMPS

CHRISTMAS TREE SHRIMP   CLARET SHRIMP   CLARET SHRIMP

CLARET SHRIMP   CLARET TAIL BANN SPECIAL   CLARET TAIL BANN SPECIAL - Dropper

COLONEL CHRISTIE SHRIMP   COOLRAW KILLER   COOLRAW KILLER, ORANGE

COOLRAW KILLER, LONG

TAIL: Yellow bucktail with 3 or 4 strands of pearl Crystal Hair. Long yellow hackle, wound around.
REAR BODY: Yellow floss
RIB: Oval silver
CENTRE HACKLE: Yellow
FRONT BODY: Yellow floss
RIB: Oval silver
WINGS: Jungle cock
FRONT HACKLE: Orange
HEAD: Black

COOLRAW KILLER, LONG VARIANT - Roulston

TAIL: Yellow bucktail with 3 or 4 strands of gold Crystal Hair.
REAR BODY: Yellow floss
RIB: Oval silver
CENTRE HACKLE: Yellow
FRONT BODY: Yellow floss
RIB: Oval silver
WINGS: Jungle cock
FRONT HACKLE: Orange dyed badger
HEAD: Black

COOLRAW KILLER, CLARET (McCormick's Folly) - Roulston

TAIL: Claret bucktail with 3 or 4 strands of gold Crystal Hair.
REAR BODY: Claret floss
RIB: Oval gold
CENTRE HACKLE: Claret
FRONT BODY: Black floss
RIB: Oval silver
WINGS: Jungle cock
FRONT HACKLE: Orange dyed badger
HEAD: Black

COPPER SHRIMP - Westcott

TAIL: None
BODY: Copper Lite-Brite
RIB: Medium to wide oval gold
COLLAR HACKLE: Long hot orange hen
CHEEKS: Jungle cock
HEAD: Black

COPPER SUNSET SHRIMP - McPhail

TUBE: 1/2" to 2" copper slipstream
BODY: None. Use orange silicone tubing to hold hook in place
WING: Yellow and orange bucktail and strands of copper Twinkle
CHEEKS: Jungle cock dyed hot orange
HEAD: Black

CRYSTAL TAIL AGIVEY RED SHRIMP (Low water) - Atkins

REAR BODY: Red holographic Mylar
RIB: Fine oval silver
TAIL: Tied at centre joint, four strands red Krystalflash
FRONT BODY: Red Lite-Brite
RIB: Fine oval silver
FRONT HACKLE: Scarlet
HEAD: Black

CRYSTAL TAIL GOLD SHRIMP (Low water) - Atkins

REAR BODY: Silver Mylar
RIB: Fine oval silver
TAIL: Tied at centre joint, four strands orange Krystalflash
FRONT BODY: Gold Lite-Brite
RIB: Fine oval silver
FRONT HACKLE: Golden yellow
HEAD: Red

CURRY'S BLUE SHRIMP - Joe Curry

TAG: Flat silver tinsel
TAIL: GP yellow rump feather, wound
REAR BODY: Embossed silver tinsel
RIB: Oval silver
VEILINGS: Orange toucan at sides of body
CENTRE HACKLE: Orange cock
FRONT BODY: Embossed silver tinsel
RIB: Oval silver
VEILINGS: Orange toucan at sides of body
WINGS: Roofed jungle cock
FRONT HACKLE: Orange or golden olive cock
HEAD: Red

CURRY'S BUG - Pat Curry

TAG: Flat silver tinsel
TAIL: GP red breast feather, wound
REAR BODY: Orange seal's fur
RIB: Oval silver
VEILINGS: White pheasant neck feathers dyed ruby red at sides of body
CENTRE HACKLE: Cream cock
FRONT BODY: Black seal's fur
RIB: Oval silver
VEILINGS: White pheasant neck feathers dyed ruby red at sides of body
WINGS: Roofed jungle cock
FRONT HACKLE: Red game
HEAD: Red

CURRY'S GOLD SHRIMP - Pat Curry

TAG: Flat silver tinsel
TAIL: GP yellow rump feather, wound
REAR BODY: Broad oval gold tinsel
RIB: Oval gold
VEILINGS: White pheasant neck feathers dyed golden olive at sides of body
CENTRE HACKLE: Golden olive cock
FRONT BODY: Broad oval gold tinsel
RIB: Oval gold
VEILINGS: White pheasant neck feathers dyed golden olive at sides of body
WINGS: Roofed jungle cock
FRONT HACKLE: Golden olive
HEAD: Red

CURRY'S GOLD SHRIMP - Malone

TAG: Flat silver tinsel
TAIL: GP yellow rump feather, wound
REAR BODY: Embossed silver tinsel
RIB: Oval silver
VEILINGS: Orange toucan at sides of body
CENTRE HACKLE: Orange cock
FRONT BODY: Embossed silver tinsel
RIB: Oval silver
VEILINGS: Orange toucan at sides of body
WINGS: Roofed jungle cock
FRONT HACKLE: Orange or golden olive
HEAD: Red

CURRY'S RED SHRIMP - Pat Curry

TAG: Flat silver tinsel
TAIL: GP red breast feather, wound
REAR BODY: Red floss
RIB: Oval silver
VEILINGS: White pheasant neck feathers dyed ruby red at sides of body
CENTRE HACKLE: Badger cock
FRONT BODY: Black floss
RIB: Oval silver
VEILINGS: White pheasant neck feathers dyed ruby red at sides of body
WINGS: Roofed jungle cock
FRONT HACKLE: Orange or golden olive
HEAD: Red

COOLRAW KILLER, LONG   COOLRAW KILLER, VARIANT   COOLRAW KILLER, CLARET

COPPER SHRIMP   COPPER SUNSET SHRIMP   CRYSTAL TAIL AGIVEY RED SHRIMP

CRYSTAL TAIL GOLD SHRIMP   CURRY'S BLUE SHRIMP   CURRY'S BUG

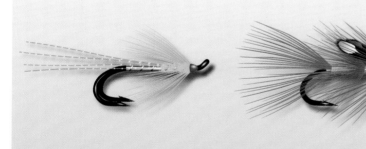

CURRY'S GOLD SHRIMP, ORIGINAL   CURRY'S GOLD SHRIMP   CURRY'S RED SHRIMP, ORIGINAL

CURRY'S RED SHRIMP - Malone

TAG: Flat silver tinsel
TAIL: GP red breast feather, wound
REAR BODY: Red floss
RIB: Oval silver
VEILINGS: Indian crow at sides of body
CENTRE HACKLE: Badger cock
FRONT BODY: Black floss
RIB: Oval silver
VEILINGS: Indian crow at sides of body
WINGS: Roofed jungle cock
FRONT HACKLE: Long grey badger
HEAD: Red

CURRY'S RED SHRIMP - modern

TAG: Flat silver tinsel
TAIL: GP red breast feather, wound
REAR BODY: Red floss, wool or seal's fur
RIB: Oval silver
VEILINGS: Red hackle tips or swan strips,
above & below
CENTRE HACKLE: Badger cock
FRONT BODY: Black floss, wool or seal's fur
RIB: Oval silver
VEILINGS: Red hackle tips or swan strips,
above & below
WINGS: Roofed jungle cock
FRONT HACKLE: Badger cock
HEAD: Red

DALBY DRIBBLER - Hansen

TAG: Hot orange floss
TAIL: 4 strands pearl Lureflash Mobile
REAR HACKLE: Chocolate brown
BODY: Lureflash Superbug yarn black/orange
RIB: Copper wire
FRONT HACKLE: Chocolate brown
HEAD: Black

DANCER SHRIMP

TAG: Flat silver tinsel
TAIL HACKLE: Dark blue dun hackle, wound
REAR BODY: Claret seal's fur
RIB: Oval gold
VEILINGS: Yellow toucan, above & below
CENTRE HACKLE: Short claret cock
FRONT BODY: Black seal's fur
RIB: Oval gold
WINGS: Roofed jungle cock
FRONT HACKLE: Long claret cock
HEAD: Red

DONEGAL BLUE SHRIMP
- Joe McDonald

TAG: Oval silver tinsel
TAIL: GP red breast feather, wound
REAR BODY: Blue seal's fur
RIB: Heavy oval silver
CENTRE HACKLE: Blue cock
FRONT BODY: Black seal's fur
RIB: Heavy oval silver
WINGS: Roofed jungle cock
FRONT HACKLE: Badger cock
HEAD: Black

DUNT - Kelson

TAG: Silver twist and light blue silk
TAIL: GP topping and teal
BODY: Yellow, orange and red-claret seal's fur
in equal divisions
RIB: Silver lace and flat silver tinsel
BODY HACKLE: Black heron over claret fur
THROAT: Teal
WINGS: Two strips brown turkey with black
bars and white tips
CHEEKS: Jungle cock, drooping over throat
hackle
HEAD: Black

EAGLE, GREY - Kelson

TAG: Silver twist
TAIL: GP red breast feather
BODY: Yellow, light blue and scarlet seal's fur
in equal divisions
RIB: Silver lace and flat silver tinsel
BODY HACKLE: Grey eagle from blue fur
THROAT: Widgeon or teal
WINGS: Two strips mottled grey turkey
HEAD: Black

EAGLE, WHITE AVON

TAG: Fine oval gold
TAIL: GP topping and widgeon strands
BODY: Flat silver tinsel
RIB: Oval silver tinsel
THROAT: White eagle under widgeon or teal
WINGS: Golden pheasant red sword feathers,
back to back. GP topping over
CHEEKS: Jungle cock
HEAD: Black

EAGLE, YELLOW - Kelson

TAG: Silver twist
TAIL: GP red breast feather
BODY: Yellow, scarlet and light blue seal's fur
in equal divisions
RIB: Silver lace and flat silver tinsel
BODY HACKLE: Eagle dyed yellow over
scarlet fur
THROAT: Widgeon or teal
WINGS: Two strips mottled grey turkey with
black bars and white tips
HEAD: Black

EASKEY GOLD SHRIMP

TAG: Oval gold tinsel
TAIL: GP red breast feather, wound
REAR BODY: Gold tinsel
RIB: Oval gold
CENTRE HACKLE: Hot orange cock
FRONT BODY: Gold tinsel
RIB: Oval gold
WINGS: Roofed jungle cock
FRONT HACKLE: Red dyed cock
HEAD: Black

EVANS' SPECIAL

BODY: Flat silver tinsel
RIB: Oval silver
HACKLE: Orange dyed squirrel tail
WING: Yellow bucktail
OVERWING: Lesser covert feathers over
jungle cock wing
EYES: Jungle cock
HEAD: Black

EXCALIBER

TAIL: #5 Glo-Brite floss
RIB: Oval silver
BODY: #8 Glo-Brite yarn
PALMER HACKLE: Light cree cock saddle
WING: Red-brown squirrel tail
HEAD: Orange

CURRY'S RED SHRIMP   CURRY'S RED SHRIMP, MODERN   DALBY DRIBBLER

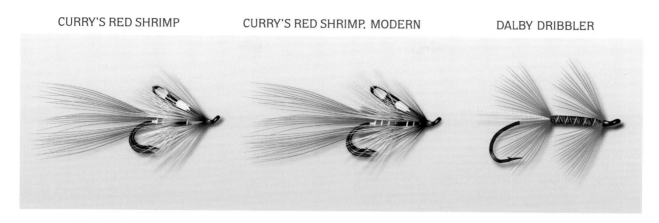

DANCER SHRIMP   DONEGAL BLUE SHRIMP   DUNT

EAGLE, GREY   EAGLE, WHITE AVON   EAGLE, YELLOW

EASKEY GOLD SHRIMP   EVANS' SPECIAL   EXCALIBER

FAUGHAN PURPLE SHRIMP - Atkins

TAG: Oval gold tinsel
TAIL: GP red breast feather, wound
REAR BODY: Yellow floss or seal's fur
RIB: Oval gold
CENTRE HACKLE: Hot orange cock
FRONT BODY: Purple floss or seal's fur
RIB: Oval gold
FRONT HACKLE: Red dyed cock
HEAD: Black

FAUGHAN SHRIMP

TAG: Oval gold tinsel
TAIL: GP red breast feather, wound
REAR BODY: Pale orange floss
RIB: Oval gold
CENTRE HACKLE: Burnt orange cock
FRONT BODY: Claret floss
RIB: Oval gold
WINGS: Roofed jungle cock
FRONT HACKLE: Rich claret cock
HEAD: Black

FAUGHAN SHRIMP, LIGHT

TAG: Oval silver tinsel
TAIL: GP red breast feather, wound
REAR BODY: Golden olive/dirty yellow seal's fur
RIB: Oval silver
VEILING: GP tippet strands, top only
CENTRE HACKLE: Short brown or red game cock
FRONT BODY: Black seal's fur
RIB: Oval silver
VEILING: GP tippet strands, top only
FRONT HACKLE: Long blue under badger cock
HEAD: Black

FINDHORN SHRIMP

TAIL: Sparse orange bucktail with strands of orange Crystal Hair
BODY: Red Lurex
RIB: Fine oval silver
WING: Natural grey squirrel under a whole GP tippet feather
HEAD: Black

FINN GOLD SHRIMP - Bonner

TAG: Oval gold tinsel
TAIL: GP red breast feather, wound
REAR BODY: Flat gold Mylar
RIB: Oval gold
CENTRE HACKLE: Hot orange cock
FRONT BODY: Flat gold Mylar
RIB: Oval gold
WINGS: Jungle cock
FRONT HACKLE: Rich yellow
HEAD: Red

FINN GOLD SHRIMP (Low water) - Atkins

REAR BODY: Gold Mylar
RIB: Fine oval gold
TAIL: Tied at centre joint, GP red breast feather
FRONT BODY: Gold Lite-Brite
RIB: Fine oval gold
FRONT HACKLE: Badger dyed orange
HEAD: Black

FLAG WING SHRIMP - Shumakov

TAG: Fine oval silver
TAIL: Two strands holographic tinsel, GP red breast feather, wound
BUTT: Glo-Brite red floss
BODY: Black floss
RIB: Pearl Flashabou
WING: Two small bunches of yellow polar bear fibres under and over body, two GP tippet feathers back to back, mounted vertically
HEAD: Black

FLUORESCENT GREEN SHRIMP

TAG: Oval gold tinsel
TAIL: GP red breast feather, wound
REAR BODY: Fluorescent green floss
RIB: Oval gold
CENTRE HACKLE: Creamy badger cock
FRONT BODY: Fluorescent green floss
RIB: Oval gold
WINGS: Roofed jungle cock
FRONT HACKLE: Creamy badger
HEAD: Red

FOXFORD SHRIMP

TAG: Oval silver tinsel
TAIL: GP red breast feather, wound
REAR BODY: Black seal's fur
RIB: Oval silver
CENTRE HACKLE: Badger cock
FRONT BODY: Fiery brown seal's fur
RIB: Oval silver
WINGS: Roofed jungle cock or eyes on smaller sizes
FRONT HACKLE: Rich ginger
HEAD: Red

FRANCIS SHRIMP, BLACK TUBE

TUBE: Aluminium or brass, 1/2" or larger
TAIL: 3 white hackle stems, 3 red game hackle stems
ROSTRUM: Bunch brown calf hair
BODY: Black wool, carrot shaped
RIB: Oval gold
BODY HACKLE: Red game
HEAD: Yellow

FRANCIS SHRIMP, RED TUBE

TUBE: Aluminium or brass, 1/2" or larger
TAIL: 3 white hackle stems, 3 red game hackle stems
ROSTRUM: Bunch brown calf hair
BODY: Red wool, carrot shaped
RIB: Oval gold
BODY HACKLE: Red game
HEAD: Red

Note: a further variant has an olive green body and a black head

FRANCIS SHRIMP, ICELANDIC

HOOK: Gold treble
TAIL: 3 white hackle stems, 3 red game hackle stems
ROSTRUM: Bunch pheasant tail feather fibres
BODY: Wool, carrot shaped - red, black or olive
RIB: Oval gold
BODY HACKLE: Red game
HEAD: Red, yellow or black

FAUGHAN PURPLE SHRIMP   FAUGHAN SHRIMP   FAUGHAN SHRIMP, LIGHT

FINDHORN SHRIMP   FINN GOLD SHRIMP   FINN GOLD SHRIMP (Low water)

FLAG WING SHRIMP   FLUORESCENT GREEN SHRIMP   FOXFORD SHRIMP

FRANCIS SHRIMP, BLACK TUBE   FRANCIS SHRIMP, RED TUBE   FRANCIS SHRIMP, ICELANDIC

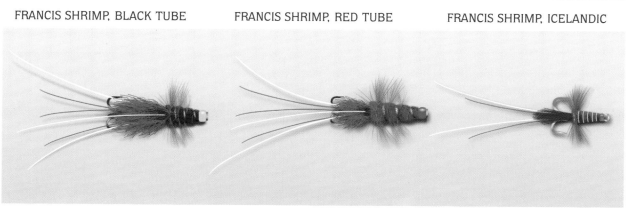

GARDENER - Kelson

TAG: Gold twist and crimson silk
TAIL: GP topping and GP tippet strands
BODY: Yellow, green and dark blue seal's fur
in equal divisions
RIB: Flat silver tinsel
BODY HACKLE: GP topping from yellow fur
THROAT: Black heron, very long
WINGS: Two strips cinnamon turkey
CHEEKS: Jungle cock, drooping over throat
hackle
HEAD: Black

GENERAL PRACTITIONER - Drury

TAIL: Hot orange bucktail, 2" beyond bend of
hook. Two small GP red neck feathers one
above other, concave to concave
RIB: Fine oval gold
BODY: orange seal's fur
BODY HACKLE: Hot orange cock
MID BODY: GP red neck feather convex side
up. GP tippet feather clipped to Vee-shape over
to represent eyes
3/4 BODY: Another GP red neck feather
convex side up - omit on smaller hook sizes
FRONT BODY: Another GP red neck feather
convex side up.
HEAD: Red

GENERAL PRACTITIONER - Atkins

TAG: Flat gold
TAIL: 6 - 8 strands orange bucktail four
strands pearl Krystalflash. Small GP red breast
feather, convex side up, above
BODY: Equal mix, orange & magenta seal's
fur in three equal divisions. Each division with
GP tippet feather followed by GP red breast
feather over
RIB: Fine oval gold
BODY HACKLE: GP red breast feather
HEAD: Red

GENERAL PRACTITIONER, HELMSDALE

TAIL: Strands hot orange bucktail
BODY: Orange seal's fur
RIB: Fine oval silver
BODY HACKLE: Palmered hot orange
WING: Sparse bunch GP tippet feathers to
hook bend
FRONT HACKLE: Silver badger to hook barb
EYES: Small jungle cock
HEAD: Black

GENERAL PRACTITIONER, IRISH

TAG: Oval gold
TAIL: GP red breast feather, wound. Short GP
tippet in Vee-shape over
REAR BODY: Orange seal's fur
REAR HACKLE: Hot orange palmered
RIB: Fine oval gold
VEILING: Short GP tippet feather, top only
FRONT BODY: Hot orange seal's fur
FRONT HACKLE: Hot orange palmered
RIB: Fine oval gold
VEILING (Wing): Short GP red breast
feather tied flat
HEAD: Red or Black

GENERAL PRACTITIONER, OYKEL

TAIL: Orange bucktail with GP red breast
feather over
BODY: Orange floss
BODY HACKLE: Hot orange palmered
RIB: Fine oval gold
WING: GP red breast feather tied flat, over GP
tippet feather
HEAD: Red

GENERAL PRACTITIONER, PURPLE

TAIL: Purple bucktail with two purple dyed GP
red breast feathers, concave to concave, over
BODY: Purple seal's fur in three sections
BODY HACKLE: Purple cock
RIB: Fine oval gold
BACK: Overlapping GP breast feathers dyed
purple, convex side up, in three sections
EYES: GP tippet feather Vee-form, dyed
purple over first back section
HEAD: Purple

GENERAL PRACTITIONER SPECIAL TUBE, RED

TAIL: Fibres of gold Crystal Hair
BODY: Red seal's fur
BODY HACKLE: Red dyed cock hackle
RIB: Fine oval gold
BACK: Up to six overlapping GP tippet
feathers dyed red, gradually smaller towards
head. Number of feathers depending upon
tube length
HEAD: Red

GENERAL PRACTITIONER SPECIAL TUBE, YELLOW

TAIL: Fibres of gold Crystal Hair
BODY: Yellow seal's fur
BODY HACKLE: Yellow dyed cock hackle
RIB: Fine oval gold
BACK: Up to six overlapping GP tippet
feathers dyed yellow, gradually smaller towards
head. Number of feathers depending upon
tube length
HEAD: Yellow

GHOST SHRIMP

TAG: Oval silver tinsel
TAIL: GP red breast feather, wound
REAR BODY: Yellow floss
RIB: Oval silver
VEILINGS: Orange hackle points, above and
below
CENTRE HACKLE: White cock
FRONT BODY: Black floss
RIB: Oval silver
VEILINGS: Orange hackle points, above and
below
WINGS: Roofed jungle cock
FRONT HACKLE: Badger cock
HEAD: Black

GINGER SHRIMP - Begley

TAG: Oval silver tinsel
TAIL: GP red breast feather, wound
REAR BODY: Flat copper Mylar
RIB: Oval silver
CENTRE HACKLE: Light to medium red
game or light furnace cock
FRONT BODY: Yellow seal's fur
RIB: Oval gold
WINGS: Roofed jungle cock
FRONT HACKLE: Light to medium red game
or ginger cock
HEAD: Black

GLENTANA - Kelson

TAG: Silver twist
TAIL: GP red breast feather
BODY: 1/3rd light orange seal's fur, 2/3rds
light claret seal's fur
RIB: Silver lace and flat silver tinsel
HACKLE: Black heron over claret fur
THROAT: Widgeon
WINGS: Two strips cinnamon turkey with light
tips
HEAD: Black

GARDENER	GENERAL PRACTITIONER, DRURY	GENERAL PRACTITIONER, ATKINS

GP, HELMSDALE	GENERAL PRACTITIONER, IRISH	GENERAL PRACTITIONER, OYKEL

GENERAL PRACTITIONER, PURPLE	GP SPECIAL TUBE, RED	GP SPECIAL TUBE, YELLOW

GHOST SHRIMP	GINGER SHRIMP	GLENTANA

GLENTIES SHRIMP

TAG: Oval silver tinsel
TAIL: GP yellow rump feather dyed hot orange,wound or two turns long hot orange hackle under a GP red breast feather on larger flies
REAR BODY: Yellow floss
RIB: Oval silver
CENTRE HACKLE: Hot orange cock
FRONT BODY: Black floss
RIB: Oval silver
WINGS: Roofed jungle cock
FRONT HACKLE: Hot orange under silver badger cock
HEAD: Red

GLOW BUTT SPEY - Saastamoinen

TAG: Fine oval silver tinsel, lacquered
BUTT: Orange floss, lacquered
BODY: Rear 2/3rds black Crystal Seal, front 1/3rd burnt orange Crystal Seal dubbing
RIB: Oval silver tinsel
BODY HACKLE: Long black heron
THROAT: Black heron
WING: 2 burnt orange cock hackles, back to back. 2 strands red Flashabou, one per side, black fox tail over
HEAD: Black with orange stripe

GOLD BUG

TAG: Oval gold tinsel
TAIL: GP red breast feather wound
REAR BODY: Flat gold tinsel
RIB: Oval gold
CENTRE HACKLE: Hot orange cock
FRONT BODY: Flat gold tinsel
RIB: Oval gold
WINGS: Roofed jungle cock
FRONT HACKLE: Brown or dark red game cock
HEAD: Black

GOLD REEACH - Knox

TAG: orange silk
BODY: Black Berlin wool
RIB: Three strands flat gold tinsel with three strands fine gold beading equi-spaced between
HACKLE: Red game cock hackle
THROAT: Two turns of teal or guinea fowl
WINGS: Two strips bronze mallard with grey roots and dark points, tied low, keel fashion
HEAD: Black

GOLD RIACH - Kelson

BODY: Three turns orange Berlin wool, followed by black wool
RIB: narrow gold tinsel, gold twist & silver twist, equi-spaced, wound in reverse direction
HACKLE: Red Spey cock wound in opposite spiral to cross over ribbing
THROAT: Two turns of teal
WINGS: Two strips bronze mallard with grey roots and dark points, tied low, keel fashion
HEAD: Black

GOLD SHRIMP

TAG: Oval gold tinsel
TAIL: Long badger cock dyed orange-red, wound
REAR 2/3rds BODY: Flat gold tinsel
JOINT: Black ostrich herl
FRONT 1/3rd BODY: Flat gold tinsel
RIB: Oval gold (front body only)
FRONT HACKLE: Red-orange cock under long badger cock
HEAD: Black

GOLDEN OLIVE SHRIMP

TAG: Oval silver tinsel
TAIL: GP red breast feather, wound
REAR BODY: Golden olive seal's fur
RIB: Oval silver
CENTRE HACKLE: Golden olive cock
FRONT BODY: Golden olive seal's fur
RIB: Oval silver
WINGS: Roofed jungle cock
FRONT HACKLE: Light to medium red game cock
HEAD: Black

GOLDEN OLIVE SHRIMP, SILVER BODY

TAG: Oval silver tinsel
TAIL: GP red breast feather wound
REAR BODY: Flat silver tinsel
RIB: Oval silver
CENTRE HACKLE: Rich yellow cock
FRONT BODY: Flat silver tinsel
RIB: Oval silver
WINGS: Roofed jungle cock
FRONT HACKLE: Rich golden olive
HEAD: Black

GOLDEN SHRIMP - Toohey

TAIL: Yellow, orange and a small amount of brown bucktail
BODY: Rich yellow seal's fur
RIB: Oval gold
WINGS: Natural barred squirrel dyed orange
COLLAR HACKLE: Hot orange
EYES: Jungle cock
HEAD: Red

GREEN PETER SHRIMP - O'Reilly

TAG: Oval gold tinsel
TAIL: GP red breast feather, wound
REAR BODY: Red wool or seal's fur
RIB: Oval gold
CENTRE HACKLE: Grizzle cock
FRONT BODY: Green olive seal's fur
RIB: Oval gold
WINGS: Roofed jungle cock
FRONT HACKLE: Ginger cock
HEAD: Black

GREY HERON - Gillespie

BODY: Rear half, yellow seal's fur. Front half black seal's fur
RIB: Oval silver - wound opposite spiral over hackle
BODY HACKLE: Long grey Chinese hen hackle, two full turns at rear of body then palmered forward
THROAT: Two turns natural guinea fowl
WINGS: Bronze mallard, tied flat, keel fashion
HEAD: Black

GREY PALMER GRUB - Pryce-Tannatt

TAG: Silver tinsel
BODY: Peacock herl
RIB: Flat silver tinsel - wound opposite spiral over palmer hackle
BODY HACKLE: Grizzle hackle from first turn of ribbing, two turns at head
HEAD: Black

GLENTIES SHRIMP	GLOW BUTT SPEY	GOLD BUG

GOLD REEACH	GOLD RIACH	GOLD SHRIMP

GOLDEN OLIVE SHRIMP	GOLDEN OLIVE SHRIMP, SILVER	GOLDEN SHRIMP

GREEN PETER SHRIMP	GREY HERON, GILLESPIE	GREY PALMER GRUB

GREY THUNDER SHRIMP - Malone

TAG: Flat gold tinsel
TAIL: GP red breast feather dyed orange,
wound
REAR BODY: Black floss
RIB: Flat gold tinsel
CENTRE HACKLE: Red-orange cock
FRONT BODY: Darkest claret seal's fur, well
picked out
FRONT HACKLE: Long black cock dyed
claret under long grey duck flank
HEAD: Black

HAIR BACK PRAWN

TAIL: Bunch orange bucktail
EYES: Nylon with ends heat-blobbed and
blackened
TAIL HACKLE: Long orange cock
BODY: Orange seal's fur
RIB: Broad oval gold
BACK: Tufts of orange dyed squirrel hair tied
in at regular intervals
BEARD HACKLE: Orange hair
HEAD: Red

HAIRY DEEP PURPLE SPEY - Mackenzie

TAG: Oval silver tinsel
BODY: Dark purple dubbing
RIB: Oval silver tinsel (flat on larger sizes)
BODY HACKLE: Natural red squirrel,
palmered from 2nd turn of ribbing
WING: Grey squirrel tail, dyed bright red
COLLAR HACKLE: Grey squirrel dyed purple
HEAD: Black

HAIRY DURHAM RANGER PRACTITIONER - Mackenzie

TAG: Oval silver tinsel
TAIL: Four strands pearl Crystal Hair
1st. hackle - bleached squirrel dyed yellow
2nd hackle - bleached squirrel dyed red
EYES: Black burnt nylon
RIB: Oval silver tinsel over both bodies
REAR BODY: Mix yellow and orange dub
REAR WING: Natural white tipped squirrel
MID HACKLE: Bleached squirrel dyed orange
FR. BODY: Mix fiery brown and black dub
FRONT WING: Grey squirrel dyed orange
COLLAR HACKLE: Squirrel dyed blue
HEAD: Black

HAIRY MAC'S PURPLE PRACTITIONER - Mackenzie

TAG: Oval silver tinsel
TAIL: Four strands pearl Crystal Hair,
1st. hackle - bleached squirrel dyed purple
2nd hackle - bleached squirrel dyed red
EYES: Black burnt nylon
RIB: Oval silver tinsel over both bodies
REAR BODY: Flat pearl Mylar
REAR WING: Grey squirrel dyed purple
MID HACKLE: Natural grey squirrel
FRONT BODY: Purple dubbing
FRONT WING: Grey squirrel dyed purple
COLLAR HACKLE: Grey squirrel dyed purple
HEAD: Black

HAIRY MAC'S PURPLE SHRIMP - Mackenzie

TAG: Oval silver tinsel
TAIL: Four strands pearl Crystal Hair
Hair hackle, grey squirrel dyed purple
RIB: Oval silver tinsel over both bodies
REAR BODY: Flat pearl Mylar
MID HACKLE: Natural grey squirrel
FRONT BODY: Purple dubbing
WING: Grey squirrel dyed purple
COLLAR HACKLE: Grey squirrel dyed purple
HEAD: Black

HAIRY MAC'S PURPLE SPEY - Mackenzie

TAG: Oval silver tinsel
BODY: Purple dubbing
RIB: Oval silver tinsel (flat on larger sizes)
BODY HACKLE: Natural grey squirrel dyed
purple, palmered from 2nd turn of ribbing
WING: Grey squirrel tail, dyed dark red
COLLAR HACKLE: Natural grey squirrel with
white tips
HEAD: Black

HAIRY SOL DUC PRACTITIONER - Mackenzie

TAG: Oval silver tinsel
TAIL: Four strands pearl Crystal Hair,
1st. hackle - Grey squirrel dyed yellow
2nd hackle - bleached squirrel dyed orange
EYES: Black burnt nylon
RIB: Oval silver tinsel over both bodies
REAR BODY: Fluo./hot orange dubbing
REAR WING: Bleached squirrel dyed orange
MID HACKLE: Bleached squirrel dyed orange
FRONT BODY: Hot orange dubbing
FRONT WING: Grey squirrel dyed orange
COLLAR HACKLE: Black squirrel
HEAD: Red

HAIRY SOL DUC SHRIMP - Mackenzie

TAG: Oval silver tinsel
TAIL: Four strands pearl Crystal Hair
Hackle: grey squirrel dyed yellow
RIB: Oval silver tinsel over both bodies
REAR BODY: Hot orange dubbing
MID HACKLE: Natural grey squirrel
FRONT BODY: Hot orange dubbing
WING: Bleached squirrel dyed orange
COLLAR HACKLE: Black squirrel
HEAD: Red

HAIRY SOL DUC SPEY - Mackenzie

TAG: Oval silver tinsel
BODY: Fluoresent or hot orange dubbing
RIB: Oval silver tinsel (flat on larger sizes)
BODY HACKLE: Bleached grey squirrel dyed
yellow, palmered from 2nd turn of ribbing
WING: Bleached grey squirrel, dyed orange
COLLAR HACKLE: Black squirrel
HEAD: Black

NOTE: body can also be in two parts:
rear half - fluorescent orange floss
front half - fluorescent or hot orange dubbing
body hackle palmered over front half

HAIRY WIGGLE (SOL DUC) PRACTITIONER - Mackenzie

TAG: Oval silver tinsel
TAIL: Four strands pearl Crystal Hair,
1st. hackle - Grey squirrel dyed yellow
2nd hackle - bleached squirrel dyed orange
EYES: Black burnt nylon
RIB: Oval silver tinsel over rear body
REAR BODY: Fluo. or hot orange dubbing
REAR WING: Bleached squirrel dyed orange
MID HACKLE: Bleached squirrel dyed
orange, black squirrel over
FRONT BODY (HEAD): Spun deer hair, rear
half black, front half orange. Incoporating hair
lip - well varnished.

HELMSDALE COPPER KING

TAIL: Bunch of GP red breast feather fibres,
length same as overall hook length
BODY: Old gold Mylar
RIB: Oval silver
FRONT HACKLES: 1st. Yellow, 2mm past
hook bend. 2nd GP red breast feather to end
of tail
CHEEKS: Jungle cock
HEAD: Black

GREY THUNDER SHRIMP   HAIR BACK PRAWN   HAIRY DEEP PURPLE SPEY

HAIRY DURHAM RANGER GP   HAIRY MAC'S PURPLE GP   HAIRY MAC'S PURPLE SHRIMP

HAIRY MAC'S PURPLE SPEY   HAIRY SOL DUC PRACTITIONER   HAIRY SOL DUC SHRIMP

HAIRY SOL DUC SPEY   HAIRY WIGGLE SOL DUC GP   HELMSDALE COPPER KING

HIGHLAND SHRIMP - McPhail

TUBE: 1/2 to 2" copper slipstream
BODY: None, use green silicone tubing to hold hook in place
WING: Orange and green bucktail and strands of green holographic tinsel
CHEEKS: Jungle cock dyed green
HEAD: Red

HORSTSOCKEN - Dupo

TAG: Oval gold tinsel
TAIL: GP red breast feather fibres
REAR HACKLE: Medium brown cock
REAR BODY: Hot orange floss
FRONT BODY: Black dubbing
BODY HACKLE: Brown cock palmered over black dubbing
WING: GP red breast feather fibres or brown hair
FRONT HACKLES: One turn brown cock hackle, dyed blue guinea fowl over
HEAD: Red

HOT GUNN LITE-BRITE SHRIMP - McPhail

TAG: Gold blue Lite-Brite
TAIL: GP red breast feather dyed black, wound
BODY: Yellow Lite-Brite
WING: Natural grey squirrel dyed orange
FRONT HACKLE: Black dyed cock
HEAD: Red

HOWARD'S CLARET SHRIMP - Reilly

TAG: Oval gold tinsel
TAIL: GP red breast feather dyed claret, wound
BODY: Rich dark claret seal's fur
RIB: Medium flat gold tinsel
WINGS: Large jungle cock
FRONT HACKLE: Bunch of claret or scarlet hair tied in top and bottom. Optionally dark claret cock
HEAD: Black

HUTCHY SHRIMP

TAG: Oval silver tinsel
TAIL: GP red breast feather, wound
REAR BODY: Pheasant tail fibres, wound
RIB: Fine oval gold
HACKLE: Hot orange cock palmered over rear body
CENTRE HACKLE: Badger cock
FRONT BODY: Black floss
RIB: Oval gold
FRONT HACKLES: Hot orange cock with badger cock over
EYES: Small jungle cock, above and below hook
HEAD: Black

IQ SHRIMP - Saastamoinen

TAIL: Burnt orange fox tail as long as hook shank, two strands pearl Flashabou
BODY: Mix 5/6ths. burnt orange, 1/6th. orange Crystal Seal
RIB: Oval gold tinsel
WING: Underwing - burnt orange fox tail with two strands pearl Flashabou
Overwing - GP tippet dyed burnt orange extending to hook bend
FRONT HACKLE: Burnt orange cock tied as collar
HEAD: Red

IQ SHRIMP, ORANGE - Saastamoinen

TAIL: Orange fox tail as long as hook shank, two strands pearl Flashabou
BODY: Orange Crystal Seal
RIB: Oval gold tinsel
WING: Underwing - orange fox tail with two strands pearl Flashabou
Overwing - GP tippet dyed orange extending to hook bend
FRONT HACKLE: Hot orange cock tied as collar
HEAD: Red

JOHN ANTHONY SHRIMP - O'Donnell

TAG: Oval gold tinsel
TAIL: GP red breast feather, wound
REAR BODY: Black floss
RIB: Oval gold tinsel
CENTRE HACKLE: Medium red game
FRONT BODY: Black floss or seal's fur
RIB: Fine oval gold tinsel
WINGS: Jungle cock (optional)
FRONT HACKLE: Medium red game
HEAD: Black

JOHN ANTHONY SHRIMP (Variant) - O'Donnell

TAG: Oval gold tinsel
TAIL: GP red breast feather dyed purple, wound
REAR BODY: Embossed gold or silver tinsel
RIB: Oval gold tinsel
CENTRE HACKLE: Medium red game
FRONT BODY: Black floss or seal's fur
RIB: Fine oval gold tinsel
WINGS: Jungle cock (optional)
FRONT HACKLE: Medium red game
HEAD: Black

JUDY of the BOGS

TAG: Flat gold tinsel
TAIL: GP topping dyed orange
TAIL HACKLE: Grey heron feather
BODY: Black floss
RIB: Oval gold tinsel
VEILINGS: At middle of body, GP toppings dyed orange at sides
WINGS: Roofed jungle cock
FRONT HACKLE: Long black henny (soft) cock or black heron
HEAD: Black

JUNCTION SHRIMP (Waddington) - Brown

BODY: Rear half yellow floss, front half black floss
RIB: Oval gold tinsel over both body parts
CENTRE HACKLE: Orange bucktail
WING: White bucktail
HEAD: Red

JUNCTION SHRIMP (Variant) - Purvis

TAIL: Long orange bucktail with two strands pearl Crystalflash
BODY: Rear half flat gold tinsel, front half black floss
RIB: Oval gold tinsel over black floss
CENTRE HACKLE: White cock
FRONT HACKLE: Orange cock
HEAD: Orange

| HIGHLAND SHRIMP | HORSTSOCKEN | HOT GUNN LITE-BRITE SHRIMP |

| HOWARD'S CLARET SHRIMP | HUTCHY SHRIMP | IQ SHRIMP |

| IQ SHRIMP, ORANGE | JOHN ANTHONY SHRIMP | JOHN ANTHONY SHRIMP (Variant) |

| JUDY of the BOGS | JUNCTION SHRIMP (Waddington) | JUNCTION SHRIMP (Variant) |

JUNER SHRIMP - Downey

TAG: Oval gold tinsel
TAIL: GP red breast feather, wound
REAR BODY: Red seal's fur or floss
RIB: Oval or fine flat gold
CENTRE HACKLE: Yellow
FRONT BODY: Purple seal's fur or floss
RIB: Oval or fine flat gold
FRONT HACKLE: Purple cock
HEAD: Black

KEACHIE'S KRILL - Keachie

TAG: Oval silver tinsel
TAIL: GP red breast feather, wound
REAR BODY: Flat Veniard pearl tinsel, wound
over a bed of black tying silk
RIB: Oval silver tinsel
CENTRE HACKLE: Light claret cock
FRONT BODY: Flat Veniard pearl tinsel,
wound over a bed of black tying silk
RIB: Oval silver tinsel
FRONT HACKLE: Orange cock
HEAD: Red

KILBARRY AUTUMN SHRIMP - Lock

TAG: Oval silver tinsel
TAIL: Red calf tail with strands of green
Crystal Hair
REAR BODY (2/3rds): Red floss
RIB: Oval silver tinsel
CENTRE HACKLE: Red cock
FRONT BODY (1/3rd): Black floss
RIB: Oval silver tinsel
FRONT HACKLE: Badger cock
CHEEKS: Jungle cock, drooping
HEAD: Black

KILBARRY SUMMER SHRIMP - Lock

TAG: Oval silver tinsel
TAIL: Orange calf tail with strands of green
Crystal Hair
REAR BODY (2/3rds): Gold floss
RIB: Oval silver tinsel
CENTRE HACKLE: Orange cock
FRONT BODY (1/3rd): Black floss
RIB: Oval silver tinsel
FRONT HACKLE: Badger cock
CHEEKS: Jungle cock
HEAD: Black

KINGFISHER SHRIMP

TAG: Flat gold tinsel
TAIL: Long red game hackle, wound
REAR BODY: Yellow floss
RIB: Flat copper tinsel
CENTRE HACKLE: Orange cock
FRONT BODY: Claret floss
RIB: Oval gold tinsel
WINGS: Jungle cock
FRONT HACKLES: Light blue cock under
long crow
SIDES: Kingfisher neck feathers
HEAD: Black

KNOCKDOLIAN SHRIMP

TAG: Fine oval silver
TAIL: Long GP red breast feather, wound
BODY: Flat silver tinsel
RIB: Oval silver tinsel
FRONT HACKLE: Hot orange cock or hen to
reach hook bend
CHEEKS: Jungle cock
HEAD: Red

KRAFLA - Gislasson

TAIL: Three stripped grizzle hackle stalks
BODY: One or two cock hackles palmered
closely forward and then clipped to a carrot
shape

COLOUR COMBINATIONS:
Red & white hackles, wound together
Black & red hackles, wound together
Black & green hackles, wound together
Black & yellow hackles, wound together
Black hackle
Rear half blue hackle, front half white hackle

KYLIE SHRIMP - Donaldson

TAG: Silver wire
TAIL: Sparse orange bucktail with strands of
orange twinkle. GP red breast feather over
BUTT: Black floss
REAR BODY: Flat copper tinsel
RIB: Silver wire
CENTRE HACKLE: Orange cock
FRONT BODY: Black floss
FRONT HACKLES: Orange cock false hackle,
above & below. Blue guinea fowl as throat
WINGS: Long jungle cock, back to back
OVERWING: Orange cock hackle fibres
HEAD: Red

LADY CAROLINE - Kelson

TAIL: Strands GP red breast feather
BODY: Mixed brown & olive green Berlin wool
- 1/3rd olive green, 2/3rds brown
RIB: Narrow gold tinsel, gold twist & silver
twist equi-spaced
BODY HACKLE: Long grey heron, wound
alongside gold tinsel
THROAT: Two turns GP red breast feather
WINGS: Bronze mallard with light roots and
brown tips
HEAD: Black

LADY ETHNA

TAIL: Six strands of pearl Krystalflash, same
length as normal tail
BUTT: Fluorescent green floss
BODY: Flat silver Mylar
RIB: Copper wire or oval copper tinsel
FRONT HACKLES: Long grey mallard flank
with silver badger cock over
HEAD: Red

LADY EWE SHRIMP - Mateer

TAG: Flat silver
TAIL: Black bucktail
BODY: Rear half blue Lurex, front half silver
Lurex
RIB: Fine oval silver
WING: Silver Twinkle under black bucktail
THROAT: Blue dyed guinea fowl
HEAD: Black

LAGGAN PRAWN - MacAffer

TAIL: Purple bucktail
BODY: Mix fiery brown & pink fluorescent
seal's fur
RIB: Fine oval silver
BODY HACKLE: Dark brown cock
WING: GP red breast feather fibres under
brown roebuck hair
HEAD: Black

JUNER SHRIMP	KEACHIE'S KRILL	KILBARRY AUTUMN SHRIMP

KILBARRY SUMMER SHRIMP	KINGFISHER SHRIMP	KNOCKDOLIAN SHRIMP

KRAFLA	KYLIE SHRIMP	LADY CAROLINE

LADY ETHNA	LADY EWE SHRIMP	LAGGAN PRAWN

LATEX PRAWN - Riding

ROSTRUM: Latex flange with a Vee cut in trailing edge. GP red breast feather over.
FEELERS: Orange bucktail
EYES: Black beads on twisted copper wire
TOP JAW: shorter rounded latex flange
BODY: Orange seal's fur, well picked out
BACK: Three overlapping latex flanges
TAIL: Fourth latex flange of back extending well over hook eye with a GP red breast feather under

LEMON & PURPLE SHRIMP

TAG: Oval gold tinsel
TAIL: GP red breast feather, wound but sleek
REAR BODY: Yellow seal's fur
RIB: Oval gold tinsel
CENTRE HACKLE: Yellow cock
FRONT BODY: Purple seal's fur
RIB: Oval gold tinsel
FRONT HACKLES: Purple under silver badger cock
HEAD: Red

LEMON GREY SHRIMP - McDonald

TAG: Oval silver tinsel
TAIL: Grizzle cock, wound together with a GP yellow rump feather
REAR BODY: Grey wool or dubbing
RIB: Oval silver tinsel
CENTRE HACKLE: Grizzle cock
FRONT BODY: Grey wool or dubbing
RIB: Oval silver tinsel
FRONT HACKLE: Yellow cock
WINGS: Jungle cock
HEAD: Black

LIME SHRIMP - McPhail

TUBE: 1/2" to 2" copper slipstream
BODY: None, use yellow silicone tubing to hold hook in place
WING: Lime and black bucktail and strands of lime Flashabou
CHEEKS: Jungle cock dyed lime green
HEAD: Lime green

LIVING SHRIMP, FIRE ORANGE - Bonner

TAIL: Hot orange dyed bucktail or polar bear plus four strands orange Krystalflash
BODY: Rear half, silver Mylar or flat tinsel Front half, well blended mix SLF hank. 50% fluorescent orange 50% crimson
RIB: Fine oval silver tinsel
WING: well blended mix SLF hank. 50% orange 50% crimson plus four to six strands orange Krystalflash
FRONT HACKLE: Hot orange genetic hen
CHEEKS: Small jungle cock
HEAD: Red

LIVING SHRIMP, FLAME RED - Bonner

TAIL: Red dyed bucktail or polar bear plus four strands orange Krystalflash
BODY: Rear half, old gold Mylar or flat tinsel Front half, well blended mix SLF hank. 75% fluorescent orange 25% crimson
RIB: Fine oval gold tinsel
WING: well blended mix SLF hank. 75% fluorescent orange 25% crimson plus four to six strands orange Krystalflash
FRONT HACKLE: Flame red genetic hen
CHEEKS: Small jungle cock
HEAD: Red

LIVING SHRIMP, GOLDEN GLOW - Bonner

TAIL: Golden olive dyed bucktail or polar bear plus four strands orange Krystalflash
BODY: Rear half, old gold Mylar or flat tinsel Front half, well blended mix SLF hank. 70% yellow 30% hot orange
RIB: Fine oval gold tinsel
WING: well blended mix SLF hank. 70% yellow 30% hot orange plus four to six strands orange Krystalflash
FRONT HACKLE: Rich deep golden olive hen
CHEEKS: Small jungle cock
HEAD: Red

LIVING SHRIMP, SUNSET ORANGE - Bonner

TAIL: Sunset orange dyed bucktail or polar bear plus four strands orange Krystalflash
BODY: Rear half, old gold Mylar or flat tinsel Front hal hot orange SLF hank
RIB: Fine oval gold tinsel
WING: well blended mix SLF hank. 50% yellow 50% hot orange plus four to six strands orange Krystalflash
FRONT HACKLE: Sunset orange genetic hen
CHEEKS: Small jungle cock
HEAD: Red

LOCHDHU

TAIL HACKLE: Natural guinea fowl
BODY: Flat silver tinsel
RIB: Oval silver tinsel
BODY HACKLE: Black cock palmered
FRONT HACKLE: Three turns natural guinea fowl
HEAD: Black

LONG TAIL SHRIMPS - Currie

TAIL: Slim bunch fine bucktail or other fine mobile hair, twice hook length
BODY: Flat Mylar or tinsel
WING: Slim bunch fine bucktail or other mobile hair, well swept back, length to half of tail
THROAT: Sparse hairs to match wing
HEAD: Black

RECOMMENDED COLOURS:
#1 - gold body, black wing, orange tail
#2 - gold body black wing, yellow tail
#3 - silver body, claret wing, yellow tail
#4 - silver body, black wing, yellow tail

M SOCKEN

TAG: Oval silver tinsel & red floss
TAIL HACKLE: GP red breast feather, wound
BODY: In two halves, black dubbing
CENTRE HACKLE: Silver badger cock
WING: Golden pheasant tail
FRONT HACKLE: Silver badger, longer than centre joint
HEAD: Black

MAGENTA SHRIMP

TAG: Oval Silver tinsel
TAIL: GP red breast feather, wound
REAR BODY: Red seal's fur
RIB: Oval silver tinsel
CENTRE HACKLE: Light magenta cock
FRONT BODY: Black seal's fur
RIB: Oval silver tinsel
WINGS: Jungle cock
FRONT HACKLE: Badger cock
HEAD: Black

LATEX PRAWN   LEMON & PURPLE SHRIMP   LEMON GREY SHRIMP

LIME SHRIMP   LIVING SHRIMP, FIRE ORANGE   LIVING SHRIMP, FLAME RED

LIVING SHRIMP, GOLDEN GLOW   LIVING SHRIMP, SUNSET ORANGE   LOCHDHU

LONG TAIL SHRIMPS   M SOCKEN   MAGENTA SHRIMP

MAGPIE SPEY - Riding

TAG: Silver Lurex
BUTT: Yellow floss
TAIL: Two GP toppings
REAR BODY: Floss or Lurex
RIB: Oval silver tinsel
BODY HACKLES: Magpie tail feather fibres tied in as bunches at three equi-spaced positions, above and below shank
THROAT: Few strands magpie fibres, overlaid with teal or widgeon
WING: Bronze mallard, folded in two, tied flat
HEAD: Black

McCLURE SHRIMP - McPhail

TAG: Oval Gold tinsel
TAIL: GP red breast feather, wound
REAR BODY: Flat gold tinsel
RIB: Gold wire
CENTRE HACKLE: Hot orange cock or hen
FRONT BODY: Black floss
RIB: Oval gold tinsel
THROAT: Yellow calf hair
WING: Black squirrel
FRONT HACKLE: Badger cock
HEAD: Black

MEGAN BOYD SHRIMP

TAG: Red floss
TAIL: GP red breast feather, wound but slim
REAR BODY: Yellow floss
RIB: Oval gold tinsel
CENTRE HACKLE: Yellow cock, well swept back
FRONT BODY: Black floss
RIB: Oval silver tinsel
FRONT HACKLE: Furnace cock, well swept back
CHEEKS: Jungle cock tied flat
HEAD: Black

MIA FLY - Hansen

TAG: Holographic tinsel
REAR HACKLE: Large fiery brown cock
BODY: Equal mix SLF fiery claret #21, claret Polar Dub, chocolate brown hair
RIB: Copper wire
FRONT HACKLE: Fiery brown cock, smaller than tail hackle
HEAD: Black

MILLENNIUM SHRIMP - Atkins

TAG: Flat gold tinsel
TAIL: GP yellow rump feather, wound
REAR BODY: Gold Lite-Brite
RIB: Oval gold tinsel
CENTRE HACKLE: Yellow cock
FRONT BODY: Gold Lite-Brite
RIB: Oval gold tinsel
FRONT HACKLE: Blue cock
HEAD: Red

MOONSHINE - Pryce-Tannatt

TAG: Silver tinsel
TAIL: GP topping with a pair small jungle cock feathers, back to back
REAR BODY: Silver tinsel
RIB: Fine oval silver tinsel
VEILINGS: Pair blue chatterer feathers back to back, above & below shank
FRONT BODY: Black silk floss
RIB: Medium oval gold tinsel
BODY HACKLE: Black heron over black floss
THROAT: Natural guinea fowl
WINGS: Narrow cinammon turkey tail strips, tied flat
HEAD: Black

MORRUM

TAG: Oval silver tinsel & orange floss
BODY: Black dubbing
RIB: Oval silver tinsel over body hackle
BODY HACKLE: GP red breast feather or orange cock
THROAT: GP red breast fether with pintail or teal over
WINGS: Underwing GP tippet feather, overwing GP tail feather slips
HEAD: Black

MORRUM, SPEY

TAG: Oval silver tinsel & orange floss
BODY: Black dubbing
RIB: Oval silver tinsel over body hackle
BODY HACKLE: Long brown heron or GP red breast feather
THROAT: Pintail or teal
WINGS: Underwing GP tippet feather, overwing GP tail feather slips tied flat
HEAD: Red

MOURNE CLARET SHRIMP

TAG: Oval gold tinsel
TAIL: GP red breast feather, wound
REAR BODY: Very dark claret seal's fur
RIB: Oval gold tinsel
CENTRE HACKLE: Very dark claret cock
FRONT BODY: Black seal's fur
RIB: Oval silver tinsel
FRONT HACKLE: Badger cock
EYES: Small jungle cock
HEAD: Black

MOURNE GOLD SHRIMP - McDonald

TAG: Oval gold tinsel
TAIL: GP red breast feather, wound
REAR BODY: Oval gold tinsel
CENTRE HACKLE: Hot orange cock
FRONT BODY: Oval gold tinsel
WINGS: Jungle cock
FRONT HACKLE: Black cock
EYES: Small jungle cock
HEAD: Red

MOURNE ORANGE & GOLD SHRIMP

TAG: Oval gold tinsel
TAIL: GP red breast feather, wound
REAR BODY: Orange seal's fur
RIB: Oval gold tinsel
CENTRE HACKLE: Hot orange cock
FRONT BODY: Black seal's fur
RIB: Oval silver tinsel
FRONT HACKLE: Badger cock
EYES: Small jungle cock
HEAD: Black

MOURNE PURPLE & GOLD SHRIMP

TAG: Oval gold tinsel
TAIL: GP red breast feather, wound
REAR BODY: Purple seal's fur
RIB: Oval gold tinsel
CENTRE HACKLE: Purple cock
FRONT BODY: Black seal's fur
RIB: Oval silver tinsel
FRONT HACKLE: Badger cock
EYES: Small jungle cock
HEAD: Black

MAGPIE SPEY   McCLURE SHRIMP   MEGAN BOYD SHRIMP

MIA FLY   MILLENNIUM SHRIMP   MOONSHINE

MORRUM   MORRUM, SPEY   MOURNE CLARET SHRIMP

MOURNE GOLD SHRIMP   MOURNE ORANGE & GOLD SHRIMP   MOURNE PURPLE & GOLD SHRIMP

MOURNE RAT

TAG: DFM red wool & silver tinsel
TAIL: GP red breast feather, wound
REAR BODY: Yellow floss
RIB: Oval silver tinsel
CENTRE HACKLE: Black cock
FRONT BODY: Red floss
RIB: Oval silver tinsel
FRONT HACKLE: Black cock
EYES: Small jungle cock
HEAD: Red

MOURNE RED SHRIMP

TAG: Oval gold tinsel
TAIL: GP red breast feather, wound
REAR BODY: Very dark red seal's fur
RIB: Oval gold tinsel
CENTRE HACKLE: Very dark red cock
FRONT BODY: Black seal's fur
RIB: Oval silver tinsel
FRONT HACKLE: Badger cock
EYES: Small jungle cock
HEAD: Black

MOURNE SILVER SHRIMP - McDonald

TAG: Oval silver tinsel
TAIL: GP red breast feather, wound
REAR BODY: Oval silver tinsel
CENTRE HACKLE: Red cock
FRONT BODY: Oval silver tinsel
WINGS: Jungle cock
FRONT HACKLE: Badger cock
HEAD: Black

NAMELESS SHRIMP

TAG: Red floss ribbed with fine oval silver
TAIL: GP topping, curving downwards
BUTT: Black ostrich herl
REAR BODY: Red floss
RIB: Fine oval silver tinsel
CENTRE WING: Slim bunch GP tippet fibres,
two grizzle or cree hackles back to back, small
jungle cock eye each side
FRONT BODY: Yellow floss
RIB: Fine oval silver tinsel
THROAT: Small bunch brown hackle fibres,
natural guinea fowl over
WING: Bronze mallard
HEAD: Red

NEPHIN SHRIMP

TAG: Oval silver tinsel
TAIL: GP red breast feather, wound
BODY: Black floss
RIB: Wide oval silver tinsel
WING: One jungle cock feather on top
FRONT HACKLE: Dark orange cock
HEAD: Black

NESS SHRIMP, HAIRY - Mackenzie

TAG: Oval silver tinsel
TAIL: Hair hackle of brown bucktail dyed red
or grey squirrel tail dyed maroon
REAR BODY: Orange seal's fur
RIB: Oval silver tinsel
CENTRE HACKLE: Bleached squirrel dyed
orange
FRONT BODY: Black seal's fur
RIB: Oval silver tinsel
WING: Bunch of white tipped grey squirrel or
silver fox fur
FRONT HACKLES: Bleached squirrel dyed
yellow, blck dyed squirrel over
HEAD: Black

OCEAN BLUE LITE-BRITE SHRIMP - McPhail

TAG: Silver blue Lite-Brite
TAIL: GP red breast feather dyed black,
wound
BODY: Ocean blue Lite-Brite
WING: Natural grey squirrel dyed Kingfisher
blue
FRONT HACKLE: Black cock
HEAD: Red

OCTOPUS SHRIMP

TAG: Oval silver tinsel
TAIL: GP red breast feather, wound
REAR BODY: Yellow floss
RIB: Oval silver tinsel
CENTRE HACKLE: White cock with a sparse
veiling of Crystal Hair fibres all round
FRONT BODY: Black seal's fur
RIB: Oval silver tinsel
FRONT HACKLE: Light brown or red game
cock
HEAD: Red

O'HARA SHRIMP - McPhail

TUBE: 1/2" to 2" copper slipstream
BODY: None, use red silicone tubing to hold
hook in place
WING: Red and black bucktail and strands of
red holographic tinsel
CHEEKS: Jungle cock dyed red
HEAD: Red

OMOE BRUSH - Bonde

TAIL: Four strands clear Flashabou with GP
red breast feather over
BODY: In three equal segments. Lureflash
Superbug yarn in tobacco or rusty red dubbing
BODY HACKLES: Between each body
segment a wound GP red breast feather hackle
FRONT HACKLE: GP red breast feather
HEAD: Red

Note: Version from Martin Joergensen uses
hackles which extend well beyond hook gape

OPOSSUM SHRIMP - Joergensen

ANTENNAE: Tuft of light opossum hair with
some longer guard hairs
EYES: Monofilament with burnt blobbed ends
BODY: Underbody weighting - lead. Black
dubbing under natural opossum hair
SHELLBACK: Light brown latex or Shellback
RIB: Copper wire or monofilament
LEGS: Bunch of barred wood duck fibres, tied
as throat. Use butts to form a small fan shaped
head projecting fowards over hook eye
HEAD: Tan tying thread

ORANGE & GOLD SHRIMP

TAG: Oval gold tinsel
TAIL: GP red breast feather, wound
REAR BODY: Medium or wide oval gold
tinsel
CENTRE HACKLE: Hot orange cock
FRONT BODY: Black seal's fur
RIB: Oval gold tinsel
FRONT HACKLE: Badger cock
HEAD: Black

Note: Orange & Copper Shrimp - replace
gold tinsel with copper tinsel

MOURNE RAT	MOURNE RED SHRIMP	MOURNE SILVER SHRIMP

NAMELESS SHRIMP	NEPHIN SHRIMP	NESS SHRIMP, HAIRY

OCEAN BLUE LITE-BRITE SHRIMP	OCTOPUS SHRIMP	O'HARA SHRIMP

OMOE BRUSH	OPOSSUM SHRIMP	ORANGE & GOLD SHRIMP

173

ORANGE & GOLD LITE-BRITE SHRIMP - McPhail

TAG: Gold Lite-Brite
TAIL: GP red breast feather dyed hot orange, wound
BODY: Gold Lite-Brite
WING: Natural grey squirrel dyed hot orange
FRONT HACKLE: Badger cock dyed hot orange
HEAD: Orange

ORANGE HACKLE SHRIMP - Greenhalgh

THREAD: Orange or red
TAIL: Bunch hot orange bucktail, few strands orange Crystal Hair, three times hook length
BODY: Orange floss
RIB: Oval gold
THORAX: Fluorescent hot orange fur
FRONT HACKLE: Hot orange cock
HEAD: Red

ORANGE MALLARD SHRIMP - Greenhalgh

THREAD: Black
TAIL: GP red breast feather, wound, few strands orange Crystal Hair
BODY: Rear fi fluorescent red floss, front fi black floss
RIB: Oval silver
FRONT HACKLE: Grey mallard flank or breast dyed hot orange
HEAD: Black

ORANGE PARTRIDGE SHRIMP - Greenhalgh

THREAD: Orange
BODY: Orange floss
RIB: Finest oval gold
FRONT HACKLE: Two turns brown partridge
HEAD: Red

ORANGE SHRIMP - Toohey

TAIL: Orange bucktail, as overall hook length
REAR BODY: Flat gold Mylar
RIB: Fine oval gold
CENTRE HACKLE: Short hot orange cock
FRONT BODY: Red floss
RIB: Fine oval gold
WING: Natural barred grey squirrel dyed orange to halfway along tail
THROAT: Natural barred grey squirrel dyed orange, half wing density, same length as wing
SIDES: Bleached squirrel dyed orange, sparse, slightly shorter than wing
CHEEKS: Jungle cock
HEAD: Red

ORANGE SHRIMP - Westcott

TAG: Oval gold
TAIL: GP red breast feather, wound
BODY: Orange floss
RIB: Oval gold
FRONT HACKLE: Long hot orange hen hackle
CHEEKS: Jungle cock
HEAD: Black

O'REILLY SHRIMP - O'Reilly

TAG: Oval silver
TAIL: GP red breast feather, wound
REAR BODY: Red floss
RIB: Oval silver
CENTRE HACKLE: Badger cock
FRONT BODY: Black floss
RIB: Oval silver
FRONT HACKLE: Hot orange cock
HEAD: Red

OWENEA SHRIMP

TAG: Oval gold
REAR BODY: Flat gold tinsel
RIB: Fine oval gold
CENTRE HACKLE: Long GP yellow rump feather, natural or dyed orange, tied as tail
FRONT BODY: Black seal's fur
RIB: Oval silver
WINGS: Jungle cock
FRONT HACKLE: Badger cock
HEAD: Red

OWENMORE SHRIMP

TAG: Oval silver
TAIL: Long red bucktail
REAR BODY: Orange floss
RIB: Oval silver
CENTRE WING: Long orange bucktail, strands pearl Crystal Hair
FRONT BODY: Black floss
RIB: Oval silver
FRONT HACKLE: Red cock
CHEEKS: Jungle cock
HEAD: Red

OWENMORE SHRIMP - Tolan

TAG: Oval silver
TAIL: GP red breast feather, wound
REAR BODY: Yellow floss
RIB: Oval silver
CENTRE WING: Red cock
FRONT BODY: Black floss
RIB: Oval silver
FRONT HACKLE: Purple cock
CHEEKS: Jungle cock
HEAD: Red

Note: The centre hackle may also be orange rather than red (this form from the river Roe)

PADDY SHRIMP - McDonald

TAG: Oval silver
TAIL: GP red breast feather, wound
REAR BODY: Yellow floss or seal's fur
RIB: Oval silver
CENTRE WING: Dyed green cock
FRONT BODY: Green floss or seal's fur
RIB: Oval silver
WINGS: Jungle cock
FRONT HACKLE: Badger cock
HEAD: Black

PARSON SHRIMP

TAG: Oval gold
TAIL: Long yellow hackle
BODY: Yellow floss
RIB: Oval gold
WINGS: Jungle cock
FRONT HACKLE: Golden olive cock
CHEEKS: Kingfisher
HEAD: Black

ORANGE & GOLD LITE-BRITE SHRIMP   ORANGE HACKLE SHRIMP   ORANGE MALLARD SHRIMP

ORANGE PARTRIDGE SHRIMP   ORANGE SHRIMP   ORANGE SHRIMP

O'REILLY SHRIMP   OWENEA SHRIMP   OWENMORE SHRIMP

OWENMORE SHRIMP   PADDY SHRIMP   PARSON SHRIMP

PARSON SHRIMP (Moy variant)

TAG: Oval gold
TAIL: Long yellow hackle
BODY: Yellow floss
RIB: Oval silver
FRONT HACKLE: Golden olive cock
CHEEKS: Jungle cock
HEAD: Black

PEACOCK SHRIMP, RED - Roulston

TAIL: Red bucktail or squirrel, 2 or 3 strands
gold Crystal Hair
REAR BODY: Flat copper
RIB: Oval gold
VEILINGS: Sparse blue peacock neck feather
fibres, above and below
CENTRE WING: Dyed red cock
FRONT BODY: Peacock herl
RIB: Oval silver
VEILINGS: As rear veilings
FRONT HACKLE: Claret cock
CHEEKS: Jungle cock
HEAD: Black

PEACOCK SHRIMP, YELLOW - Roulston

TAIL: Yellow bucktail or squirrel, 2 or 3
strands silver Crystal Hair
REAR BODY: Flat silver
RIB: Oval silver
VEILINGS: Sparse blue peacock neck feather
fibres, above and below
CENTRE WING: Dyed red cock
FRONT BODY: Bronze peacock herl
RIB: Oval silver
VEILINGS: As rear veilings
FRONT HACKLE: Badger cock
CHEEKS: Jungle cock
HEAD: Black

PEARL & MAGENTA SHRIMP

TAIL: Pearl Krystalflash
REAR BODY: Flat pearl Mylar
RIB: Oval silver
CENTRE HACKLE: Yellow cock
FRONT BODY: Flat pearl Mylar
RIB: Oval silver
FRONT HACKLE: Magenta cock
HEAD: Red

PEARL & ORANGE SHRIMP

TAIL: Pearl Krystalflash
REAR BODY: Flat pearl Mylar
RIB: Oval silver
CENTRE HACKLE: Yellow cock
FRONT BODY: Flat pearl Mylar
RIB: Oval silver
FRONT HACKLE: Hot orange cock
HEAD: Red

PENYBONT (Variant)

TAIL: GP tippet fibres
BODY: Dirty yellow seal's fur
RIB: Oval silver
BODY HACKLE: Brown hen palmered along
body
WING: GP tippet feather enclosed by grey
heron wing slips
HEAD: Black

PINK & PURPLE PRAWN

TAG: Fluorescent pink floss
TAIL: White bucktail dyed pink
BODY: Purple floss
RIB: Oval silver
BODY HACKLE: Pink cock palmered, two
turns at throat
WING: Brown bucktail
HEAD: Black

POLYTHENE PRAWN

FEELERS: Orange bucktail
EYES: Monofilament, heat blobbed and
blackened
ROSTRUM: Swathe of orange swan
UNDERBODY: Orange-red wool
OVERBODY: Clear polythene, wound
TAIL VANES: Polythene, fanned out over
hook eye
HEAD: Red

PRAWN FLY, TUBE

TUBE: 1" to 2" plastic or brass
FEELERS: GP red breast feathers
BODY: Orange seal's fur
RIB: Oval gold
BODY HACKLE: Orange cock, palmered
WING: GP tippet feather, vee-shaped, as long
as body
THROAT: Long GP red breast feather
HEAD: Red

PRAWN, RED

FEELERS: Equal mix, brown, red and black
bucktail, trimmed to length
EYES: Black glass beads on monofilament
UNDERBODY: Red floss
OVERBODY: Fluorescent red floss
BODY HACKLE: Two red game cock hackles
palmered and swept back and down
SHELLBACK: Clear polythene strip
RIB: 10lb. clear monofilament
HEAD: Red

PURGATORY SHRIMP - McDonald

TAG: Oval silver
TAIL: GP red breast feather, wound
REAR BODY: Heavy oval silver tinsel
CENTRE HACKLE: Hot orange cock
FRONT BODY: Hot orange seal's fur
RIB: Oval silver
WINGS: Jungle cock
FRONT HACKLE: Yellow cock
HEAD: Red

PURPLE & GOLD SHRIMP

TAG: Oval gold
TAIL: GP red breast feather, wound
REAR BODY: Flat or oval gold tinsel
RIB: Oval gold
CENTRE HACKLE: Purple cock
FRONT BODY: Black floss
RIB: Oval gold
FRONT HACKLE: Silver badger cock
HEAD: Black

PARSON SHRIMP, VARIANT	PEACOCK SHRIMP, RED	PEACOCK SHRIMP, YELLOW

PEARL & MAGENTA SHRIMP	PEARL & ORANGE SHRIMP	PENYBONT, VARIANT

PINK & PURPLE PRAWN	POLYTHENE PRAWN	PRAWN FLY, TUBE

PRAWN, RED	PURGATORY SHRIMP	PURPLE & GOLD SHRIMP

PURPLE & GOLD SHRIMP, DONEGAL

TAG: Oval gold
TAIL: GP red breast feather, wound
REAR BODY: Flat or oval gold tinsel
RIB: Oval gold
CENTRE HACKLE: Purple cock
FRONT BODY: Red floss
RIB: Oval gold
FRONT HACKLE: Silver badger cock
HEAD: Red

PURPLE BUG

TAG: Oval gold
TAIL: GP red breast feather, wound
REAR BODY: Flat or oval gold tinsel
RIB: Oval gold
VEILINGS: Red hackle tips or swan strips
CENTRE HACKLE: Purple cock
FRONT BODY: Flat or oval gold tinsel
RIB: Oval gold
FRONT HACKLE: Furnace cock
HEAD: Black

PURPLE SHRIMP #1- McDonald

TAG: Oval gold
TAIL: GP red breast feather, wound
REAR BODY: Purple floss or seal's fur
RIB: Oval gold
CENTRE HACKLE: Purple cock
FRONT BODY: Purple floss or seal's fur
RIB: Oval gold
WINGS: Jungle cock
FRONT HACKLE: Purple cock
HEAD: Black

PURPLE SHRIMP #2 - McDonald

TAG: Oval gold
TAIL: Long purple cock hackle, wound
REAR BODY: Purple seal's fur
RIB: Oval gold
CENTRE HACKLE: Purple cock
FRONT BODY: Purple seal's fur
RIB: Oval gold
WINGS: Jungle cock dyed fiery brown or natural
FRONT HACKLE: Purple cock
HEAD: Purple

QUINN SHRIMP

TAG: Oval silver
TAIL: GP red breast feather, wound
REAR BODY: Flat silver tinsel
RIB: Silver wire
VEILINGS: Bright blue hen hackle fibres at sides of body
CENTRE HACKLE: Pale magenta cock
FRONT BODY: Flat silver tinsel
RIB: Silver wire
VEILINGS: As rear veilings
WINGS: Jungle cock, back to back
FRONT HACKLES: Magenta cock with grey badger over
HEAD: Black

QUINN SHRIMP, MODERN

TAG: Oval silver
TAIL: GP red breast feather, wound
REAR BODY: Flat silver tinsel
RIB: Oval silver
CENTRE HACKLE: Pale magenta cock
FRONT BODY: Flat silver tinsel
RIB: Oval silver
WINGS: Jungle cock, back to back
FRONT HACKLES: Magenta cock with badger cock over
HEAD: Black

RAEKEN - Gislasson

TAIL: Two bright orange hackles, mounted one above the other, convex side to convex
REAR BODY: Pinky-orange floss
RIB: Fine oval gold
CENTRE VEILINGS: Above hook - GP tippet feather reaching to hook bend
Below hook - light bright orange hackle fibres reaching to hook barb
FRONT BODY: Pinky-orange floss
RIB: Fine oval gold
WING: Orange hackle fibres, to end of tippet feather
THROAT: Orange hackle fibres to hook barb
HEAD: Red

RAT SHRIMP - McDonald

TAG: Oval silver
TAIL: Natural grey squirrel tail
BODY: Gold Mylar twist
WING: Jungle cock
FRONT HACKLE: Badger cock
HEAD: Red ostrich herl

RED & GOLD SHRIMP

TAG: Oval gold
TAIL: GP red breast feather, wound
BODY: Flat gold tinsel
RIB: Oval gold tinsel
VEILINGS: Red dyed hackle tips, above and below
WINGS: Jungle cock, back to back
FRONT HACKLES: Orange cock with badger cock over
HEAD: Red

RED & GOLD SHRIMP - Bonner

TAG: Oval gold
TAIL: GP red breast feather, wound
REAR BODY: Flat old gold Mylar
RIB: Oval gold
CENTRE HACKLE: Red dyed cock
FRONT BODY: Flat gold Mylar
RIB: Oval gold
WINGS: Jungle cock, back to back
FRONT HACKLE: Furnace cock
HEAD: Red

RED DEVIL SHRIMP - McPhail

TUBE: 1/2" to 2" copper slipstream
BODY: None, use red silicone tubing to hold hook in place
WING: Red bucktail and strands of gold/pink Reflections
CHEEKS: Jungle cock
HEAD: Red

RIDINGS PRAWN

TAG: Silver tinsel & scarlet floss
TAIL: GP topping
BUTT: Black ostrich herl or black chenille
REAR BODY: Pink wool ribbed oval silver
CENTRE JOINT: Two ginger cock hackles with vee-notch in tips. Back to back curving outwards enclosed by two small jungle cock feathers. Sparse guinea fowl hackle. Bunch of GP tippet fibres tied as beard hackle
FRONT BODY: Yellow wool, ribbed oval silver, small ginger hackle palmered.
SHOULDER HACKLE: Bunch guinea fowl
WINGS: Bronze or grey mallard, dressed flat but curved upwards
HEAD: Red

PURPLE & GOLD SHRIMP, DONEGAL PURPLE BUG PURPLE SHRIMP #1

PURPLE SHRIMP #2 QUINN SHRIMP QUINN SHRIMP, MODERN

RAEKEN RAT SHRIMP RED & GOLD SHRIMP

RED & GOLD SHRIMP, BONNER RED DEVIL SHRIMP RIDINGS PRAWN

ROE GOLD SHRIMP - Atkins

TAG: Oval gold
TAIL: GP red breast feather, wound
REAR BODY: Flat gold Mylar
RIB: Oval gold
CENTRE HACKLE: Hot orange cock
FRONT BODY: Flat gold Mylar
RIB: Oval gold
FRONT HACKLE: Purple cock
HEAD: Black

ROE PURPLE SHRIMP - Atkins

TAG: Oval gold
TAIL: GP red breast feather, wound
REAR BODY: Yellow floss or seal's fur
RIB: Oval gold
CENTRE HACKLE: Hot orange cock
FRONT BODY: Purple floss or seal's fur
RIB: Oval gold
FRONT HACKLE: Claret magenta
HEAD: Black

Note: Claret magenta - ginger hackle dyed
dark rich magenta, which produces claret on
the dark side and magenta on the light side

ROE ROYAL SHRIMP - Atkins

TAG: Oval gold
TAIL: GP red breast feather, wound
REAR BODY: Dark claret seal's fur
RIB: Oval gold
CENTRE HACKLE: Hot orange cock
FRONT BODY: Dark claret seal's fur
RIB: Oval gold
FRONT HACKLE: Claret magenta
HEAD: Black

Note: Claret magenta - ginger hackle dyed
dark rich magenta, which produces claret on
the dark side and magenta on the light side

ROEBUCK, GOLD - MacAffer

TAG: Orange floss
TAIL: GP topping
BODY: Flat gold tinsel
RIB: Oval gold
BODY HACKLE: Dark brown cock
THROAT HACKLE: Orange cock
WING: Brown roebuck hair
HEAD: Black

ROEBUCK, SILVER - MacAffer

TAG: Yellow floss
TAIL: GP topping
BODY: Flat silver tinsel
RIB: Oval silver
BODY HACKLE: Yellow cock
THROAT HACKLE: Blue jay
WING: Brown roebuck hair
HEAD: Black

ROSS LITE-BRITE SHRIMP - McPhail

TAG: Silver Lite-Brite
TAIL: GP red breast feather, wound
BODY: Rear fi silver Lite-Brite, front fi red Lite-Brite
WING: Natural grey squirrel
FRONT HACKLE: Grizzle cock
HEAD: Red

ROY WILSON SHRIMP - Wilson

TAG: Oval silver
TAIL: Long dyed red hackle or two turns red
hackle under a GP red breast feather, wound
REAR BODY: Flat silver tinsel
RIB: Oval silver
CENTRE HACKLE: Yellow cock
FRONT BODY: Flat silver tinsel
RIB: Oval silver
FRONT HACKLE: Medium or light blue cock
HEAD: Black

SAM'S BADGER - Bremner

TAIL: Long yellow bucktail
REAR BODY: Flat gold tinsel
RIB: Oval copper
CENTRE HACKLE: Orange cock
FRONT BODY: Flat copper tinsel
RIB: Oval gold
WING: Natural badger hair at top and bottom,
not sides
HEAD: White varnish

SANDY'S SHRIMP - Leventon

TAIL: Slim bunch long black marabou
BODY: Wound orange marabou
RIB: Oval gold
FRONT HACKLE: Long black hen
CHEEKS: Jungle cock
HEAD: Black

SECRET WEAPON - Heaney

TAG: Oval silver
TAIL: GP red breast feather, wound
REAR BODY: Yellow floss
RIB: Oval silver
VEILINGS: Scarlet ibis or cock-of-the-rock,
above and below (modern version - red hackle
tips or swan strips)
CENTRE HACKLE: Badger henny cock
FRONT BODY: Black floss
RIB: Oval silver
VEILINGS: As rear
FRONT HACKLE: Long badger henny cock
HEAD: Red

SHADOW SHRIMP, BLUE & GOLD - Bonner

TAIL: Silver fox body guard hair dyed fiery
brown, strands of orange Krystal Flash
REAR BODY: Flat gold Mylar
RIB: Fine oval gold
VEILING: GP tippet Vee-form, tips varnished
CENTRE HACKLE: Dyed blue webby saddle
hackle
FRONT BODY: Flat gold Mylar
RIB: Fine oval gold
WING: Fiery brown shadow fox fur
FRONT HACKLE: Light furnace genetic cock
saddle
HEAD: Red

SHADOW SHRIMP, BLUE & SILVER - Bonner

TAIL: Silver fox body guard hair dyed fiery
brown, strands of smolt blue Krystal Flash
REAR BODY: Flat silver Mylar
RIB: Fine oval silver
VEILING: GP tippet Vee-form, tips varnished
CENTRE HACKLE: Dyed blue webby saddle
hackle
FRONT BODY: Flat silver Mylar
RIB: Fine oval silver
WING: Orange shadow fox fur
FRONT HACKLE: Silver badger genetic cock
saddle
HEAD: Black or red

ROE GOLD SHRIMP	ROE PURPLE SHRIMP	ROE ROYAL SHRIMP

ROEBUCK, GOLD	ROEBUCK, SILVER	ROSS LITE-BRITE SHRIMP

ROY WILSON SHRIMP	SAM'S BADGER	SANDY'S SHRIMP

SECRET WEAPON	SHADOW SHRIMP, BLUE & GOLD	SHADOW SHRIMP, BLUE & SILVER

SHADOW SHRIMP, FINN - Bonner

TAIL: Silver fox body guard hair dyed yellow, strands of pearl or yellow Krystal Flash
REAR BODY: Flat gold Mylar
RIB: Fine oval gold
VEILING: GP tippet Vee-form, tips varnished
CENTRE HACKLE: Dyed orange webby saddle hackle
FRONT BODY: Flat gold Mylar
RIB: Fine oval gold
WING: Orange shadow fox fur
FRONT HACKLE: Silver badger dyed yellow
HEAD: Red

SHADOW SHRIMP, ORANGE & GOLD - Bonner

TAIL: Silver fox body guard hair dyed orange, strands of orange Krystal Flash
REAR BODY: Flat old gold Mylar
RIB: Fine oval gold
VEILING: GP tippet Vee-form, tips varnished
CENTRE HACKLE: Dyed hot orange webby saddle hackle
FRONT BODY: Flat old gold Mylar
RIB: Fine oval gold
WING: Orange shadow fox fur
FRONT HACKLE: Silver badger dyed hot orange
HEAD: Red

SHADOW SHRIMP, RED & GOLD - Bonner

TAIL: Silver fox body guard hair dyed fiery brown, strands of orange Krystal Flash
REAR BODY: Flat old gold Mylar
RIB: Fine oval gold
VEILING: GP tippet Vee-form, tips varnished
CENTRE HACKLE: Dyed red webby saddle hackle
FRONT BODY: Red floss
RIB: Fine oval gold
WING: Fiery brown shadow fox fur
FRONT HACKLE: Light furnace
HEAD: Red

SHADOW SHRIMP, SILVER - Bonner

TAIL: Natural silver fox body guard hair, strands of pearl Krystal Flash
REAR BODY: Flat silver Mylar
RIB: Fine oval silver
VEILING: GP tippet Vee-form, tips varnished
CENTRE HACKLE: Dyed orange webby saddle hackle
FRONT BODY: Flat silver Mylar
RIB: Fine oval silver
WING: Orange shadow fox fur
FRONT HACKLE: Silver badger
HEAD: Red

SHRIMP #1 - Dupo

TAIL: GP red breast feather, wound
REAR BODY: Red seal's fur
RIB: Oval silver
CENTRE HACKLES: White cock under red cock
FRONT BODY: Black seal's fur
RIB: Oval silver
WING: Jungle cock, back to back - above and below
FRONT HACKLE: Black cock
HEAD: Red

SHRIMP #2 - Dupo

TAIL: GP red breast feather, wound
REAR BODY: Green Lurex
RIB: Oval silver
CENTRE HACKLES: Green dyed cock
FRONT BODY: Black floss
RIB: Oval silver
FRONT HACKLE: Black cock
HEAD: Black

SHRIMP FLY

TAG: Oval silver
TAIL: GP red breast feather, wound
REAR BODY: Red wool or floss
RIB: Oval silver tinsel
CENTRE HACKLE: Hot orange cock
FRONT BODY: Black floss
RIB: Oval silver tinsel
WING: Jungle cock, roofed
FRONT HACKLE: Silver badger
HEAD: Red

SHRIMP FLY - Evans

FEELERS: Orange bucktail
BODY: Orange wool
RIB: Oval silver tinsel
BODY HACKLE: Orange cock, palmered
RIB: 20 - 30lb. monofilament
BACK: Red raffia
EYES: Metallic chain beads, painted black
HEAD: Red

SILK CUT SHRIMP - Wren

TAIL: Long purple bucktail, strands purple Crystal Hair
BODY: Flat pearl Lurex wound over wet varnished tying silk. Varnish over Lurex
WING: GP tippet feather dyed purple, tied to lie horizontally
FRONT HACKLE: Purple hen or cock, long and full
HEAD: Black

SILVER BLUE SHRIMP

TAG: Oval silver
TAIL: GP red breast feather, wound
REAR BODY: Flat silver tinsel
RIB: Oval silver tinsel
CENTRE HACKLE: Light blue cock
FRONT BODY: Flat silver tinsel
RIB: Oval silver tinsel
WING: Jungle cock, roofed
FRONT HACKLE: Silver badger
HEAD: Red

SILVER COOT SPEY - Andreassen

BODY: Flat silver tinsel
RIB: Oval silver tinsel
BODY HACKLE: Natural coot wing feather, palmered alongside ribbing for front 3/5ths of body
WING: Bronze mallard, tied flat, keel fashion
HEAD: Black

SILVER SHRIMP

TAG: Oval silver
TAIL: GP red breast feather, wound
REAR BODY: Flat silver tinsel
RIB: Oval silver tinsel
VEILINGS: Orange hackle tips or orange swan strips, above and below
CENTRE HACKLE: Silver badger cock
FRONT BODY: Flat silver tinsel
RIB: Oval silver tinsel
VEILINGS: Orange hackle tips or orange swan strips, above and below
WING: Jungle cock, roofed
FRONT HACKLE: Silver badger cock
HEAD: Black

SHADOW SHRIMP, FINN   SHADOW SHRIMP, ORANGE & GOLD   SHADOW SHRIMP, RED & GOLD

SHADOW SHRIMP, SILVER   SHRIMP #1 - Dupo   SHRIMP #2 - Dupo

SHRIMP FLY   SHRIMP FLY, EVANS   SILK CUT SHRIMP

SILVER BLUE SHRIMP   SILVER COOT SPEY   SILVER SHRIMP

SILVER SHRIMP - Bonner

TAG: Oval silver
TAIL: GP red breast feather, wound
REAR BODY: Flat silver tinsel
RIB: Oval silver tinsel
CENTRE HACKLE: Orange cock
FRONT BODY: Flat silver tinsel
RIB: Oval silver tinsel
WING: Jungle cock
FRONT HACKLE: Grizzle cock
HEAD: Red

SILVER WILKINSON SPEY

TAG: Oval silver
TAIL: GP tippet feather
BUTT: Orange wool
BODY: Flat silver tinsel
BODY HACKLE: Long magenta spey hackle palmered along body
RIB: Oval silver tinsel, over body hackle in opposite spiral
SHOULDER HACKLE: Long blue hackle
WINGS: Jungle cock
HEAD: Red

SLANEY BADGER

TAG: Oval silver tinsel & red Glo-Brite #3 fluorescent floss
TAIL: GP red breast feather, wound. Two small jungle cock feathers
REAR BODY: Red floss
RIB: Oval silver tinsel
CENTRE HACKLE: Grizzle cock
FRONT BODY: Black floss
RIB: Oval silver tinsel
WING: Pearl Mobile under badger hair
FRONT HACKLE: Grizzle cock
HEAD: Red

SPRING GRUB - Kelson

TAG: Oval silver tinsel & light blue silk
TAIL: Ibis feather and blue macaw, married
REAR HACKLE: Furnace hackle dyed orange
REAR BODY: Yellow silk ribbed with black chenille
CENTRE HACKLE: Vulturine guinea fowl (natural blue)
FRONT BODY: Black silk ribbed with oval silver tinsel
FRONT HACKLE: coch-y-bondhu with guinea fowl dyed orange over
HEAD: Black

STEWART SHRIMP

TAG: Oval silver tinsel & red Glo-Brite #3 fluorescent floss
TAIL: GP red breast feather, wound. Two small jungle cock feathers
REAR BODY: Red floss
RIB: Oval silver tinsel
CENTRE HACKLE: Grizzle cock
FRONT BODY: Black floss
RIB: Oval silver tinsel
WING: Pearl Mobile under badger hair
FRONT HACKLE: Grizzle cock
HEAD: Red

SUNBURST SHRIMP, LITE-BRITE - McPhail

TAG: Gold Lite-Brite
TAIL: GP red breast feather dyed red, wound
BODY: Yellow Lite-Brite
WING: Natural grey squirrel dyed flame red
FRONT HACKLE: Badger cock dyed sunburst yellow
HEAD: Orange

SWINFORD BLUE SHRIMP

TAG: Oval silver
TAIL: GP red breast feather, wound
REAR BODY: Red wool or floss
RIB: Oval silver tinsel
CENTRE HACKLE: Hot orange cock
FRONT BODY: Black floss
RIB: Oval silver tinsel
WING: Jungle cock, roofed
FRONT HACKLE: Medium or light blue cock
HEAD: Red

TAIL FIRE - Evans

TAG: Orange floss
REAR BODY: Yellow floss
RIB: Oval gold tinsel
CENTRE HACKLE: GP red breast feather, wound as tail
FRONT BODY: Black floss
RIB: Oval gold tinsel
THROAT: Yellow hackle fibres
WING: Black hair
CHEEKS: Jungle cock
HEAD: Black

THUNDER SPEY - Dupo

TAG: Oval silver and red floss
BODY: Black floss
RIB: Oval silver tinsel
BODY HACKLE: GP red breast feather, palmered
COLLAR HACKLE: Guinea fowl, dyed blue
CHEEKS: Jungle cock
HEAD: Black

TIPPET GRUB - Kelson

TAG: Gold tinsel and scarlet seal's fur
REAR HACKLE: GP tippet wound as hackle followed by a furnace hackle
REAR BODY: Green Berlin wool
CENTRE HACKLE: GP tippet wound as hackle followed by a furnace hackle
FRONT BODY: Green Berlin wool
FRONT HACKLE: GP tippet wound as hackle followed by a furnace hackle
HEAD: Black

Note: Hackles increase in size towards head

TIPPET SHRIMP, IRISH

TAG: Oval gold
TAIL: GP red breast feather, wound
REAR BODY: Golden olive or rich yellow seal's fur
RIB: Oval gold tinsel
VEILING: GP tippet strands, on top only
CENTRE HACKLE: Creamy badger cock
FRONT BODY: Purple seal's fur
RIB: Oval gold tinsel
VEILING: GP tippet strands, on top only
FRONT HACKLE: Creamy badger cock
HEAD: Red or black

TODD'S SHRIMP - Todd

REAR BODY: Oval gold tinsel
CENTRE HACKLE: GP red breast feather, wound as tail
FRONT BODY: Black floss or seal's fur
RIB: Oval gold tinsel
WINGS: Jungle cock
FRONT HACKLE: Soft orange cock
HEAD: Black

SILVER SHRIMP, BONNER

SILVER WILKINSON SPEY

SLANEY BADGER

SPRING GRUB

STEWART SHRIMP

SUNBURST SHRIMP, LITE-BRITE

SWINFORD BLUE SHRIMP

TAIL FIRE - Evans

THUNDER SPEY - Dupo

TIPPET GRUB

TIPPET SHRIMP, IRISH

TODD'S SHRIMP

ULLSOCK

TAIL: Red wool or GP tippet
TAIL HACKLE: Brown cock
REAR BODY: Black floss or wool
CENTRE HACKLE: Brown cock
FRONT BODY: Black floss or wool
FRONT HACKLE: Brown cock
HEAD: Black

Note: Hackles increase in size towards head

UMBRELLA - Joergensen

TAIL: Red or yellow GP body feather
REAR BODY: Flat silver tinsel
RIB: Oval silver tinsel
REAR WING: Red or yellow GP body feather
CENTRE HACKLE: Furnace, brown or badger cock
FRONT BODY: Opossum or polar fox dubbing, orange or yellow to match GP feathers
FRONT HACKLE: Furnace, brown or badger cock
HEAD: Tan

USK GRUB - Bates

TAG: Fine round silver tinsel
TAIL: Bunch GP red breast feather fibres
REAR BODY: Hot orange seal's fur
RIB: Fine oval silver tinsel
CENTRE HACKLE: Small hot orange hackle, followed by small white hackle
FRONT BODY: Black seal's fur
RIB: Oval silver tinsel
WINGS: Pair long jungle cock feathers, extending length of body, tied flat
FRONT HACKLE: Coch-y-bondhu cock
HEAD: Red

USK GRUB - Modern

TAG: Silver tinsel
TAIL: Bunch GP red breast feather, wound
REAR BODY: Orange seal's fur
RIB: Oval silver tinsel
CENTRE HACKLE: White cock under orange cock
FRONT BODY: Black seal's fur
RIB: Oval silver tinsel
WINGS: Pair long jungle cock feathers, extending length of body
HEAD: Black

USK GRUB - Original

TAG: Silver tinsel
TAIL: Bunch GP red breast feather, wound
REAR BODY: Orange seal's fur
RIB: Oval silver tinsel
CENTRE HACKLE: White cock under orange cock
FRONT BODY: Black seal's fur
RIB: Oval silver tinsel
WINGS: Pair long jungle cock feathers, extending length of body
FRONT HACKLE: Furnace cock
HEAD: Black

WADE'S ARCTIC SHRIMP, GOLD - Wade

TAIL: 4 to 6 strands pearl or orange Krystal Flash in the centre of a bunch of orange arctic fox fur
BODY: Old gold Mylar
RIB: Oval gold tinsel
WING: Orange arctic fox fur to extend about 1/4 length along tail
FRONT HACKLE: Badger cock dyed orange
HEAD: Red

WADE'S ARCTIC SHRIMP, GREEN - Wade

TAIL: 4 to 6 strands yellow Krystal Flash in the centre of a bunch of yellow arctic fox fur
BODY: Silver Mylar
RIB: Oval silver tinsel
WING: Green arctic fox fur to extend about 1/4 length along tail
FRONT HACKLE: Orange cock
HEAD: Black

WADE'S ARCTIC SHRIMP, ORANGE - Wade

TAIL: 4 to 6 strands pearl or orange Krystal Flash in the centre of a bunch of orange arctic fox fur
BODY: Old gold Mylar
RIB: Oval silver tinsel
WING: Orange arctic fox fur to extend about 1/4 length along tail
FRONT HACKLE: Silver badger cock
HEAD: Red

WADE'S ARCTIC SHRIMP, YELLOW - Wade

TAIL: 4 to 6 strands pearl or orange Krystal Flash in the centre of a bunch of rich yellow arctic fox fur
BODY: Gold Mylar
RIB: Oval gold tinsel
WING: Yellow arctic fox fur to extend about 1/4 length along tail
FRONT HACKLE: Badger cock dyed rich yellow
HEAD: Black

WELSH SHRIMP - Jones

TAG: Yellow floss
TAIL: GP topping
BUTT: Black ostrich herl
BODY: Yellow floss
RIB: Oval silver
WING: GP red breast feather with jungle cock each side
FRONT HACKLE: White cock
HEAD: Black

WELSH SHRIMP (Variant)

TAG: Yellow floss
TAIL: GP red breast feather, wound
REAR BODY: Yellow floss
RIB: Oval silver
CENTRE HACKLE: Badger cock
FRONT BODY: Black floss
RIB: Oval silver tinsel
WING: Jungle cock, back to back
FRONT HACKLE: Orange cock
HEAD: Black

WHEATSHEAF SHRIMP - Mullen

TAG: Oval gold
TAIL: GP red breast feather, wound
REAR BODY: Gold tinsel
RIB: Oval gold
CENTRE HACKLE: Brown cock
FRONT BODY: Yellow floss
RIB: Oval gold tinsel
FRONT HACKLE: Golden olive cock
CHEEKS: Jungle cock
HEAD: Red

ULLSOCK	UMBRELLA	USK GRUB- Bates

USK GRUB, MODERN	USK GRUB, ORIGINAL	WADE'S ARCTIC SHRIMP, GOLD

WADE'S ARCTIC SHRIMP, GREEN	WADE'S ARCTIC SHRIMP, ORANGE	WADE'S ARCTIC SHRIMP, YELLOW

WELSH SHRIMP	WELSH SHRIMP (Variant)	WHEATSHEAF SHRIMP

WHITE SHRIMP

TAG: Oval gold
TAIL: GP red breast feather, wound
REAR BODY: Orange seal's fur
RIB: Oval gold
CENTRE HACKLE: Hot orange cock
FRONT BODY: Black seal's fur
RIB: Oval silver tinsel
WINGS: Jungle cock, roofed
FRONT HACKLE: Silver badger cock
HEAD: Black

WHITE SHRIMP, Burns

TAG: Oval gold
TAIL: GP red breast feather, wound
REAR BODY: Orange seal's fur
RIB: Oval gold
CENTRE HACKLE: Hot orange cock
FRONT BODY: Black seal's fur
RIB: Oval silver tinsel
WINGS: Jungle cock, roofed
FRONT HACKLE: Silver badger cock
HEAD: Black

WILKINSON SHRIMP, DARK

TAG: Oval silver
TAIL: GP red breast feather, wound
REAR BODY: Flat silver tinsel
RIB: Oval silver
CENTRE HACKLE: Rich kingfisher blue cock
FRONT BODY: Flat silver tinsel
RIB: Oval silver tinsel
WINGS: Jungle cock, roofed
FRONT HACKLE: Dark claret cock
HEAD: Red

WILKINSON SHRIMP, GOLD

TAG: Oval gold
TAIL: GP red breast feather, wound
REAR BODY: Flat gold Mylar
RIB: Oval gold
CENTRE HACKLE: BLue cock
FRONT BODY: Flat gold Mylar
RIB: Oval gold tinsel
FRONT HACKLE: Hot orange cock
HEAD: Red

WILKINSON SHRIMP, LIGHT

TAG: Oval silver
TAIL: GP red breast feather, wound
REAR BODY: Flat silver tinsel
RIB: Oval silver
CENTRE HACKLE: Magenta blue cock
FRONT BODY: Flat silver tinsel
RIB: Oval silver tinsel
WINGS: Jungle cock, roofed
FRONT HACKLE: Medium blue cock
HEAD: Red

WYE BUG, AGIVEY #1

TAG: Oval silver
TAIL: GP red breast feather, wound
REAR BODY: Orange seal's fur
RIB: Oval silver
CENTRE HACKLE: Hot orange cock
FRONT BODY: Black seal's fur
RIB: Oval silver tinsel
WINGS: Jungle cock, roofed
FRONT HACKLE: Light brown or red game cock
HEAD: Black

WYE BUG, AGIVEY #2

TAG: Oval silver
TAIL: GP red breast feather, wound
REAR BODY: Orange seal's fur
RIB: Oval silver
CENTRE HACKLE: Hot orange cock
FRONT BODY: Black seal's fur
RIB: Oval silver tinsel
WINGS: Jungle cock, roofed
FRONT HACKLE: Black cock
HEAD: Black

WYE BUG, AGIVEY #3

TAG: Oval silver
TAIL: GP red breast feather, wound
REAR BODY: Red seal's fur
RIB: Oval silver
FRONT BODY: Black seal's fur
RIB: Oval silver tinsel
WINGS: Jungle cock, roofed
FRONT HACKLES: Long hot orange hen
under light brown or red game cock
HEAD: Black

WYE BUG, AGIVEY #4

TAG: Oval silver
TAIL: GP red breast feather, wound
REAR BODY: Red floss
RIB: Oval silver
CENTRE HACKLE: Hot orange cock
FRONT BODY: Black floss
RIB: Oval silver tinsel
WINGS: Jungle cock, roofed
FRONT HACKLE: Light brown or red game cock
HEAD: Black

WYE BUG, AGIVEY #5

TAG: Oval silver
TAIL: GP red breast feather, wound
REAR BODY: Orange seal's fur
RIB: Oval silver
CENTRE HACKLE: Smaller GP red breast feather
FRONT BODY: Black seal's fur
RIB: Oval silver tinsel
WINGS: Jungle cock, roofed
FRONT HACKLE: Black cock
HEAD: Black

WYE BUG, DONEGAL

TAG: Oval silver
TAIL: GP red breast feather, wound
REAR BODY: Orange seal's fur
RIB: Oval silver
REAR VEILINGS: Dyed red hackle tips or
swan strips, above and below
CENTRE HACKLE: Hot orange cock
FRONT BODY: Black seal's fur
RIB: Oval silver tinsel
WINGS: Jungle cock, roofed
FRONT HACKLE: Furnace or dark
Greenwell's cock
HEAD: Red

WYE BUG, McHAFFIE #1

TAG: Oval silver
TAIL: GP red breast feather, wound
REAR BODY: Red seal's fur
RIB: Oval silver
CENTRE HACKLES: White under orange
cock
FRONT BODY: Black seal's fur
RIB: Oval silver tinsel
WINGS: Jungle cock, roofed
FRONT HACKLES: Orange under Furnace or
dark Greenwell's cock
HEAD: Red

WHITE SHRIMP — WHITE SHRIMP - Burns — WILKINSON SHRIMP, DARK

WILKINSON SHRIMP, GOLD — WILKINSON SHRIMP, LIGHT — WYE BUG, AGIVEY #1

WYE BUG, AGIVEY #2 — WYE BUG, AGIVEY #3 — WYE BUG, AGIVEY #4

WYE BUG, AGIVEY #5 — WYE BUG, DONEGAL — WYE BUG, McHAFFIE #1

WYE BUG, McHAFFIE #2

TAG: Oval silver
TAIL: GP red breast feather, wound
REAR BODY: Orange seal's fur
RIB: Oval silver
CENTRE HACKLE: Orange cock
FRONT BODY: Black seal's fur
RIB: Oval silver tinsel
WINGS: Jungle cock, roofed
FRONT HACKLES: Orange under red game cock
HEAD: Red

YABBIE - Betts

TAIL: Red squirrel or goat hair with strands of red Twinkle, very long
BODY: Red floss
RIB: Oval silver
FRONT HACKLE: Orange cock with badger cock over
HEAD: Red

YELLOW SHRIMP

TAG: Oval silver
TAIL: GP red breast feather, wound
REAR BODY: Yellow seal's fur
RIB: Oval silver
CENTRE HACKLE: Yellow cock
FRONT BODY: Black seal's fur
RIB: Oval silver tinsel
WINGS: Jungle cock, roofed
FRONT HACKLE: Silver badger cock
HEAD: Red

WYE BUG, IRISH ORIGINAL

TAG: Oval silver
TAIL: Long furnace cock, wound
REAR BODY: Orange seal's fur
RIB: Oval silver
CENTRE HACKLE: Orange cock
FRONT BODY: Black seal's fur
RIB: Oval silver tinsel
WINGS: Jungle cock, roofed
FRONT HACKLE: Furnace cock
HEAD: Black

YELLOW AND SILVER SHRIMP

TAIL: Long furnace cock, wound
REAR BODY: Flat silver tinsel
RIB: Oval silver
CENTRE HACKLE: Yellow cock
FRONT BODY: Black seal's fur
RIB: Oval silver tinsel
FRONT HACKLE: Silver badger cock
CHEEKS: Jungle cock
HEAD: Red

YELLOW SHRIMP (Low water) - Atkins

REAR BODY: Golden yellow floss
RIB: Fine oval silver
TAIL: Tied at centre joint. GP red breast feather
FRONT BODY: Orange Lite-Brite
RIB: Fine oval silver
FRONT HACKLE: Golden yellow hen
HEAD: Red

WYE GRUB - Kelson

TAG: Silver twist and red silk
TAIL: Yellow macaw and strands of ibis
REAR HACKLE: Jungle cock cheeks, back to back with badger hackle dyed yellow
REAR BODY: Yellow seal's fur
RIB: Oval silver
CENTRE HACKLE: As rear
FRONT BODY: Yellow seal's fur
RIB: Oval silver tinsel
FRONT HACKLE: Jungle cock cheeks, back to back with badger hackle dyed yellow. Two turns guinea fowl dyed yellow over
HEAD: Black

YELLOW PIGLET, Piggott

TAIL: Long yellow bucktail with strands of yellow Crystal Hair
REAR BODY: Medium oval gold tinsel
CENTRE HACKLE: Orange cock
FRONT BODY: Medium oval gold tinsel
FRONT HACKLE: Yellow cock
CHEEKS: Jungle cock
HEAD: Black

WYE BUG, McHAFFIE #2   WYE BUG, IRISH ORIGINAL   WYE GRUB - Kelson

YABBIE - Betts   YELLOW AND SILVER SHRIMP   YELLOW PIGLET - Piggott

YELLOW SHRIMP   YELLOW SHRIMP (Low water)

ALL NIGHT SPEY - Silvey

BODY: Purple floss underbody with a mix of purple and black Lite-Brite dubbing over
RIB: Flat silver & oval silver tinsel
BODY HACKLE: Black marabou
COLLAR HACKLE: Natural guinea fowl
FRONT HACKLE: Silver badger cock
WINGS: Black and purple goose, married
HEAD: Black

AMETHYST SPEY - LeMert

TAG: Fine oval tinsel & red floss
BODY: Four strands peacock sword fibres
RIB: Narrow oval silver tinsel
BODY HACKLE: Blue heron or blue-eared pheasant
COLLAR HACKLE: Purple hackle
THROAT: Red hackle
WING: Mallard dyed purple, tented and tied low
HEAD: Red

AS SPECIFIED #1 SPEY - Lingren

TAG: Flat gold tinsel
TAIL: Purple chinese hen neck hackle
BODY: Rear half, purple floss; front half, purple dubbing
RIB: Medium oval gold tinsel
BODY HACKLE: Black Spey hackle, sparse
COLLAR HACKLE: Teal
WING: Bronze mallard, tented and tied low
HEAD: Red

BARNETT'S SHRIMP

TAIL: GP red breast feather with strands of orange Krystal Flash
EYES: Black plastic
REAR BODY: Pink dubbing
RIB: Flat silver tinsel
CENTRE HACKLE: GP red breast feather fibres, above shank only, teal hackle over
FRONT BODY: Black dubbing
RIB: Flat silver tinsel
COLLAR HACKLE: Guinea fowl dyed blue
HEAD: Black

BLUE KNIGHT SPEY - Bartsch

TAG: Fine oval tinsel & red floss
UNDERBODY: Flat silver tinsel
BODY: Rear half - Silver Doctor blue floss. Front half - blue dubbing
RIB: Flat gold tinsel
BODY HACKLE: Blue Spey hackle
COLLAR HACKLE: Purple chinese neck feather with teal over
WING: Bronze mallard, tented and tied low
HEAD: Black

BONNE-AVENTURE - LeBlanc

TAG: Fine oval tinsel & emerald green floss
TAIL: GP topping, amherst pheasant crest over (1/2 as long), peacock sword fibres over
BUTT: Black ostrich herl
BODY: Rear half - embossed silver tinsel ribbed with three turns emerald green tinsel. Front half - Four clumps of rabbit fur, top & bottom. Green, then blue, red & black, each a little longer than last. Rib between clumps with flat embossed silver tinsel followed by grey heron hackle
COLLAR HACKLE: Guinea fowl, dyed blue
CHEEKS: Long jungle cock, drooping
HEAD: Black

BORDEN'S PRAWN - Borden

EYES: Bead-chain eyes, black apart from purple and black variants which have pearl eyes
ROSTRUM: Hareline Dubbin
ANTENNAE: GP tippet dyed, 10-12 strands Krystal Flash
BODY: Rabbit strip, cut side to side, wound so that fibres lie back naturally
BACK: GP rump feathers dyed, two on #6 hook, three on larger sizes
Colour combinations:

Name	Rostrum	Antennae	Body	Krystal Flash	Back feathers
Red	Fluo red	Red	Red	Pearl	Fluo red
Orange	Hot orange	Hot orange	Hot orange	Fluo fire orange	Fluo orange
Crayfish	Hot orange	Rusty orange	Crayfish	Fluo fire orange	Fluo orange
Yellow	Yellow	Natural	Yellow	Hot yellow	Natural
Hot pink	Fluo hot pink	Hot pink	Hot pink	Fluo shrimp pink	Hot pink
Purple	Purple	Purple	Purple	Dark purple	Purple
Black	Black	Red	Black	Pearl	Fluo red

BOULDER CREEK - Kinney

BODY: Black floss
RIB: Chartreuse Mylar tinsel
BODY HACKLE: Black saddle hackle
THROAT: Kingfisher blue hackle with guinea fowl over
WING: Two GP red flank feathers, back to back
TOPPING: Two GP toppings
HEAD: Black

BROWN LEGGED SHRIMP

BODY: Oval silver tinsel
THROAT HACKLE: Brown hackle
WING: Grey bucktail. Tie in at head and tie down again at rear, forming back and tail
HEAD: Black

BUCKTAIL SHRIMP

TAIL: 5-6 fibres red duck primary feather
UNDERBODY: wool
BODY: Red floss covering underbody
RIB: Wide black tying thread
WING: White bucktail. Tie in at head and tie down again at rear, forming back
WING: Light brown bucktail, dyed red duck primary strips each sise
HEAD: Black

CAR BODY - Kinney

BODY: Black dubbing
RIB: Chartreuse Mylar tinsel
BODY HACKLE: Deep purple saddle hackle
THROAT: Kingfisher blue hackle
WING: Two GP rump feathers dyed deep purple, back to back
HEAD: Black

ALL NIGHT SPEY - Silvey   AMETHYST SPEY - LeMert   AS SPECIFIED #1 SPEY - Lingren

BARNETT'S SHRIMP   BLUE KNIGHT SPEY - Bartsch   BONNE-AVENTURE - LeBlanc

BORDEN'S PRAWN - Borden   BOULDER CREEK - Kinney

BROWN LEGGED SHRIMP   BUCKTAIL SHRIMP   CAR BODY - Kinney

CDC SHRIMP - Schweitzer

TAIL: GP tippet feather, vee-shaped
BODY: Yellow seal's fur
RIB: Oval gold tinsel
BODY VEILINGS: Four white CDC feathers tied in around body at head, extending slightly beyond hook bend
THROAT: White saddle hackle
WING: GP yellow rump feather
HEAD: Black

CDC WING SPEY - Schweitzer

TAG: Flat gold tinsel
BODY: Rear 2/3rds fluorescent chartreuse floss. Front 1/3rd Olive-gold seal's fur
RIB: Flat gold tinsel
WING: Two white CDC feathers, extending slightly beyond hook bend
COLLAR HACKLE: 3 turns black dyed pheasant rump followed by 2-3 turns guinea fowl dyed green
HEAD: Black

COURTESAN - Glasso

BODY: Fluorescent orange floss
RIB: Flat silver tinsel
BODY HACKLE: Long brown saddle hackle
WING: Four matching hot orange hackle tips, extending to hook bend
HEAD: Black

DANNY'S SHRIMP - Ripley

TAG: Flat silver tinsel
TAIL: Shrimp pink or orange hackle fibres
REAR BODY: Pink Phentex yarn
RIB: Oval silver tinsel
CENTRE HACKLE: Badger cock
FRONT BODY: Black Phentex yarn
RIB: Oval silver tinsel
FRONT VEILINGS: Few fibres orange hackle at sides
FRONT HACKLE: Badger cock
WING: Shrimp pink or orange hackle fibres, extending to end of body
HEAD: Red

DEEP PURPLE SPEY - Johnson

BODY: Deep purple mohair
RIB: Flat silver tinsel
BODY HACKLE: Dark brown pheasant rump feather
COLLAR HACKLE: Deep purple dyed hen hackle
WING: GP red breast feathers, back to back
HEAD: Black

DEREK'S SUMMER SPEY - Tay

TAG: Gold Mylar
BODY: Grey wool
RIB: Flat gold Mylar followed by oval gold tinsel
WING: GP red breast feather tied flat-wing style
COLLAR HACKLE: GP red breast feather with ring-necked pheasant rump over
HEAD: Black

DEUCE SPEY - Bartsch

HOOK: Alec Jackson Spey - gold
BODY: Rear half - burnt orange floss. Front half - orange dubbing
RIB: Medium oval gold followed by narrow oval silver tinsel
BODY HACKLE: Yellow Spey hackle
COLLAR HACKLE: Black Spey hackle
THROAT: Teal
WING: Bronze mallard
HEAD: Black

DILEAS - MacLeod

TAG: Fine oval gold tinsel
TAIL: Orange bucktail
REAR BODY (2/3rds): Red floss
RIB: Oval gold tinsel
CENTRE JOINT: Small bunch black bear on top, GP tippet vee-shaped tied underneath curving upwards
FRONT BODY: Orange floss
RIB: Oval gold tinsel
FRONT HACKLES: Orange hen and black hen separated by chartreuse floss
HEAD: Black

DRAGON'S TOOTH - Kinney

TAG: Fine oval silver tinsel
BODY: Purple dubbing or wool
RIB: Flat silver tinsel followed by narrow oval silver tinsel
BODY HACKLE: Deep purple saddle hackle
THROAT HACKLE: Pintail
WING: GP red breast feathers, back to back, veil with GP yellow rump feather both sides
HEAD: Black

DUNMORE SHRIMP - Deane

TAG: Fine oval gold tinsel
TAIL: GP red breast feather, wound
REAR BODY: Rust Dazl-Tron dubbing, tie in eyes after two turns
EYES: 7lb monofilament burn blobbed, black
RIB: Fine oval gold tinsel
CENTRE HACKLE: Fiery brown cock
FRONT BODY: Black Dazl-Tron dubbing
RIB: Oval gold tinsel
WING: Two GP red breast feathers, tied flat, four strands hot orange Krystal Flash over
FRONT HACKLE: Yellow cock
HEAD: Black

ESTUARY SHRIMP - Les Johnson

TAIL: Dyed calf tail and strands of pearl Flashabou
BODY: Dubbing as below
RIB: Tinsel as below
BODY HACKLE: Dyed cock as below
WING: Dyed calf tail as below and pearl Flashabou
TOPPING: Few hair strands as below
HEAD: As below
Colour combinations:

Name	Tail	Body	Rib	Body Hackle	Wing	Topping	Head
Black	Black	Black	Pearl	Sparse black	Black	Hot orange calf	Red
Orange	Orange	Orange	Pearl	Orange	Orange	White polar bear	Orange
Pink	Pink	Pink	Pearl	Pink	Pink	White polar bear	Red
Green	Lime green	Lime green	Pearl	Lime green	Lime green	White polar bear	Green
Tan	Brown squirrel	Gold tinsel	none	Grey pheasant	Brown Squirrel	Grey pheasant	White

CDC SPEY SHRIMP - Schweitzer   CDC SHRIMP - Schweitzer   COURTESAN - Glasso

DANNY'S SHRIMP - Ripley   DEEP PURPLE SPEY - Johnson   DEREK'S SUMMER SPEY - Tay

DEUCE SPEY - Bartsch   DILEAS - MacLeod   DRAGON'S TOOTH - Kinney

DUNMORE SHRIMP - Deane   ESTUARY SHRIMP - Les Johnson

EYE OPENER DEE - Silvey

TAG: Flat gold tinsel
TAIL: GP topping with GP tippet over
BODY: Rear half - Purple SLF. Front half - Claret SLF
RIB: Flat gold tinsel followed by oval silver tinsel
COUNTER RIB: Fine holographic tinsel
BODY HACKLE: Grey heron and claret saddle hackle
WING: White goose slips, tied Dee style
CHEEKS: Jungle cock, slanted downwards
HEAD: Black

FATAL ATTRACTION - Blanton

TAIL: Flashabou, equal in length to hook, colour as below
BODY: Diamond braid, colours as below
COLLAR HACKLE: Long soft saddle or hen hackle, colour as below
WING: Bucktail between two bunches of Krystal Flash. Tied in front of hackle, reaching to middle of tail
WING TOPPING: Several strands of peacock sword

Colour combinations:

Tail	Body	Hackle	Wing
Gold	Gold	Black	Orange bucktail between gold and pearl Krystal Flash
Silver	Silver	White	White bucktail between silver and pearl Krystal Flash
Copper	Copper	Chartreuse	Orange bucktail between pearl and peacock Krystal Flash

F. P. SHRIMP - Dunne

TAIL: Fluorescent orange squirrel tail and a GP red breast feather, wound
BODY: Three parts - fluorescent orange dubbing
RIB: Rear third, fluo green nylon. Middle third, fluo green nylon. Front third, red Uni-Yarn
HACKLES: At each body joint a GP red breast feather, wound with a GP red breast feather over
WING: GP red breast feathers with strands of hot orange Krystal Flash over
HEAD: Red

GABY - Boivin

TAG: Flat silver Mylar
TAIL: 4 to 6 strands lime green Krystal Flash
BODY: Rear 2/3rds lime green Krystal Flash wrapped over underbody of silver Mylar
VEILING: 4 to 6 strands lime green Krystal Flash
BODY: Front 1/3rd Fine oval silver tinsel and 4 to 6 strands black ostrich herl wound together
BODY HACKLE: Black heron over front 1/3rd
WING: Sparse black squirrel or bear
COLLAR HACKLE: Long mallard flank dyed chartreuse
HEAD: Black

GASPEY HIGHLANDER

TAG: Flat silver Mylar
TAIL: GP topping with red dyed topping over
BUTT: Black ostrich herl
BODY: Rear 1/2 - golden yellow dubbing. Front 1/2 - bright green dubbing
RIB: Fine oval silver tinsel, counterwound over body hackle
BODY HACKLE: Mallard flank dyed fluorescent green over green body
THROAT: Fluorescent yellow hen hackle
WING: GP tippet with bronze mallard over
COLLAR HACKLE: Long mallard flank dyed chartreuse
HEAD: Black

GENERAL PRACTITIONER, SIMPLIFIED

TAIL: Orange calf tail with orange Krystal Flash over
BODY: Red-orange SLF dubbing
RIB: Flat gold tinsel
BODY HACKLE: Orange saddle hackle
WING: GP tippet with GP red breast feather over
HEAD: Red

GENERAL PRACTITIONER, BLACK - Lingren

TAIL: Black squirrel tail with small GP red breast feather over
BODY: Black mohair or wool, lead wire weighting under
RIB: Medium oval silver tinsel
BODY HACKLE: Black cock hackle, palmered and trimmed on top
EYES: GP tippet feather tied in about 1/3rd along body
BACK: Black cock or hen spade feathers tied in at eye position and front
WING: GP tippet with GP red breast feather
HEAD: Black

GENERAL PRACTITIONER, BLACK MARABOU - Gallagher

TAIL: Bunch Krafty fur between sparse black polar bear hairs. Two bunches GP tippet fibres tied in each side
BODY: Black seal's fur
RIB: Medium pearl Mylar
BODY HACKLE: Black saddle hackle, palmered
BACK: Black marabou plumes tied in halfway along body and at head
HEAD: Black

GENERAL PRACTITIONER, ED'S BLACK - Taylor

TAG: Silver Mylar tinsel
TAIL: Black hair
BODY: Black wool
RIB: Flat silver Mylar tinsel
EYES: Small jungle cock tied in 1/3rd along body
BODY HACKLE: Black cock
THROAT: Long teal, dyed orange
WING: Five strands copper Flashabou, black hair over
HEAD: Black

G.P. GREEN - Freeman

TAG: Oval silver tinsel and green dubbing
TAIL: Bunch bucktail dyed fluorescent green with GP body feather dyed green over
BODY: Green Highlander SLF dubbing
RIB: Oval silver tinsel
EYES: GP tippet feather dyed green
BODY HACKLE: Highlander green cock hackle
THROAT: Highlander green cock hackle
BACK: Green saddle feather with green dyed GP body feather over, tied in halfway along body and at head
HEAD: Green
Blue version: change green elements to blue

GENERAL PRACTITIONER, HAIRWING - Melanson

TAG: Oval gold tinsel
TAIL: GP tippet with GP red breast feather over
BODY: Orange seal's fur
RIB: Oval gold
THROAT: Orange cock
WING: GP red breast feather fibres, extending to hook bend
HEAD: Red

EYE OPENER DEE - Silvey   FATAL ATTRACTION - Blanton

F. P. SHRIMP - Dunne   GABY - Boivin   GASPEY HIGHLANDER

GP, SIMPLIFIED   GP, BLACK - Lingren   GP, BLACK MARABOU - Gallagher

GP, ED'S BLACK - Taylor   GP, GREEN - Freeman   GP, HAIRWING - Melanson

GENERAL PRACTITIONER, IMPROVISED - Kinney

TAIL: Orange bucktail fibres with two small GP red breast feathers over
BODY: Hot orange wool in two joints. At centre tie in GP tippet feather with orange dyed pheasant rump hackle
RIB: Flat silver tinsel
THROAT: Long teal, dyed orange
WING: Two small GP red breast feathers dyed orange. Natural GP red breast feather over
HEAD: Red

GENERAL PRACTITIONER, PURPLE

TAIL: Purple bucktail fibres. Black cock hackle
BODY: Black seals fur
BODY HACKLE: Black saddle hackle
THROAT: Long black saddle hackle
WING: GP tippet feather with black dyed GP breast feather over. Tie in at centre body and head
HEAD: Black

GENERAL PRACTITIONER, RED - Wallace

TAIL: Polar bear dyed red, two small GP red breast feathers over
BODY: Scarlet seals fur
RIB: Oval gold tinsel
BODY HACKLE: Scarlet saddle hackle
CENTRE JOINT: GP tippet feather dyed red with GP breast feather over
WING: GP red breast feather
CHEEKS: Jungle cock
HEAD: Black

GIBB'S SHRIMP

TAG: Oval silver tinsel
TAIL: GP red breast feather, wound. Blue kingfisher body feather on each side
REAR BODY: Flat silver tinsel with flame red seal's fur at front
RIB: Oval silver tinsel
VEILING: Bright blue kingfisher at sides
CENTRE HACKLE: Claret saddle hackle
FRONT BODY: As rear body
RIB: Oval silver tinsel
VEILING: Bright blue kingfisher at sides
WING: Very long jungle cock, back to back
FRONT HACKLE: Long claret saddle
HEAD: Red

GLEN GRANT - Whorwood

TAIL: GP yellow body feather
BODY: Three turns yellow seal's fur, black seal's fur
RIB: Flat silver tinsel
BODY HACKLE: Grey heron
THROAT: Teal
WING: Three pairs jungle cock feathers, reducing in size towards head, teal over
HEAD: Yellow seal's fur

GOLD STREAK - Howell

TAG: Flat gold tinsel
BODY: Rear half - orange floss. Front half - Hot orange seal's fur
RIB: Oval gold tinsel
BODY HACKLE: Grey heron
THROAT: Guinea fowl dyed orange
WING: Bronze mallard
HEAD: Black

GOLDEN SPEY - Bartsch

TAG: Flat silver tinsel
BODY: Underbody - flat silver tinsel. Rear half - yellow floss. Front half - black dubbing
RIB: Large oval silver tinsel
CENTRE JOINT: Pair GP tippet feathers, back to back
BODY HACKLE: Blue-eared pheasant dyed black following rib over front body
COLLAR HACKLE: Blue-eared pheasant dyed black
TOPPING: GP topping
HEAD: Black

GOLDEN SPEY - Johnson

BODY: Fluorescent yellow floss underbody overlaid with deep yellow seal's fur
RIB: Flat embossed gold tinsel
BODY HACKLE: White-black heron breast dyed golden olive
COLLAR HACKLE: Orange dyed hen hackle
WING: Two light brown hackles, back to back. Tied low over body
HEAD: Black

GREEN BUTT SPEY

TAG: Flat silver tinsel
TAIL: Red hackle fibres
BUTT: Fluorescent green floss
BODY: Black seal's fur
RIB: Flat silver tinsel
COLLAR HACKLE: Long black spey hackle
WING: Bunch white polar bear hair
HEAD: Black

GREEN HIGHLANDER SHRIMP

TAG: Oval silver tinsel
TAIL: GP red breast feather, wound
REAR BODY: Green floss
RIB: Oval silver
CENTRE HACKLES: Green cock
FRONT BODY: Green floss
RIB: Oval silver
FRONT HACKLES: Yellow cock
HEAD: Red

HARLEQUIN SPEY - Brocco

TAG: Oval gold tinsel and red floss
TAIL: Peacock sword fibres
BODY: Deep orange, red and purple seal's fur, equally divided
RIB: Narrow oval gold tinsel
HACKLE: GP red body feather
WING: White polar bear hair
COLLAR HACKLE: Bronze mallard
HEAD: Red

H.D. PURPLE SPEY - Bartsch

TAG: Flat silver tinsel
TAIL: Peacock sword fibres
BODY: Underbody - flat silver tinsel. Rear half - red floss. Front half - purple dubbing
RIB: Narrow oval silver tinsel
HACKLE: Purple Spey hackle
COLLAR HACKLE: Teal
WING: Bronze mallard
HEAD: Red

GP, IMPROVISED - Kinney GENERAL PRACTITIONER, PURPLE GP, RED - Wallace

GIBB'S SHRIMP GLEN GRANT GOLD STREAK - Howell

GOLDEN SPEY - Bartsch GOLDEN SPEY - Johnson GREEN BUTT SPEY

GREEN HIGHLANDER SHRIMP HARLEQUIN SPEY - Brocco H.D. PURPLE SPEY - Bartsch

HERON, BLACK & ORANGE - Veverka

BODY: Rear half - black floss. Front half - orange seal's fur
RIB: Two narrow strands oval silver tinsel with strand fluorescent floss between
HACKLE: Black and orange Spey hackle
WING: Two orange hackle tips flanked by two black hackle tips
HEAD: Black

HERON, BLUE - Veverka

BODY: Rear half - deep blue floss. Front half - blue seal's fur
RIB: Flat silver tinsel and fine oval silver tinsel
HACKLE: Grey heron hackle
THROAT: Teal
WING: Two blue hackle tips
HEAD: Black

HERON, BROWN - Glasso

BODY: Rear 2/3rds - orange floss. Front 1/3rd - hot orange seal's fur
RIB: Flat silver tinsel and fine oval silver tinsel
HACKLE: Grey heron hackle
THROAT: Teal
WING: Bronze mallard
HEAD: Red

HERON, BROWN - McNeese

BODY: Rear fl - orange floss. Front fl - hot orange seal's fur
RIB: Flat silver tinsel and fine oval gold tinsel
HACKLE: Grey heron over front body only
COLLAR HACKLE: Teal
WING: Bronze mallard reaching to end of body
HEAD: Red

HERON, GOLD - Glasso

BODY: Rear 2/3rds - flat gold tinsel. Front 1/3rd - hot orange seal's fur
RIB: Fine oval gold tinsel
HACKLE: Grey heron
THROAT: Widgeon flank
WING: Widgeon flank reaching to end of body
HEAD: Orange

HERON, GOLDEN - McNeese

TAG: Flat silver tinsel
BODY: Medium flat gold tinsel
RIB: Fine oval silver tinsel
HACKLE: Long black heron
THROAT: Widgeon flank
WING: Four golden macaw breast feathers or substitute. Thin section bronze mallard over
CHEEKS: Jungle cock
HEAD: Orange

Note: Red Heron - identical but wing of red macaw or hackle tips dyed red

HERON, GREEN - Veverka

BODY: Rear half - fluorescent green floss. Front half - green seal's fur
RIB: Flat gold tinsel and fine oval gold tinsel
HACKLE: Black heron hackle
THROAT: Hooded merganser flank
WING: Four fluorescent green hackle tips
HEAD: Red

HERON, GREY - Gobin

BODY: Rear 1/3rd - yellow floss. Front 2/3rds - black floss
RIB: Flat silver tinsel followed by oval silver tinsel
HACKLE: Long black heron
THROAT: Guinea fowl
WING: Bronze mallard
HEAD: Black

HERON, GREY - Solo

BODY: Rear 1/3rd - yellow wool. Front 2/3rds - black wool
RIB: Flat silver tinsel followed by oval silver tinsel, oval gold tinsel counterwound over body hackle
HACKLE: Long grey Chinese cock behind oval silver tinsel
THROAT: Guinea fowl
WING: Natural grey squirrel dyed dark brown
HEAD: Black

HERON, ORANGE #1 - Howell

TAG: Flat silver tinsel
BODY: Rear 1/2 - fluorescent orange floss. Front 1/2 - hot orange seal's fur
RIB: Fine oval gold tinsel
HACKLE: Long black heron
THROAT: Teal, two turns
WING: Four matching hackle tips, dyed orange
CHEEKS: Jungle cock
HEAD: Red

HERON, ORANGE #2 - Howell

TAG: Flat silver tinsel
BODY: Rear 1/2 - fluorescent orange floss. Front 1/2 - hot orange seal's fur
RIB: Fine oval gold tinsel
HACKLE: Long grey heron
THROAT: Teal, two turns
WING: Peacock secondary wing quills
HEAD: Red

HERON, ORANGE - Glasso

TAG: Flat silver tinsel
BODY: Rear 2/3rds - fluorescent orange floss. Front 1/3rd - orange seal's fur
RIB: Medium flat silver tinsel
HACKLE: Long grey heron
THROAT: Teal flank
WING: Four matching hot orange hackle tips, tied low
HEAD: Red

HERON, BLACK & ORANGE - Veverka   HERON, BLUE - Veverka   HERON, BROWN - Glasso

HERON, BROWN - McNeese   HERON, GOLD - Glasso   HERON, GOLDEN - McNeese

HERON, GREEN - Veverka   HERON, GREY - Gobin   HERON, GREY - Solo

HERON, ORANGE #1 - Howell   HERON, ORANGE #2 - Howell   HERON, ORANGE - Glasso

HERON, ORANGE - Gobin

TAG: Flat silver tinsel
BODY: Rear 1/4 - orange floss. Front 3/4 - orange seal's fur
RIB: Flat gold tinsel and oval silver tinsel. Narrow oval silver tinsel counterwound over hackle
HACKLE: Long black Spey hackle or schlappen
THROAT: Teal flank
WING: Bronze mallard
HEAD: Red

HERON, RUSTY - Veverka

TAG: Flat silver tinsel
BODY: Rear 1/2 - fluorescent orange floss. Front 1/2 - orange seal's fur
RIB: Flat silver tinsel and oval silver tinsel.
HACKLE: Grey heron
THROAT: GP red breast feather
WING: Two yellow hackle tips flanked by two orange or red hackle tips
HEAD: Red

HERON, SILVER - Glasso

TAG: Flat silver tinsel
BODY: Rear 2/3rds - flat silver tinsel. Front 1/3rd - black seal's fur
RIB: Oval silver tinsel.
HACKLE: Grey heron
THROAT: Guinea fowl
WING: Grey heron slips
HEAD: Black

HORNER'S SILVER SHRIMP - Horner

TAIL: Grey bucktail. Tie in second bunch for carapace
BODY: Oval silver tinsel over floss underbody. Space tinsel and palmer hackle in the spaces. Bring carapace bucktail forward over back and tie in at head
HACKLE: Grizzle hackle
HEAD: Large black with painted eye

HORNEY SHRIMP - Butorac

TAIL: Salmon marabou, 1.5" (38mm) long
EYES: Modelling pins with black heads
BODY: Fluorescent salmon chenille
BODY HACKLE: Light orange hackle
WING/BACK: Red marabou slicked back with head cement
HEAD: Flame red floss

ICE BLUE SPEY - Bartsch

BODY: Rear 1/2 - blue tinsel. Front 1/2 - black dubbing
RIB: Small oval silver tinsel
HACKLE: Black Spey hackle
COLLAR: Teal
WING: Bronze mallard
HEAD: Black

JOE'S SHRIMP

TAG: Oval gold tinsel
TAIL: Hot orange bucktail, strands of orange Krystal Flash. GP red breast feather over
EYES: Large black beads
BODY: Orange dubbing
RIB: Small oval silver tinsel
REAR HACKLE: GP red breast feather
FRONT HACKLE: GP red breast feather
WING: Pair GP red breast feathers
HEAD: Red

JONES' SPECIAL - LeBlanc

TAG: Oval silver tinsel
BODY: Pearl UNI Axxel Flash
RIB: Small oval silver tinsel, seven turns
WING: White bucktail under pearl blue Krystal Flash. Light brown bucktail over
HACKLE: Grey heron followed by silver pheasant, both tied collar fashion
CHEEKS: Jungle cock
HEAD: White & blue

K.C's STEELHEAD SPEY - Chandler

TAG: Silver Mylar tinsel
BODY: Black floss or yarn
RIB: Silver Mylar tinsel
THORAX: Black ostrich herl
WING: White bucktail under pearl blue Krystal Flash. Light brown bucktail over
COLLAR HACKLE: Black Spey hackle
HEAD: Black

KISPIOX SHRIMP - Craig

BODY: Underbody wrap - 20 turns 3/0 lead wire. Flame orange fluorescent yarn, left long at rear to represent rostrum
RIB: Heavy copper or gold wire
EYES: Silver bead-chain eyes
BODY HACKLE: Orange saddle hackle, long at rear
BACK: Orange Krystal Flash covered with heavy clear plastic. Krystal flash left 1" (25mm) long at tail to represent feelers
HEAD: Red

LADY CAROLINE - Solo

TAIL: GP red breast feather fibres
BODY: Blend 1/3rd olive green and 2/3rds light brown wool
RIB: Flat gold tinsel followed by oval gold tinsel, oval silver tinsel counterwound over body hackle
HACKLE: Long grey Chinese cock behind oval gold tinsel
THROAT: GP red breast feather
WING: Natural grey squirrel dyed dark brown
HEAD: Black

LAPOINTE SHRIMP

TAG: Oval gold tinsel and pale yellow floss
TAIL: GP tippet, 6 to 10 strands, tied upright
BODY: Pink floss
RIB: Flat gold tinsel
THROAT: Few turns yellow hackle before wing, few turns olive-green hackle after wing
WING: Small bunch silver monkey hair with small bunch of mixed brown and white bucktail over
HEAD: Black

HERON, ORANGE - Gobin   HERON, RUSTY - Veverka   HERON, SILVER - Glasso

HORNER'S SILVER SHRIMP   HORNEY SHRIMP - Butorac   ICE BLUE SPEY - Bartsch

JOE'S SHRIMP   JONES' SPECIAL - LeBlanc   K.C's STEELHEAD SPEY - Chandler

KISPIOX SHRIMP - Craig   LADY CAROLINE - Solo   LAPOINTE SHRIMP

LEMON GREY SPEY

TAG: Oval silver tinsel
BODY: Rear 1/2 - light grey seal's fur. Front 1/2 - lemon yellow seal's fur
RIB: Flat silver tinsel
BODY HACKLE: Long grey heron or substitute
THROAIndexT: Yellow hackle
WING: Small bunch red brown bucktail with dark brown bucktail over
HEAD: Black

LESTER THE LOBSTER

TAIL: Orange bucktail and 2 to 4 strands orange Krystal Flash
EYES: Black beads on monofilament
BODY: Orange wool, tapered
RIB: Oval copper tinsel, over body but beneath back
BODY HACKLE: Orange, palmered
BACK: Orange surveyor's tape 1/8" to 1/4" (3 to 6mm) wide, depending upon hook size
RIB 2: 4lb monofilament over everything
HEAD: Red with vee-shaped tail extending over hook eye

LOGAN'S SILVER TIP SPEY - McLeod

TAG: Flat silver Mylar
BODY: Rear 1/3rd - flat silver Mylar. Front 2/3rds - black wool
RIB: Oval silver tinsel
BODY HACKLE: Grey heron or marabou
THROAT: Teal
WING: Bronze mallard
HEAD: Black

MACKENZIE - Boudreau

TAG: Oval gold tinsel
TAIL: 2 GP red breast feathers, wound
BUTT: Orange ostrich herl
REAR BODY (2/3rds): Flat copper tinsel
RIB: Oval gold tinsel
FRONT BODY (1/3rd): Orange wool
RIB: Flat gold holographic tinsel and oval gold tinsel
BODY HACKLE: Over front 1/3rd of body only, heron hackle
COLLAR HACKLE: Guinea fowl
WING: Teal or bronze mallard
EYES: Jungle cock
HEAD: Red

MARABOU SPEY - Farrar

BODY: Rear 1/3rd - flat gold Mylar. Front 2/3rds - half and half red and then orange dubbing
BODY HACKLE: Half and half orange and then red marabou
THROAT: GP red breast feather
WING: Bronze mallard
HEAD: Red

MATEPEDIA SPEY - Sturrock

TAG: Oval silver tinsel and chartreuse floss
BODY: Peacock herl
RIB: Oval silver tinsel
BODY HACKLE: Long grey heron or substitute
COLLAR HACKLES: GP red breast feather under teal
WING: Bronze mallard
HEAD: Red

MICKEY MOUSE SPEY - Whyet

TAG: Silver Mylar
BODY: Black floss
RIB: Emerald green floss and oval silver tinsel
THORAX: Black ostrich herl
COLLAR HACKLE: Black Spey hackle
CHEEKS: Jungle cock
HEAD: Black

MIDNIGHT SPEY - Noble

TAG: Flat silver Tinsel
BODY: Rear 1/2 - purple floss. Front 1/2 - purple seals fur
RIB: Flat silver tinsel
BODY HACKLE: From 2nd tinsel turn. Purple pheasant flank or Spey hackle
THROAT HACKLE: Blue schlappen
UNDERWING: Purple goose primary 1/4" (6mm) long, solely to support wing
WING: From bottom to top - 5 fibres green, 5 fibres blue, married, 7-8 fibres purple over to give married appearance
HEAD: Red

MILWAUKEE SPEY - Blumreich

TAG: Flat silver Tinsel
BODY: Rear 1/2 - hot pinl seal's fur. Front 1/2 - black seals fur
RIB: Flat silver tinsel
BODY HACKLE: Over black body, hot pink Spey hackle or marabou
THROAT: Mallard flank dyed hot pink
WING: Narrow strips black goose, set low and tented
HEAD: Black

MOISIE GRUB

TAIL: GP topping
REAR BODY: Yellow floss
CENTRE HACKLE: Short black cock
FRONT BODY: Black herl
FRONT HACKLE: Natural guinea fowl under grizzle cock
HEAD: Black

OCTOBER SPEY - Stetzer

BODY: Hot orange seal's fur or goat
RIB: Oval gold tinsel and fine gold wire
BODY HACKLE: Black heron
THROAT HACKLE: Mallard or teal flank, dyed hot orange
WING: Bronze mallard
HEAD: Red

ORANGE CDC SHRIMP - Schweitzer

HOOK: Alec Jackson Spey - gold
TAG: 10 turns fine round gold tinsel and Pearsall's orange silk
TAIL: 3 peacock sword plumes extending to hook bend
BODY: Orange seal's fur
RIB: Oval gold tinsel
BODY VEILINGS: Four orange CDC feathers tied in around body at head, extending to slightly beyond hook bend
COLLAR HACKLE: GP red rump feather
TOPPING: Strands peacock sword feathers
HEAD: Black

LEMON GREY SPEY   LESTER THE LOBSTER   LOGAN'S SILVER TIP SPEY - McLeod

MACKENZIE - Boudreau   MARABOU SPEY - Farrar   MATEPEDIA SPEY - Sturrock

MICKEY MOUSE SPEY - Whyet   MIDNIGHT SPEY - Noble   MILWAUKEE SPEY - Blumreich

MOISIE GRUB   OCTOBER SPEY - Stetzer   ORANGE CDC SHRIMP - Schweitzer

ORANGE LEGGED SHRIMP

BODY: Oval silver tinsel
THROAT HACKLE: Orange hackle
WING: Grey bucktail. Tie in at head and tie
down again at rear, forming back and tail
HEAD: Black

ORANGE SHRIMP

TAG: Gold tinsel
TAIL: Red hackle fibres
BODY: Orange wool or chenille
HACKLE: Orange
WING: White bucktail
HEAD: Black

ORANGE SHRIMP - McNeese

TAG: Gold tinsel
TAIL: Red hackle fibres
BODY: Orange wool or chenille
RIB: Flat gold tinsel
BODY HACKLE: Orange, palmered
COLLAR HACKLE: GP red breast feather
WING: White bucktail
EYES: Jungle cock
HEAD: Black

ORANGE SPEY - Strobel

TAG: Flat gold tinsel, 1/3rd body length
BODY: Orange seal's fur
RIB: Flat gold tinsel
BODY HACKLE: Grey heron over seal's fur
WING: White hackle tips
COLLAR HACKLE: Guinea fowl dyed orange
HEAD: Red

ORANGE SPEY - Bartsch

TAG: Flat gold tinsel
BODY: Underbody - flat gold tinsel. Rear 1/2 -
orange floss. Front 1/2 - orange dubbing
RIB: Oval gold tinsel
BODY HACKLE: Long natural blue-eared
pheasant
COLLAR HACKLE: Teal
WING: Bronze mallard
HEAD: Red

OUT TO LUNCH - LeBlanc

TAG: Embossed silver tinsel
TAIL: Five or six peacock sword fibres
BODY: Embossed silver tinsel
RIB: Emerald green oval tinsel
WING: Lime green or olive Krystal Flash
COLLAR HACKLE: Very long yellow heron
followed by black heron about half as long
CHEEKS: Jungle cock
HEAD: Black

PETE'S SHRIMP - McVey

TAIL: Fluorescent orange polar bear hair, long
and sparse
BUTT: Black chenille
BODY: Fluorescent flame chenille
BODY HACKLE: Long hot orange hackle
WING: GP tippet feather under GP red breast
feather
HEAD: Black

PHEASANT SHRIMP - Silvey

TAIL: GP red breast feather
BUTT: Black chenille
BODY: Fluorescent flame chenille
BODY HACKLE: Long hot orange hackle
WING: GP tippet feather under GP red breast
feather
HEAD: Black

PINK SHRIMP

TAIL: Two matching fluorescent pink saddle
hackle tips
BODY: Oval silver tinsel
BODY HACKLE: Fluorescent pink saddle
hackle
BACK: Fluorescent pink bucktail tied in at tail,
brought forward and tied off at head
HEAD: White

POLAR SHRIMP - Brooks

TAG: Flat gold tinsel
TAIL: GP red breast feather tip
BODY: Bright orange seal's fur
RIB: Flat gold tinsel
BODY HACKLE: Hot orange saddle hackle
from 2nd turn of tinsel
WING: Soft white hair, extending to tag
COLLAR HACKLE: GP red breast feather to
hook bend
HEAD: Red

POLAR SHRIMP, DARK - Gobin

TAG: Oval silver tinsel
BODY: Rear 1/2 - rose red floss. Front 1/2 -
rose red seal's fur
RIB: Flat silver tinsel and narrow oval silver
tinsel
BODY HACKLE: Rose red hackle
THROAT: Guinea fowl, one turn
WING: Bronze mallard
HEAD: Black

Note: Rose red - 2/3rds hot orange, 1/3rd
magenta

POLAR SHRIMP, LIGHT - Gobin

TAG: Oval silver tinsel
BODY: Rear 1/2 - deep orange red floss.
Front 1/2 - hot orange seal's fur
RIB: Narrow oval silver tinsel
BODY HACKLE: Hot orange hackle
THROAT: Pintail, one turn
WING: White goose
HEAD: Black

ORANGE LEGGED SHRIMP

ORANGE SHRIMP

ORANGE SHRIMP - McNeese

ORANGE SPEY - Strobel

ORANGE SPEY - Bartsch

OUT TO LUNCH - LeBlanc

PETE'S SHRIMP - McVey

PHEASANT SHRIMP - Silvey

PINK SHRIMP

POLAR SHRIMP - Brooks

POLAR SHRIMP, DARK - Gobin

POLAR SHRIMP, LIGHT - Gobin

POLAR SHRIMP - Tolley

TAIL: Orange hackle fibres
BODY: Rear 1/2 - flat gold tinsel. Front 1/2 -
orange polar bear underhair
WING: White polar bear with orange hackle
tip over
COLLAR HACKLE: Orange hackle
HEAD: Black

POLAR SPEY - Blumreich

BODY: Hot orange SLF
RIB: Oval gold tinsel
BODY HACKLE: Red-tipped orange marabou
THROAT: Mallard flank, dyed red
WING: Narrow strips of white goose
HEAD: Black

POMPIER SHRIMP

TAIL: Long yellow hair
BODY: Black floss
RIB: Oval gold tinsel
WING: GP tippet in vee-form
COLLAR HACKLE: Bright green cock
HEAD: Red

PRAWN FLY - Johnson/Shreeve

BODY: Pale purple floss, veiled with light pink
seal's fur
RIB: Narrow embossed pink tinsel
BODY HACKLE: White-black heron
COLLAR HACKLE: Pale pink heron
WING: Narrow strips of dyed light blue goose
HEAD: Black

PRISMATIC SPEY - Noble

TAG: Flat gold tinsel
BODY: Rear 1/2 - hot orange floss. Front 1/2
- hot tangerine (50% red, 50% orange) seal's
fur
RIB: Flat gold tinsel
BODY HACKLE: Yellow schlappen
COLLAR HACKLE: Hot orange
UNDERWING: Hot orange goose primary
1/4" (6mm) long, solely to support wing
WING: From bottom to top - 3 fibres
magenta, 2 purple, 2 green, 2 blue and 2
orange fibres, married. Single strip of red over
to give married appearance
HEAD: Flame red

PURPLE & PINK SPEY - Silvey

BODY: Purple floss
RIB: Oval silver and oval pink tinsel
BODY HACKLE: Purple marabou
THORAX: 50% mix. purple & pink SLF
COLLAR HACKLE: GP breast feather, dyed
pink
WING: Whiting hen cape dyed pink
HEAD: Black

PURPLE BRAT - McNeese

TAG: Flat silver tinsel
TAIL: GP topping, dyed red
RIB: Oval silver tinsel
BODY: Rear 1/3rd - fluorescent orange floss
and then fluorescent red floss. Front 2/3rds -
hot purple seal's fur
BODY HACKLE: Long hot purple from 3rd
turn of rib
WING: Hot orange polar bear with a few
strands of orange Krystal Flash, purple polar
bear over
CHEEKS: Jungle cock
HEAD: Black

PURPLE HEART SPEY #1 - Veverka

BODY: Rear 1/2 - fluorescent red floss. Front
1/2 - purple seal's fur
RIB: Oval silver tinsel
BODY HACKLE: Purple Spey hackle
THROAT: Black hackle
WING: Two red hackle tips flanked by two
purple hackle tips
HEAD: Black

PURPLE HEART SPEY #2 - Veverka

BODY: Rear 1/2 - red floss. Front 1/2 - blue
SLF salmon fly dubbing
RIB: Oval silver tinsel
BODY HACKLE: Purple Spey hackle
THROAT: GP red breast feather
WING: Purple goose quill
HEAD: Red

PURPLE KING

BODY: Deep purple floss
RIB: Strand of deep purple floss with oval
silver tinsel. Gold thread counterwound over
body hackle
BODY HACKLE: Black schlappen
THROAT: Guinea fowl
WING: Bronze mallard
HEAD: Black

PURPLE PERIL SPEY

TAG: Flat silver tinsel
TAIL: Purple hackle fibres
BODY: Purple seal's fur
RIB: Oval silver tinsel
BODY HACKLE: Purple marabou
THROAT: Black spey hackle
WING: Brown bucktail
HEAD: Black

PURPLE PRINCE - McNeese

TAG: Flat silver tinsel
TAIL: GP topping and Indian crow substitute
BODY: Rear 1/2 - fluorescent red floss. Front
1/2 - fluorescent orange seal's fur
RIB: Oval silver tinsel
BODY HACKLE: Hot purple pintail flank
THROAT: Long pintail flank
UNDERWING: Hot orange hackle tips
WING: GP flank dyed purple, two GP toppings
over
CHEEKS: Jungle cock
HEAD: Black

POLAR SHRIMP - Tolley

POLAR SPEY - Blumreich

POMPIER SHRIMP

PRAWN FLY - Johnson/Shreeve

PRISMATIC SPEY - Noble

PURPLE & PINK SPEY - Silvey

PURPLE BRAT - McNeese

PURPLE HEART SPEY #1 - Veverka

PURPLE HEART SPEY #2 - Veverka

PURPLE KING

PURPLE PERIL SPEY

PURPLE PRINCE - McNeese

PURPLE SPEY - McNeese

BODY: Rear 1/3rd - fluorescent orange floss over flat silver tinsel. Front 2/3rds - purple seal's fur
RIB: Oval silver tinsel
BODY HACKLE: Long black heron
THROAT: Long pintail flank
WING: GP flank dyed purple, two GP toppings dyed purple over
CHEEKS: Jungle cock
HEAD: Black

PURPLE SPEY - Strobel

TAIL: Clump of rabbit fur dyed purple
BODY: Rear 2/3rds - flat silver tinsel. Front 1/3rd - purple seal's fur
BODY HACKLE: Purple Spey hackle over purple seal's fur
COLLAR HACKLE: Blue-eared pheasant with black dyed pheasant over
HEAD: Purple

PURPLE SPEY - Gobin

TAIL: Clump of rabbit fur dyed purple
BODY: Rear 1/4 - hot pink floss. Front 3/4 - deep purple floss
RIB: Oval silver tinsel
BODY HACKLE: Purple dyed schlappen
THROAT: Guinea fowl
WING: Bronze mallard
HEAD: Black

PURPLE SPEY - Schweitzer

TAIL: Clump of rabbit fur dyed purple
BODY: Rear 2/3rds - flat gold tinsel. Front 1/3rd - red-purple seal's fur
BODY HACKLE: Blue-eared pheasant
COLLAR HACKLE: Guinea fowl dyed red-purple
HEAD: Black

RALLAYE - LeBlanc

TAG: Flat gold tinsel
TAIL: GP topping with GP red breast feather fibres over
BODY: Rear 1/2 - black floss. Front 1/2 - black seal's fur
RIB: Rear 1/2 - oval gold tinsel. Front 1/2 - Flat gold tinsel and gold twist
BODY HACKLE: Very long black heron over front half of body
THROAT: Teal
WING: Two sections orange goose, one section mottled goose
CHEEKS: Jungle cock
HEAD: Black

RAY'S SPEY - Plourde

TAG: Oval gold tinsel
TAIL: GP red breast feather, wound
REAR BODY: Peach floss
RIB: Fine oval gold tinsel
CENTRE HACKLE: GP yellow body feather
FRONT BODY: Deep purple floss
RIB: Medium oval gold tinsel
FRONT HACKLE: GP red breast feather
WINGS: Jungle cock, back to back
HEAD: Black

RED & PURPLE SPEY - Bartsch

TAG: Flat silver tinsel
RIB: Oval silver tinsel
UNDERBODY: Flat silver tinsel
BODY: Rear 1/2 - red floss. Front 1/2 - purple seal's fur
HACKLE: Long purple marabou
COLLAR HACKLE: Two GP feathers dyed black
HEAD: Black

RED DOG - Brooks

TAG: Flat silver tinsel
RIB: Wide flat silver tinsel and medium oval silver tinsel
BODY: Bright red Berlin wool
BODY HACKLE: Heron dyed brown or brown Spey hackle
COLLAR HACKLE: Teal
WING: Bronze mallard
HEAD: Red

RED SHRIMP - Johnson

BODY: Fluorescent orange floss veiled with red seal's fur
RIB: Flat silver tinsel
BODY HACKLE: Brown pheasant rump feather
COLLAR HACKLE: Red hen hackle
WING: Red dyed hackle tips or turkey strips dyed red with GP topping over
HEAD: Red

RED SHRIMP - Schweitzer

BODY: Build up underbody of floss and cover with oval silver tinsel
BACK: Tie in red bucktail fibres at head, stretch over back and tie down again at tail position to form carapace
RIB: Rib body with black tying thread
HEAD: Black

REIFF'S SHRIMP - Reiff

UNDERBODY: Burnt orange seal's fur
EYES: Insect mounting pins coloured black
BODY: Fluorescent orange floss veiled with red seal's fur
CARAPACE: Tie in red polar bear hair fibres at head, stretch over back and tie down again at tail position to form carapace
RIB: Red tying thread
THROAT: Red polar bear hair to hook point
HEAD: Red

ROYAL SPEY - Johnson

TAG: Silver tinsel overlaid with cerise floss
BODY: Peacock herl and fluorescent pink wool
BODY HACKLE: White-black heron dyed fluorescent pink over pink body section
COLLAR HACKLE: Fluorescent pink hen
WING: Two light blue hackle tips set low over body
CHEEKS: Lady Amherst pheasant tippets dyed blue
HEAD: Black

PURPLE SPEY - McNeese   PURPLE SPEY - Strobel   PURPLE SPEY - Gobin

PURPLE SPEY - Schweitzer   RALLAYE - LeBlanc   RAY'S SPEY - Plourde

RED & PURPLE SPEY - Bartsch   RED DOG - Brooks   RED SHRIMP - Johnson

RED SHRIMP - Schweitzer   REIFF'S SHRIMP - Reiff   ROYAL SPEY - Johnson

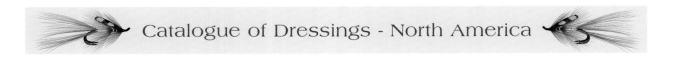

RIVER SHRIMP SERIES - Madore

Orange version
TAIL: Orange polar bear with strands of Krystal Flash
BODY: Rear 50% - hot orange dubbing. Front 50% - peacock herl
RIB: Oval silver tinsel
BODY HACKLE: Orange cock, palmered
WING: Three laquered GP tippet feathers, the first to reach end of body, the second reaching 2/3rds along body , the third at head to reach 1/3rd body
HEAD: Black

Colour variants:

Name	Tail	Body	Body hackle	Wing	Head
Black	Black squirrel	Black dubbing	Black	Laquered black and white jungle cock	Black
Blue	Blue dyed grey squirrel	50% and 50% blue and black dubbing	Blue	Laquered blue hackle tips	Black
Green	Green dyed grey squirrel	50% and 50% green and black dubbing	Green	Laquered green hackle tips	Black
Yellow	Yellow polar bear	50% and 50% yellow and black dubbing	Yellow	Yellow feather strip, jungle cock cheeks	Red

RVI - Brooks

TAG: Flat silver tinsel
TAIL: GP red breast feather fibres
BODY: Rear 1/3rd - silver tinsel or pearl Flashabou. Front 2/3rds - orange seal's fur
RIB: Flat silver tinsel
BODY HACKLE: Teal flank palmered over seal's fur
WING: Four GP red breast feathers tied low and tented, extending to tip of tail
HEAD: Red

SAUK RIVER SHRIMP - Jackson

TAIL: Orange bucktail, at least as long as hook
BODY: Red ostrich herl twisted into a rope and wound. Body in four segments
BODY HACKLES: Orange saddle hackle, each larger towards head
COLLAR HACKLE: Orange saddle
HEAD: Red

SANDY CANDY SPEY - Silvey

BODY: Fuschia or hot pink floss
RIB: Pearl Mylar
BODY HACKLE: Schlappen hackle dyed hot pink
THORAX: Fiery orange SLF
COLLAR HACKLE: Orange schlappen
WING: Goose slips dyed hot pink
CHEEKS: Jungle cock
HEAD: Red

SEA LICE - MacLeod

TAG: Fine oval gold tinsel
TAIL: GP topping
BODY: Orange wool
RIB: Small oval gold tinsel
BODY HACKLE: Large GP red breast feather, wound. Tied in at centre of body
COLLAR HACKLE: Large pheasant rump feather
WING: Bronze mallard
HEAD: Red

SEAN'S PRAWN - Gallagher

TAIL: Hot orange Krafty fur with strands of polar bear
EYES: Black chain beads
BODY: Sparse hot orange dubbing
RIB: Small oval gold tinsel
BODY HACKLE: Orange cock
BACK: Three GP red breast feathers. First one tied in halfway along body, last at head
COLLAR HACKLE: Deep cerise saddle hackle
HEAD: Red

SHRIMP FLY - Clarke

TAIL: Hot orange polar bear with a small bunch of orange marabou over
EYES: Black plastic beads
BODY: Orange Crystal chenille
BACK: Clear plastic tubing cut in half and shaped
RIB: Dark brown monofilament
HEAD: Orange

SILVER STREAK - Howell

TAG: Flat silver tinsel
BODY: Flat silver tinsel
RIB: Small oval gold tinsel
BODY HACKLE: Long grey heron hackle
THROAT HACKLE: Guinea fowl dyed blue
WING: Bronze mallard
HEAD: Red

SILVEY'S PRAWN - Silvey

TAIL: Red Super hair
EYES: Black blobbed monofilament
TAIL HACKLE: Hot orange dyed GP tippet
BODY: Hot orange rabbit strip, cut across skin, wound so that fur lies backwards
THROAT HACKLE: Hot orange dyed GP tippet feather
WING: GP red breast feather dyed hot orange
HEAD: Red

Other colours:
Red, black, purple, pink, white

SKAGIT SPEY, BLACK - Farrar

TAG: Flat gold tinsel
REAR BODY (1/4): Orange floss over underbody of flat gold tinsel
REAR BODY VEILING: 6 to 8 strands orange polar bear hair
FRONT BODY (3/4): Black seal's fur
RIB: Fine oval silver tinsel over front body
BODY HACKLE: Black marabou palmered over front body
THROAT: Teal
WING: Bronze mallard
CHEEKS: Jungle cock
HEAD: Black

RIVER SHRIMP SERIES - Madore

RVI - Brooks   SAUK RIVER SHRIMP - Jackson   SANDY CANDY SPEY - Silvey

SEA LICE - MacLeod   SEAN'S PRAWN - Gallagher   SHRIMP FLY - Clarke

SILVER STREAK - Howell   SILVEY'S PRAWN - Silvey   SKAGIT SPEY, BLACK - Farrar

SKAGIT SPEY, ORANGE - Farrar

TAG: Flat gold tinsel
REAR BODY (1/4): Orange floss over underbody of flat gold tinsel
REAR BODY VEILING: 6 to 8 strands orange polar bear hair
FRONT BODY (3/4): Hot orange seal's fur
RIB: Fine oval gold tinsel over front body
BODY HACKLE: Orange marabou palmered with one turn of red marabou at front
THROAT: GP red feather with pintail over
WINGS: Bronze mallard
CHEEKS: Jungle cock
HEAD: Red

SKAGIT SPEY, WHITE - Farrar

TAG: Flat gold tinsel
REAR BODY (1/4): Red floss
REAR BODY VEILING: 6 to 8 strands white polar bear hair
FRONT BODY (3/4): Light grey seal's fur over underbody of flat gold tinsel
RIB: Fine oval gold tinsel over front body
BODY HACKLE: Light grey marabou palmered over front body
THROAT: Mallard flank
WINGS: Bronze mallard
CHEEKS: Jungle cock
HEAD: Black

SKAGIT SPEY, YELLOW - Farrar

TAG: Flat gold tinsel
REAR BODY (1/4): Hot orange floss
REAR BODY VEILING: 6 to 8 strands white polar bear hair
FRONT BODY (3/4): Yellow seal's fur over underbody of flat gold tinsel
RIB: Fine oval gold tinsel over front body
BODY HACKLE: Light grey marabou with one turn yellow at front, palmered over front body
THROAT: Mallard flank with a small bunch of magenta hackle fibres
WINGS: Bronze mallard
CHEEKS: Jungle cock
HEAD: Black

SKYKOMISH SPEY, DARK - Gobin

TAG: Oval silver tinsel
REAR BODY: Orange floss
FRONT BODY: Red seal's fur
RIB: Fine oval silver tinsel
BODY HACKLE: Long yellow hackle
THROAT: Pheasant rump dyed black
WINGS: Bronze mallard
HEAD: Red

SKYKOMISH SPEY, LIGHT - Gobin

TAG: Oval silver tinsel
REAR BODY: Orange floss
FRONT BODY: Red seal's fur
RIB: Fine oval silver tinsel
BODY HACKLE: Long yellow hackle
THROAT: GP red breast feather
WINGS: Bronze mallard
HEAD: Red

SLF PRAWN - Silvey

TAIL: SLF hank, rainbow with Rainbow Krystal Flash
EYES: Pearl Kraft eyes
BODY: SLF hank, rainbow
MID WING: Natural mallard flank
WING: Natural mallard flank
HEAD: Brown

SOL DUC SPEY - Glasso

TAG: Oval silver tinsel
BODY: Rear 1/2 - fluorescent orange floss. Front 1/2 - orange seal's fur
RIB: Flat silver tinsel and oval silver tinsel
BODY HACKLE: Long yellow hackle
THROAT: Black
WINGS: Four orange hackle tips
HEAD: Red

SPAWNING SPEY - McNeese

TAG: Flat silver tinsel
BODY: Rear 1/3rd - fluorescent orange floss and then fluorescent red floss. Front 2/3rds - fluorescent orange seal's fur
RIB: Oval silver tinsel
BODY HACKLE: Hot orange heron from 2nd turn of rib
THROAT: Long pintail flank dyed hot purple
WINGS: Four hot purple hackle tips with GP toppings dyed hot purple over
CHEEKS: Jungle cock
HEAD: Black

SPRING SPEY - Stetzer

TAIL: GP topping
BODY: Grass green seal's fur
RIB: Oval gold tinsel and fine gold wire
BODY HACKLE: Long grey heron
THROAT: Mallard or teal flank dyed grass green
WING: Bronze mallard
HEAD: Black

SQUAMISH POACHER, VARIANT - Silvey

TAIL: Pearl blue Lite-Brite fibres
EYES: Black blobbed monofilament
LEGS: Wiggle Legs, clear with hot orange tips
BODY: Pearl blue Lite-Brite dubbing
BODY HACKLE: Orange saddle hackle
CARAPACE: Orange Edge Bright
RIB: Red wire
HEAD: Lead eyes tied in under hook shank

SSSS - Soule

TAG: Flat silver or silver holographic tinsel
BODY: Firefox peacock Lite-Brite
WING: Blue Flashabou or Krystal Flash
THROAT: Black schlappen with blue dyed guinea fowl over
EYES: Black chain bead or barbells
HEAD: Black

Other colours:
Green body, green Flashabou, guinea dyed yellow
Copper body, copper Flashabou, guinea dyed orange

ST. GEORGE'S SPEY - Burry

TAG: Oval silver tinsel
TAIL: GP red breast feather fibres
BODY: Rear 1/3rd - orange seal's fur. Front 2/3rds - light green seal's fur
RIB: Oval silver tinsel
BODY HACKLE: Grey heron over front body, extra turns at throat
WING: Bronze mallard
HEAD: Black

SKAGIT SPEY, ORANGE - Farrar   SKAGIT SPEY, WHITE - Farrar   SKAGIT SPEY, YELLOW - Farrar

SKYKOMISH SPEY, DARK - Gobin   SKYKOMISH SPEY, LIGHT - Gobin   SLF PRAWN - Silvey

SOL DUC SPEY - Glasso   SPAWNING SPEY - McNeese   SPRING SPEY - Stetzer

SQUAMISH POACHER, VARIANT   SSSS - Soule   ST. GEORGE'S SPEY - Burry

TARTAN

TAG: Gold tinsel
TAIL: GP red breast feather
BODY: Rear fi - orange pig's wool. Front fi - scarlet pig's wool
RIB: Broad flat gold tinsel
BODY HACKLE: Red game cock over first 2/3rds of body, grey heron over front 1/3rd
THROAT: Pintail or teal
WING: Long strips silver-grey turkey
HEAD: Black

TIGER PRAWN #1 - Veverka

TAG: Flat silver tinsel
TAIL: Orange bucktail
BODY: Mix of purple and orange seal's fur
RIB: Flat silver tinsel
THROAT HACKLE: Long saddle or schlappen purple to black at roots
WING: Two grizzle hackles dyed orange-red, back to back
HEAD: Red

TIGER PRAWN #2 - Veverka

TAG: Flat silver tinsel
TAIL: Orange bucktail
BODY: Orange Crystal seal's fur in two parts
RIB: Oval silver tinsel
CENTRE HACKLE: Orange-red dyed grizzly hen
THROAT HACKLE: Orange-red dyed grizzly hen
WING: Two grizzle hackles dyed orange-red, back to back
HEAD: Red

TIPPET SHRIMP - Hunter

TAG: Medium oval gold tinsel
TAIL: 10 to 12 hot orange bucktail fibres, twice hook length. 2 strands each gold and pearl Krystal Flash
REAR BODY: Danvilles #7, golden-orange chenille (take this right through to head before applying front body)
CENTRE HACKLE: Two GP tippet feathers, spread out to form veiling around rear body
FRONT BODY: SLF #17 red-orange dubbing
RIB: Oval gold tinsel
COLLAR HACKLE: GP red breast feather
HEAD: Red

TURKEY TRACKER - Hunter

BODY: Black wool or dubbing
RIB: Embossed gold tinsel
BODY HACKLE: Brown turkey hackle from 2nd. turn of rib
THROAT: One turn pintail flank with purple saddle over
WING: Two hackle tips, dyed Highlander green flanked by short GP red breast feather
HEAD: Black

USK GRUB

TAG: Flat silver tinsel and red floss
TAIL: GP red breast feather, wound
REAR BODY: Orange seal's fur
RIB: Oval silver tinsel
CENTRE HACKLE: Orange cock with badger cock over
FRONT BODY: Black seal's fur
RIB: Oval silver tinsel
WING: Jungle cock, back to back
COLLAR HACKLE: Black cock
HEAD: Black

WINTER PUNCH SPEY - Bachmann

TAG: Flat silver tinsel and red floss
TAIL: GP red breast feather, wound
BODY: Rear 1/2 - fuchia floss. Front 1/2 - lime green dubbing
RIB: Flat silver Mylar tinsel
BODY HACKLE: Large Chinese hackle, dyed hot pink from 2nd turn of rib
COLLAR HACKLE: Large Chinese hackle, dyed lime green
WING: Mallard flank feather, dyed wood duck
HEAD: Black

WINTER'S HOPE SPEY - Blumreich

TAG: Bright yellow floss
TAIL: GP topping
BUTT: Yellow ostrich herl
BODY: Bright blue floss
RIB: Oval silver tinsel
BODY HACKLE: Kingfisher blue schlappen
THROAT: Mallard flank dyed hot purple
WING: Narrow strips of hot orange goose
HEAD: Black

TARTAN   TIGER PRAWN #1 - Veverka   TIGER PRAWN #2 - Veverka

TIPPET SHRIMP - Hunter   TURKEY TRACKER - Hunter   USK GRUB

WINTER PUNCH SPEY - Bachmann   WINTER'S HOPE SPEY - Blumreich

Bibliography

Bachmann, Troy
Frontier Flies, Frank Amato Publications ,1998

Bates, Col. Joseph D.
Atlantic Salmon Flies & Fishing, Stackpole Books, 1970
The Art of the Atlantic Salmon Fly, D. R. Godine, 1987

Buckland, John
The Pocket Guide to Trout & Salmon Flies, Mitchell Beazley, 1986

Buckland, John and Oglesby, Arthur
A Guide to Salmon Flies, Crowood Press, 1990

Combs, Trey
Steelhead Fly Fishing and Flies, Lyons Press 1991, Paperback edition 1999
Steelhead Fly Fishing, Salmon Trout Steelheader, 1976

Dunham, Judith
The Atlantic Salmon Fly - The Tyers and Their Art, Chronicle Books, 1991

Francis, Francis
A Book on Angling, London, 1867

Frodin, Mikael
Classic Salmon Flies - History & Patterns, Bonanza Books, 1991

Hale, J. H.
How to Tie Salmon Flies, London, 1892 & 1919

Headley, Stan
Trout & Salmon Flies of Scotland, Merlin Unwin Books, 1997

Jorgensen, Poul
Salmon Flies - Their Character, Style and Dressing, Stackpole Books, 2nd Edition, 1999

Kelson, George Mortimer
The Salmon Fly, London, 1895

Knox, Arthur Edward
Autumns on the Spey, London, 1892

Lingren, Arthur James
Fly Patterns of British Columbia, Frank Amato Publications, 1996

Malone, E. J.
Irish Trout & Salmon Flies, Coch-Y-Bonddu Books. Paperback Ed. 1998

Marriner, Paul C.
Modern Atlantic Salmon Flies, Frank Amato Publications, 1998

Morgan, Moc
Trout & Salmon Flies of Wales, Merlin Unwin Books, 1996

O'Reilly, Peter
Trout & Salmon Flies of Ireland, Merlin Unwin Books, 1995

Patrick, Roy A.
Pacific Northwest Fly Patterns, Patrick's Fly Shop, 1948, Revised 1953, 1958

Pryce-Tannatt, Dr. Thomas
How to Dress Salmon Flies, London, 1914

Radenich, Michael D.
Tying the Classic Salmon Fly, Stackpole Books, 1997

Stetzer, Randle Scott
Flies - The Best One Thousand, Frank Amato Publications, 1992